ONLY
THE
STRONG

ALSO BY TOM COTTON

Sacred Duty: A Soldier's Tour at Arlington National Cemetery

ONLY
THE
STRONG

Reversing the Left's Plot to Sabotage
American Power

Tom Cotton

TWELVE

NEW YORK   BOSTON

Twelve

Hachette Book Group

1290 Avenue of the Americas, New York, NY 10104

twelvebooks.com

twitter.com/twelvebooks

First Edition: November 2022

Twelve is an imprint of Grand Central Publishing. The Twelve name and logo are trademarks of Hachette Book Group, Inc.

The publisher is not responsible for websites (or their content) that are not owned by the publisher.

The Hachette Speakers Bureau provides a wide range of authors for speaking events. To find out more, go to www.hachettespeakersbureau.com or call (866) 376-6591.

Library of Congress Control Number: 2022942294

ISBN: 9781538726792 (hardcover), 9781538726815 (ebook)

Printed in the United States of America

LSC-C

Printing 1, 2022

To my wife, Anna

CONTENTS

Sabotaging a Superpower

WHO COULD'VE FORESEEN, eight years ago, this strange and unexpected moment, I thought as I surveyed the scene. Soldiers and airmen huddled against the HESCOs, giant earth-filled baskets typically used for cover from gunfire, but today used for even a sliver of shade. No luck. The sun baked everything in sight as the temperature passed 110 degrees, routine for May in eastern Afghanistan. Looking over our base's perimeter wall, I saw the mud huts of Mehtar Lam, with Afghan women washing clothes and kids playing with sticks. Lacking electricity, the huts would disappear into darkness most nights.

Standing in front of our duck-and-cover bunkers and thousands of precariously stacked water bottles, improbably enough, was the Matt Poss Band, a country group from downstate Illinois. The six musicians had traveled to Afghanistan as part of a two-week tour to entertain the troops. Athletes, movie stars, and musicians visited often enough, but this was a first for our little base; most celebrities stuck close to the mega-bases like Bagram and Kandahar. But that made us appreciate the band even more. I could tell the troops really enjoyed the mix of country, rock, and blues, even if their tastes ran more toward rap and metal, judging by what I heard in the barracks. It was a welcome break after seven months in theater.

As I listened, I reflected on the eight years of choices and chances that had brought me to a concert in the foothills of Afghanistan. It was an unpredictable path, but who can ever predict the path a life will take?

In the summer of 2001, I was heading into my final year of law school, with a job already lined up after graduation. The future seemed safe, secure, and predictable. But all that changed on 9/11. I wanted to rush out and join the next day; some friends in the Army encouraged me to finish school and repay my loans. The Army and the bad guys aren't going anywhere, they said, and neither are your loans if you drop out of school. The delay frustrated me at times, but I realized they were right when I started earning a few hundred bucks a paycheck as an E-4 specialist.

I spent more than a year at Fort Benning, earning my commission as a second lieutenant, learning my craft as an infantry officer, and enduring the travails of Ranger and Airborne Schools. My buddies and I were all eager to get downrange and see combat—it's why we joined—but our commander also counseled patience. "Don't worry," he often said, "you'll all get your shot at the title."

Mine came in 2006, as soon as I left Benning. After reporting to Fort Campbell, I flew straight to Iraq on the "replacement bird"—the nickname, in typical Army gallows humor, for the airplane that takes "replacements" for casualties into a combat theater. I joined my new unit, the 101st Airborne Division, in Baghdad. By then, we were in the middle of both an insurgency and a sectarian war, making the battlefield especially complex. Thanks to our training and equipment, a little luck, and a lot of prayer, I brought all my soldiers home alive and well in time for Thanksgiving. I later joked with friends that I now drove more carefully and ate more healthily because I had left eight of my nine lives in Baghdad.

I moved next to The Old Guard at Arlington National Cemetery. This assignment was unusual because The Old Guard is a volunteer, application-only unit—and I hadn't applied. The regiment was short on officers, however, and I fit the first key criterion—I'm very tall—so the Army voluntold me. But it was also a welcome assignment. If not leading troops in combat, there's almost nothing I'd rather do than honor our fallen heroes inside Arlington.

At one point, The Old Guard was supposed to be my last assignment. I was slated to go either back to Benning for another training course or, worse yet, to a desk making PowerPoint slides. Neither appealed to me. Between Iraq and Arlington, I had already had a good run in the Army, doing what I joined to do and then some. I submitted my resignation papers in late 2007, intending to serve another year at the cemetery and then go home.

But things changed again in the spring of 2008. The Army asked for volunteers among infantry captains for an Afghanistan mission. I was intrigued. By that point, the Iraq surge had succeeded in stabilizing the country and bringing American casualties way down. Barack Obama and John McCain both campaigned on a renewed commitment to Afghanistan. Obama in particular sounded uncharacteristically tough on Afghanistan in contrast to his strident criticism of the Iraq War. It seemed like a promising time to head to Afghanistan. Moreover, pre-deployment training would last only three months, with volunteers shipping out by the early fall. Army headquarters gladly promised the deployment to me if I withdrew my resignation. I was heading back to war.

Now here I was, of all places, at a concert in Mehtar Lam. Yet my story wasn't all that unusual. Our base had soldiers and airmen from every walk of life. Many of the privates had been in elementary school or middle school on 9/11. Most were on their first combat tour, getting their first shot at the title, as my old commander put it.

I was proud of these young troops. They represented what was best about our nation: brave, patriotic, dogged, hardworking, selfless, and entirely convinced of America's righteousness. They deserved this welcome little break before the next mission.

Unfortunately, warning clouds were gathering over the mission. Four months into office, Obama had ratified George W. Bush's late decision to deploy some extra troops to Afghanistan, but hadn't yet unveiled a promised new strategy. Maybe he was too busy with his global apology tour. But news reports suggested that Obama was already souring on the war and looking for a way out of his chesty campaign promises. Vice President Joe Biden blurted out that only "5 percent of the Taliban is incorrigible," which surprised the soldiers busy fighting them. Perhaps most ominous, leaks from the White House implied that Obama was depending on Biden for advice as much as or more than his own commanders.

As the Matt Poss Band wrapped up, I worried about the troops applauding them and those who would come next. Our tour would soon end, but the war would not. Nor would the threats to our nation. I feared the new commander in chief wasn't up to the task.

TWELVE YEARS LATER, I was splashing around a pool with my boys, Gabriel and Daniel. Summer was ending and school was starting soon. They wanted one more Sunday afternoon of swimming, belly flops, and backflips. It was as far from Afghanistan as you could imagine, but Afghanistan was still very much on my mind.

It had been an eventful decade for me. Three years after leaving the Army, I was elected to the House of Representatives. Shortly after taking office, I met my wonderful wife, Anna. We got married a year later in the middle of my Senate campaign, and then started a family.

Our country had gone through even more dramatic changes. In Barack Obama's second term, American power crumbled. China grew richer and more aggressive, Russia invaded Ukraine, and ISIS rampaged across the Middle East, all while Obama refused to enforce his own red lines and rewarded Iran and Cuba. The American people repudiated Obama's weakness by electing Donald Trump. For four years, we had a reprieve from defense cuts and humiliating concessions. We defeated ISIS; killed Iran's terrorist mastermind, Qasem Soleimani; and took the first steps to stand up to China. But the reprieve ended when Joe Biden took office. Illegal immigration surged at our border, prices surged at the grocery store and the gas pump, and now the Taliban surged across Afghanistan.

Since Biden had announced our withdrawal in April, I had observed the Taliban's momentum with growing concern. When he stated in early July that a Taliban takeover was "highly unlikely," I wasn't so sure. We had abandoned Bagram Air Base, reduced air support for the Afghan military, and even withdrawn civilian mechanics who kept the Afghan Air Force flying. By early August, I knew from intelligence briefings and my own experiences that the Taliban was seizing territory it hadn't held for two decades. On August 6, the Taliban captured its first provincial capital and took more capitals every day after that. Biden insisted, "I do not regret my decision," even as he rushed thousands of troops to Kabul to evacuate our embassy. In private, intelligence officials kept revising downward their predictions of how long Kabul would hold out, but they still overestimated it. On August 15, news broke that Kabul had fallen and Afghan president Ashraf Ghani had fled the country.

As I packed up my boys for the pool that Sunday, I seethed at the president's mistakes. Joe Biden's incompetent retreat had turned into a rout, humiliating America and squandering the sacrifices of our troops. I pondered the fallout for American power and prestige, but I was about to learn that the book on Afghanistan hadn't yet closed. The ending would be far worse than I feared.

I stepped out of the pool and checked my phone. I had a voice mail from my dad, who still lived on our family farm in Dardanelle. He asked me to call him because someone needed help in Afghanistan. That's odd, I thought. Dardanelle is a small community; other than veterans, not many people would've ever traveled to Afghanistan, or even met someone who had. I called him back and listened in disbelief. He'd heard that a development worker from down the road was stuck in Kabul, trapped behind Taliban lines.

I was stunned. The State Department has the chief responsibility for the safety of our citizens overseas. Now, State could only tell them to "shelter in place" and fill out a form on its website. I called the operations desk at State for more answers. No one had any.

This was shaping up as a disaster of the first order. If an Arkansan from my neck of the woods was stuck in Taliban-occupied Afghanistan, there was no telling how many thousands of Americans were also trapped. They needed help, fast.

Knowing every second counted, I mobilized my staff for a hasty rescue mission. First things first, I directed them to help the Arkansan get to safety, if possible. Next, I posted on social media a hotline and emergency email account to urge any American trapped in Afghanistan to contact my office. "The situation is dire," I wrote, "but we'll do everything in our power to help keep you informed and to help get you out." We obviously lacked the resources of the executive branch, but at least we could offer stranded Americans a real person on the other end of the line.

Sure enough, the calls and emails flooded in by the hundreds, then the thousands. It was a race against time. Taliban fighters roamed the streets, beating civilians and searching door to door for Americans and our Afghan friends. Plus, the Biden administration was so clueless and flat-footed that we didn't know how long we had. A potential hostage crisis—or worse—was materializing before our eyes.

There was one silver lining: Congress was in the middle of its

August recess. Without votes in the Senate or committee hearings, I could dedicate my entire staff to the mission. In Arkansas and Washington, our team worked around the clock. Some were veterans of the war, others knew the State Department well, but all threw themselves into the work to save our fellow citizens. As luck would have it, one of my young aides was a mobilized reservist stationed at the Kabul airport. She acted at times as a forward liaison for our efforts.

For two weeks, my team vetted and verified requests for help and supplied information to my aide in Kabul and other military contacts on the ground that they used for rescue missions. We talked Americans through Taliban checkpoints and gave tips about which gates to use and which to avoid.

All told, we helped more than three hundred Americans and green-card holders get to safety, along with more than two hundred trusted Afghan allies. The first American we got out was the Arkansan. Within forty-eight hours of the call from my dad, we had verified his identity and location, coordinated a rescue plan with military personnel at Kabul airport, and confirmed his safe arrival at the airport, despite the frantic crowd. He was on one of the first military transports out of Afghanistan.

But for every person rescued, there were many tales of tragedy. America's final days in Afghanistan were scenes of chaos, confusion, horror, and death. Everyone remembers Afghans mobbing the runways at Kabul airport, clinging to the sides and landing gear of planes, and plummeting to their deaths on the tarmac. Taliban goons whipped and beat our citizens in the streets. Desperate moms and dads passed their babies over barbed wire at the airport gates, knowing they might never see them again. The Taliban targeted dozens of translators and other loyal allies for revenge killings.

And on August 26, four days before the last American plane took off from Kabul, the worst blow of all landed. An ISIS terrorist infiltrated the crowd outside the airport's busiest gate and detonated a suicide vest, killing thirteen of our brave troops and as many as 170 civilians. It was the deadliest day for American troops in Afghanistan in a decade and a tragic epitaph to our twenty-year struggle in that country.

JOE BIDEN'S AFGHANISTAN fiasco will live in infamy as a strategic blunder of the first order. So many people asked me at the time, "How did they let this happen?" The simple answer to our humiliation in Afghanistan is Joe Biden's rank, reprehensible incompetence.

But the deeper, unspoken questions lurking in the background were, "How did we get to this point? and "Why doesn't America win anymore?"

I wrote this book to answer those questions.

America's recent decline isn't an accident. It's decline by design. For more than a century, liberal Democrats have plotted to sabotage American power. These Democrats believe a strong and confident America brings war, arrogance, and oppression—not safety, freedom, and prosperity. They want America to pull in its horns and apologize for its sins. I don't assert these liberals are necessarily un-American or hate our country—though plenty are and do—but they genuinely believe American power is dangerous for both America and the world.

This book explores how the Democrats adopted these strange beliefs and the consequences for our nation. We'll start at the beginning, more than a century ago, when the original Progressives repudiated the Declaration of Independence and the Constitution. This little clique of liberal intellectuals, led by Woodrow Wilson, ridiculed the Founders' defense of God-given natural rights and limited government. They entrusted the nation's business not to the people, but to supposedly nonpartisan, scientific, elite "experts." On the world stage, too, they believed our affairs should be managed by so-called experts who rose above what they considered petty nationalism. For instance, Wilson eagerly advocated the surrender of American sovereignty to globalist institutions. The Progressives might wage war, as Wilson did in World War I, but only for abstractions and other nations' interests—not America's national interest.

But once the Progressives repudiated our founding principles, it was just a short slide into outright anti-Americanism. The Democrats descended deeper into radicalism in the 1960s and 1970s, when left-wing terrorists incited riots and bombed the Capitol out of hatred for our troops, our military, and our flag. "Blame America First" Democrats condemned America as an evil, imperialist power. They fought at every turn to shrink our military, undermine our allies, and appease the forces of communism. You can spot the latest generation of Blame America First Democrats today as they riot in the streets, tear down statues, agitate for socialism, and slander our country in liberal newspapers like the *New York Times*.

Behind this worldview lies a deep mistrust of our people and our republican form of government. Liberals believe the American people can't be trusted to make decisions about serious matters like war and peace. Instead, they want to undermine our sovereignty in favor of a transnational regime of lawyers, diplomats, and professors. These globalists seek to elevate the United Nations over the United States, open our borders and our markets, and trade away our freedom of action to international bureaucrats and foreign adversaries.

Liberals also want to neuter the military precisely because it guarantees American freedom of action. A strong military empowers an American president, for example, to kill Iran's terrorist mastermind in a sudden strike. Our military serves every day as a rebuke to the progressives' transnational dreams, which is one reason why leftists single out our military for condemnation. The solution for these liberals is to cut the defense budget and erode the military's hard, fighting edge.

Even when liberals feel compelled to act tough—usually for political reasons—their hearts are rarely in the fight. Timid and diffident about American power to begin with, liberals all too often lead our nation into catastrophe, from the Democrats' mismanagement of the Vietnam War to John Kennedy's dithering at the Bay of Pigs to Bill Clinton's misadventure in Somalia. Their failures usually result in dead Americans and emboldened adversaries.

This liberal mindset reached its logical conclusion during the presidencies of Barack Obama and Joe Biden. Obama, the most ideological president since Wilson, purposefully dismantled American strength around the world. With the haughtiness of a progressive professor and the hostility of a Blame America First radical, Obama apologized for America's sins, hollowed out our military, shunned our friends, and rewarded our enemies.

Though Joe Biden is no one's idea of a strategic mastermind, his impulsive and reckless approach to foreign policy may be even worse. Biden didn't just leave our people behind during his retreat from Afghanistan. His weakness enticed Vladimir Putin to invade Ukraine. And Biden has done next to nothing to protect America from our greatest threat, Communist China.

This is the story of how the radical left plots to sabotage American power.

Of course, Republicans can make mistakes; we're all human, no one's perfect. George H. W. Bush reacted too mildly to the massacre at Tiananmen Square. George W. Bush didn't dedicate enough troops during the early days of the Iraq War; I witnessed the consequences of that mistake firsthand. Donald Trump waited too long to withdraw from the Iran nuclear deal. Yet they often recover from their mistakes, as the younger

Bush did with the surge and as Trump did with the "maximum pressure" campaign against Iran. More to the point, these were *mistakes*—not a deliberate effort to rein in America and sabotage our power.

But this book comes to resurrect American power, not to administer its last rites. In the final chapters, I explain how we can take the road back to American greatness. It starts with restoring a distinctive strategy that puts America first and looks after the safety, freedom, and prosperity of our citizens. Our people deserve a government that champions their interests—not the interests of a few or the interests of some other people or some ideological abstraction. We also have to regain America's strength. We can only protect our interests by rebuilding vital elements of national strength: an indomitable military, secure borders, energy independence, and strong alliances of friends against our foes.

AMERICANS SENSE THAT something is wrong. We live in a dangerous world, and it's grown more dangerous as American power has declined. Many Americans worry that our country is fading. They worry that China will soon call the shots. They worry that their children will live worse lives than they did, which would be a tragic first in our history. And they're right to worry.

It wasn't always this way. From George Washington's presidency to the end of World War II, not even 150 years, we went from a global backwater to an undisputed global champion. We possessed the world's mightiest, most fearsome military. What's more, we built the world's largest and most dynamic economy, providing the highest standards of living ever known for the working man, with unlimited opportunity for success. And then we prevailed in the Cold War. America had fulfilled what Ronald Reagan called our "rendezvous with destiny": we had become the greatest superpower in the history of the world.

None of this was inevitable; it didn't just happen. America's greatness resulted from the individual choices of men and women, not vast impersonal forces beyond our control. In Washington's Farewell Address, he urged patience as we built the strength needed to give America "the command of its own fortunes." For generations, we followed his guidance, adding strength upon strength. This is a testament to our greatest statesmen and our brave, resourceful people.

You can see and feel this tradition of American strength at our National Mall in Washington, D.C. Stand at the base of Washington's Monument and lift your gaze. The soaring obelisk of marble and granite projects strength, reliability, permanence. Look west to Lincoln's temple. Gazing upon Washington's Monument, there sits the president who after the deadliest battle of our deadliest war still had the strength to "highly resolve that these dead shall not have died in vain—that this nation, under God, shall have a new birth of freedom—and that government of the people, by the people, for the people, shall not perish from the earth." Finally, walk across Memorial Bridge and witness the endless rows of patriot graves of Arlington. These Americans had the strength, courage, and patriotism to answer the call of duty and to give their todays for our tomorrows.

This tradition may have faded in recent times, but it's not lost or forgotten. We got to this point thanks to bad choices. Through our own new choices, we can reclaim the tradition of American strength.

And we must, if we want to guard against the gathering dangers and preserve our way of life. One day, the meek will inherit the Earth; until then, the strong will need to guard it. And even when the lion lies down with the lamb, I'd still prefer to be the lion.

Only the strong can survive in a dangerous world. Only the strong can protect the weak. Only the strong can afford to be merciful. And only the strong can preserve our freedom.

PART I

Decline by Design

CHAPTER 1

The Progressive Roots of Decline

THE 1904 WORLD'S FAIR in St. Louis was a monumental cele-
bration of America, our achievements, and our rising star in the
world. Formally known as the Louisiana Purchase Exposition, the
fair celebrated the one-hundredth anniversary of President Thomas
Jefferson's great diplomatic achievement, which doubled the size of
the United States.

The fair paid tribute to America's rapid expansion. The Census
Bureau had announced the closing of the frontier fourteen years earlier; America had achieved our destiny as a continental republic. We
were the undisputed power of the hemisphere, having evicted Spain
from Cuba and the Caribbean in the Spanish-American War.

America's technological and cultural might were on full display.
The fair began when President Teddy Roosevelt touched a golden
telegraph key in the White House, which triggered an artillery salvo
in Washington and, in St. Louis, a huge chorus from the assembled
bands, including one led by John Philip Sousa.

Millions of Americans attended this celebratory fair out of pride
for our country. Odds are, if you and I lived back then, we might
have made the trip to St. Louis with our kids. And we too would've
taken them both for the entertainment and to teach them about our

country and to honor our Founders, who had given us so great a heritage and so promising a future.

But a smaller event next door contrasted sharply with the patriotism and pride of the fair. The International Congress of Arts and Sciences gathered thousands of intellectuals to preview some of the century's worst ideas, including "scientific" racism and bureaucratic government.

These intellectuals did not celebrate America's heritage. They instead promoted foreign ideas hostile to the founding principles that had made America a mighty nation. The event catered to the intellectual fads and trends of European, and especially German, academics. The mood was heady, perhaps because the world hadn't yet seen the horrors that could result from the ideas of German philosophers like Karl Marx.

The list of American presenters at the International Congress was a who's who of left-wing scholars known as the Progressives. Their ranks included utopian dreamers, fanatical proponents of big government, and virulent racists and eugenicists. Woodrow Wilson, the arch-Progressive president of Princeton, was all of those things. Within a decade, he would also become president of the United States.

Wilson gave a lecture on history at the Congress that summarized this new Progressive ideology. He confidently announced "the dawn and the early morning hours of a new age" in which intellectuals like himself would be the "source" of "progress and reform." He called on his fellow academics to "transform society"—much like another professor-turned-politician, Barack Obama, would call for "fundamentally transforming the United States" a century later. Wilson wanted progressive intellectuals to "walk at the van" of society, echoing another foreign ideologue of his time—Vladimir Lenin—who called for "a vanguard of the proletariat."

The role of the Progressive vanguard, according to Wilson, wasn't to record history, but to *make* history and move it to a more "enlightened" plane. The Progressives didn't want to celebrate America's founding, but to overcome and replace it with their vision of utopia.

GROWING UP, I was taught to love America and to revere our Founding Fathers. You probably were too. Not long ago, it was common for families to read the Declaration on the Fourth of July and for students to memorize its preamble and the Constitution's preamble too.

While our Declaration and Constitution haven't lost any of their power or truth, they've come under neglect and attack. Too many schools don't bother to teach them. Left-wing radicals condemn them as oppressive and obsolete. The *New York Times* even tries to rewrite history altogether, claiming America was founded in 1619 on slavery instead of in 1776 on freedom.

These liberal attacks on our Constitution and founding principles might seem new. But they're not. Many of the malicious arguments we hear today are recycled versions of the same arguments the Progressives made a century ago.

In fact, the best way to understand why the left is sabotaging American power today is to go back to where it all started. And to do that, we have to start with the Progressives, who repudiated America's founding principles.

The Founders created a limited government to protect our rights and advocated a hard-nosed foreign policy to protect our safety and national interests. They designed the American form of government based on timeless and unchanging human nature. They knew that men are not angels, and we'll never have heaven on Earth. But the Progressives rejected nature as the basis of government, replacing it with a theory of historical evolution and determinism—"History" with a capital *H*. They believed that human nature changes over time and that government must change with it. They disparaged individual rights, created a sprawling bureaucratic government, and reoriented our foreign policy toward utopian fantasies.

Like a lot of bad ideas, Progressivism began as a small academic movement but quickly sprawled into a mass political movement that succeeded in electing one of its own as president: Woodrow Wilson. And progressive ideology still guides the Democratic Party today. When you hear politicians speak of "being on the right side of history" or "the arc of history," they're reflecting early Progressive thought.

Today's liberals may think these phrases sound pretty, but they reflect an ugly and anti-American ideology that laid the roots of American decline. Once Progressives repudiated the moral and political foundations of America, it was a short step to repudiating America itself. The violent hatred of America we see on the left today got its start with the Progressives' attacks on America many years ago.

THE PROGRESSIVE ATTACK ON THE FOUNDING

Progressives rejected our Founders' first principles of government. The Progressives' sharp break with the founding principles is sometimes overlooked because more than a century has passed since the Progressives began their attack. That's why it's important to return to these first principles to understand how the Progressives planted the seeds of decline.

Nature versus History

Our Founders built America on eternal principles and timeless truths. By contrast, the Progressives viewed the founding era as outdated, asserting that our founding principles had been overtaken by the progress of History and could be ignored.

These concepts can seem abstract, so it's best to begin at the beginning, with the document that literally founded America: the

Declaration of Independence. The Declaration announced to the world our independence from Great Britain. But it did much more: it laid down the principles of our new country. Abraham Lincoln honored its principal author, Thomas Jefferson, for having "the coolness, forecast, and capacity to introduce into a merely revolutionary document, an abstract truth, applicable to all men and all times." A "merely revolutionary" document! As if rebellion against the British Empire was some small thing. Lincoln understood, though, how essential that "abstract truth, applicable to all men and all times," was to our revolution, justifying the sacrifice of so many patriots.

That truth, of course, is the central claim of the Declaration: "all men are created equal." The Founders called this truth "self-evident," which is to say it carries its evidence with it and needs no additional or external proof.

What does it mean to be created equal? It doesn't mean we're alike in every respect. The Founders elaborated that our equality is moral and political. Or as Jefferson wrote for the fiftieth anniversary of the Declaration, "the mass of mankind has not been born with saddles on their backs, nor a favored few booted and spurred, ready to ride them legitimately, by the grace of God." Lincoln, the great interpreter of the Declaration, agreed, and also answered those who point out the many ways in which humans are obviously not equal:

> I think the authors of that notable instrument intended to include *all* men, but they did not intend to declare all men equal *in all respects*. They did not mean to say all were equal in color, size, intellect, moral developments, or social capacity. They defined with tolerable distinctness, in what respects they did consider all men created equal—equal in "certain inalienable rights, among which are life, liberty, and the pursuit of happiness."

7

In other words, despite our many differences, we all have the same rights, and no one by nature is entitled to rule over another.

The Founders explained that our equality is an eternal truth because it comes from God—or as the Declaration says, "the Laws of Nature and Nature's God." John Adams tied the Declaration directly to Christianity, writing that Christianity "is founded on that eternal and fundamental Principle of the Law of Nature, Do as you would be done by: and love your Neighbor as yourself." We are equal because God created us equally in His image, because we are each equally human—then, now, and always. And just as God always is and always has been, these laws of nature are also immutable and timeless.

This understanding wasn't controversial or disputed among Americans at the time. Near his death, Jefferson denied any "originality of principle or sentiment" on his part, explaining that he articulated the common sense of the American people. The goal of the Declaration was "not to find out new principles, or new arguments, never before thought of, nor merely to say things which had never been said before; but to place before mankind the common sense of the subject." He recalled that Americans were of "one opinion" and all "thought alike on these subjects," making the Declaration simply "the expression of the American mind." And despite intellectual fads on the left, you probably share this opinion; it's why we shoot fireworks, go to parades, and read the Declaration on the Fourth of July.

To the Progressives, though, this was all so much nonsense—and worse than that, it was an obstacle to "progress."

Woodrow Wilson didn't love the Declaration. In fact, he hated it. Wilson often ridiculed the Declaration and its "expression of the American mind" of the late eighteenth century. He scoffed that "the question is not whether all men are born free and equal or not. Suppose they were born so, you know they are not." I doubt many politicians would so boldly criticize the Declaration today! Nor would many politicians mock patriotic Americans, as Wilson did when he regretted that "some citizens of this country have never got beyond the Declaration of Independence." Wilson admonished, "if you want to understand the real Declaration of Independence, do not repeat the preface." Put differently, don't read the part that proclaims our equality based on timeless laws of nature and nature's God—the most important part of the document. And certainly don't believe that our equality—or anything else—has an eternal, immutable foundation that could act as a limit on the power of government.

Progressives rejected such eternal principles in favor of a belief in historical evolution. Here, they borrowed from German philosophers, especially G. W. F. Hegel. He contended that History—with a capital *H*—progressed as a kind of rational, evolutionary process with a mind of its own. Hegel's History advanced through various stages of despotism, feudalism, and monarchy before ending in "freedom" under what Hegel called the "rational State." A key implication of Hegel's theory is that knowledge and wisdom change over time. What was true for our forefathers, he claimed, wasn't necessarily true for us today.

This kind of historical relativism runs throughout the Progressives' writings about the Declaration and the founding era. Wilson objected that "the Declaration of Independence did not mention the questions of our day." He didn't see much relevance to the questions that were mentioned in the Declaration, either. "Such sentences do not afford a general theory of government to formulate policies upon. No doubt we are meant to have liberty; but each generation must form its own conception of liberty." At root, Wilson wanted to cast aside the Declaration as outdated and obsolete—to progress beyond it, one might say: "We are not bound to adhere to the doctrines held by the signers of the Declaration of Independence: we are as free as they were to make and unmake governments. We are not here to worship men or a document."

Another leading Progressive, John Dewey, was even more blunt. He ridiculed the Founders, dismissing them because "their own special interpretations of liberty, individuality, and intelligence were themselves historically conditioned, and were relevant only to their own time and places." Their "special interpretation of liberty" wasn't subject to "historic relativity," so its authors had "frozen it into a doctrine to be applied at all times under all circumstances." Of course, Lincoln and the Founders knew that permanence was a virtue of our system of government. But to the Progressives, this was a central defect.

In the end, the Progressives repudiated the Declaration for two reasons. First, by appealing to God-given nature instead of History, the Progressives thought the Founders relied on embarrassing, outdated knowledge—really, on myth or superstition. Second, the Progressives believed that this myth of God-given, inalienable rights interfered with their plans to construct a vast administrative bureaucracy—Hegel's "rational State"—to regulate the economy and private life.

In our day, this dispute between nature and History may not seem so important. After all, many people still read the Declaration on Independence Day, while well-meaning people talk about "being on the right side of history." More than a century on, the progressive view of History is a fairly common way of thinking. America has also made great progress in power, wealth, and fairness, so many tend to think progress is more or less inevitable.

Yet nature and History really are different, as Wilson stressed with one of his favorite metaphors:

The captain of a Mississippi steamboat had made fast to the shore because of a thick fog lying upon the river. The fog lay low and dense upon the surface of the water, but overhead all was clear. A cloudless sky showed a thousand points of starry light. An impatient passenger inquired the cause of the delay. "We can't see to steer," said the captain. "But all's clear overhead," suggested the passenger, "you can see the North Star." "Yes," replied the officer, "but we aren't going that way."

Here, Wilson modifies the classical metaphor of the ship of state. At sail on the high seas, the captain is free to choose his destination and navigates there by fixed, eternal principles—such as the North Star—even as he selects his course and technique accounting for circumstances such as wind, weather, and sea conditions. By contrast, Wilson's riverboat captain has not only his destination but also his course chosen for him. He must exercise some skill to avoid the banks and the shoals, but ultimately he must submit to the river current—to History. Indeed, to the Progressives, an appeal to timeless principles isn't merely outdated, but dangerous. As Wilson stated the moral of the metaphor: "Politics must follow the actual windings of the channel: if it steer by the stars it will run aground."

And the difference between nature and History genuinely makes a difference too. The twentieth century was filled with misery, bloodshed, and oppression because so many rulers thought of themselves as "agents of history" who were unbound by the supposedly obsolete morality and rights of the past. The Progressives were no exception.

Individual Rights versus the State

The Founders viewed protecting our rights as the chief purpose of government. But the Progressives viewed our rights as the chief obstacle to their plans for a new form of government.

For the Founders, our rights derived from our natural equality—the fact that no one is born with a saddle or spurs, as Jefferson put it. It's another one of those "self-evident" truths of the Declaration that the rights of human beings "are endowed by their Creator."

Neither the Declaration nor the Constitution's Bill of Rights created these rights; rather, these documents simply recognized them. These rights existed prior to any government and act as both a constraint on and an end for government. Our rights today to speak our mind, worship God, own guns, or receive due process of law are no different from our forebears' rights in the founding era. For that matter, our rights are no different from the rights of any person at any time or place, even though oppressive governments may deny those rights.

Having rejected nature as the basis of government, the Progressives believed that individual rights are not a gift from God or inherent in our nature, but rather a gift from government. And what government may give, government may take away.

The prominent Progressive intellectual Frank Goodnow—the president of Johns Hopkins University, a hotbed of Progressivism, and also the first president of the American Political Science Association—put the case very starkly. He condemned what he called the "private rights political philosophy" as a "menace" to "the necessary prerequisite of progress." According to Goodnow, individual rights are what the left today sometimes calls a "social construct":

> The rights which he possesses are, it is believed, conferred upon him, not by his Creator, but rather by the society to which he belongs. What they are is to be determined by the legislative authority in view of the needs of that society. Social expediency, rather than natural right, is thus to determine the sphere of individual freedom of action.

Goodnow frankly admitted that individual rights must succumb to the growing size and needs of government. "The sphere of government action is continually widening," he wrote hopefully, "and the actual content of individual private rights is being increasingly narrowed." As government grows, our rights recede.

For Progressives, that was all part of the plan. They wanted to build a vast administrative state that would define our rights, instead of being limited by them. The Progressives knew this was the key to building a more "efficient," collectivist society. Stripped of natural rights, "men as communities are supreme over men as individuals," as Wilson put it. By extension, Wilson added, "no line can be drawn between private and public affairs which the State may not cross at will; that omnipotence of legislation is the first postulate of all just political theory."

The "omnipotence of legislation"—the belief that lawmakers have unlimited power—fairly captures the progressive left's view of government. It explains why Democrats greatly expand the size of government every time they take power. And it explains why they believe they can dictate every aspect of our lives, from the food that we eat to how we raise our kids. Progressives don't think our rights come from God. They think government is God.

The Constitution versus Big Government

Lincoln borrowed from Proverbs when he called the Declaration "the apple of gold" and the Constitution "the picture of silver." The Constitution gave form and structure to the Declaration: "The picture was made, not to conceal, or to destroy the apple; but to adorn, and preserve it." Just as they attacked our Declaration, the Progressives unsurprisingly attacked our Constitution, as well.

In the famed *Federalist* 51, James Madison explained that the

Constitution, like the Declaration, also is based on our timeless, unchangeable human nature: men are not angels. Just as we are equal by nature, we are also fallen creatures by nature. "If angels were to govern men," Madison observed, "neither external nor internal controls on government would be necessary." Yet government must be "administered by men over men," so it must be designed not only to "enable the government to control the governed," Madison wrote, but also to "oblige it to control itself." "It may be a reflection on human nature," he acknowledged, "that such devices should be necessary to control the abuses of government. But what is government itself, but the greatest of all reflections on human nature?" Because mankind is fallen and sinful, government is necessary. Yet fallen and sinful men will run the government, so it shouldn't have unchecked power.

These reflections on human nature, I would add, are part of the reason why conservatives today are skeptical about utopian plans like "eliminating poverty" or "ending tyranny in our world." We don't dispute the nobility of the goals, but we have measured expectations about achieving them this side of heaven.

Madison's "devices" are our Constitution's indispensable features: regular elections, limited government, federalism, and the separation of powers. He wrote that regular elections are the "primary control on the government, but experience has taught mankind the necessity of auxiliary precautions." One "auxiliary precaution" is "the federal system," which delegates limited powers to the federal government, leaving most power with the states. Another is the separation of powers with its system of checks and balances between the three branches of government. Together, "a double security arises to the rights of the people." These "devices" and "controls," Madison noted, are "essential to the preservation of liberty."

But just because we're not angels doesn't mean we're devils, either.

Elsewhere in *The Federalist*, Madison elaborated on the good and the bad of human nature and what it means for our government: "As there is a degree of depravity in mankind which requires a certain degree of circumspection and distrust, so there are other qualities in human nature which justify a certain portion of esteem and confidence. Republican government presupposes the existence of these qualities in a higher degree than any other form." This sober assessment of human nature runs throughout the Founders' thinking about the Constitution.

The Progressives, by contrast, were far from sober; they were utopian. As we've seen, the Progressives believed that "History" has its own logic of progress. And just as our material conditions improved with the advance of science and technology, so too did the moral conditions of mankind. As the Progressive academic John Burgess wrote grandiosely, History was "the true and faithful record of these progressive revelations of the human reason, as they mark the line and stages of advance made by the human race towards its ultimate perfection." Adam and Eve may have been turned out of Eden, but with the superior knowledge imparted by History, the Progressives believed they could create a new garden of paradise here on earth.

In retrospect, given the horrors of the twentieth century, this view seems hopelessly naive. But farseeing observers could've seen that utopian political beliefs combined with modern technology could lead to disaster. In fact, one did. In an essay on modern warfare, Winston Churchill, a contemporary of the Progressives, contrasted scientific and technological progress on the one hand with moral progress on the other: "Mankind has never been in this position before. Without having improved appreciably in virtue or enjoying wiser guidance, it has got into its hands for the first time the tools by which it can unfailingly accomplish its own extermination." The Founders shared

Churchill's view that our nature doesn't change or improve with time—with History.

Yet the perfectibility of human nature was an article of faith for the Progressives and key to their criticism of the Constitution. As History progressed and our nature evolved for the better, government "by men over men" became less dangerous and "auxiliary precautions" were no longer needed; the government could be trusted not to abuse its power. For example, the Progressive journalist Herbert Croly eagerly looked forward to a future where "the community will be united not by any specific formulation of the law, but by the sincerity and the extent of its devotion to a liberal and humane purpose." Things like separation of powers and the Bill of Rights merely interfere with the government's ability to act. That's why "gridlock" is a left-wing term for the separation of powers.

Progressives clothed this critique in the language of science. As both an academic and a politician, Wilson criticized the Constitution as "Newtonian," or unduly mechanistic. He believed that "the Constitution was founded on the law of gravitation. The government was to exist and move by virtue of the efficacy of 'checks and balances.' The trouble with the theory is that government is not a machine, but a living thing." Wilson dismissed this "Newtonian" theory as little more than "political witchcraft."

The Founders, bound by the historical horizon of their times, couldn't see Darwin coming over that horizon. But Wilson claimed that government, as a living thing, "falls, not under the theory of the universe, but under the theory of organic life. It is accountable to Darwin, not to Newton." He stressed that "living political constitutions must be Darwinian in structure and in practice." The system of checks and balances is deadly: "No living thing can have its organs offset against each other, as checks, and live." According to

Wilson, "all that progressives ask or desire is permission—in an era when 'development,' 'evolution,' is the scientific word—to interpret the Constitution according to the Darwinian principle."

It's revealing that Wilson said Progressives only wanted to "interpret" the Constitution: what they really meant is they wanted to distort its original meaning beyond recognition. Instead of amending the Constitution to alter the separation of powers or federalism, for instance, the Progressives grafted a new system on top of the Constitution. In his very first book, Wilson admitted that he wanted to replace the "defects" of the Constitution with "single, unstinted power." Few things could be more alien to our Founders' thought than "unstinted power," but that was the Progressives' vision for the modern administrative state.

Today, we're used to the alphabet soup of bureaucracies in Washington—IRS, EPA, SEC, and on and on the list could go to include nearly every letter in the alphabet. These agencies only date back to the Progressive era. One of the first was the Federal Trade Commission, which Wilson created early in his presidency. The FTC still has sweeping power to regulate "unfair methods of competition" and "unfair or deceptive acts or practices," vague generalities that the FTC gets to define itself. Most other administrative agencies follow this model.

Suffice it to say, these bureaucracies break with the Founders' constitutional design. The agencies write their own binding regulations, they enforce their own regulations, and they judge cases involving their own regulations. As Madison put it in *Federalist* 47, they combine the legislative, executive, and judicial powers all "in the same hands," which "may justly be pronounced the very definition of tyranny."

For the Progressives, however, these agencies represent the coming of Hegel's "rational State." Wilson acknowledged that public administration is a product of "German professors" and "is a foreign science, speaking very little of the language of English or American principle." Administrative agencies, according to Wilson, must have "unstinted power" given the complexity of modern society. "Administration cannot wait upon legislation," he wrote, "but must be given leave, or take it, to proceed without specific warrant in giving effect to the characteristic life of the State."

And these bureaucracies must be insulated from political accountability to fulfill their purposes. "Bureaucracy can exist," Wilson believed, "only where the whole service of the state is removed from the common political life of the people." The Progressives didn't fear government overreach or abuse because they imagined that these agencies would be run by what Hegel called the "universal class," a group of morally pure and scientifically expert civil servants. On the contrary, Wilson was thrilled by a growing bureaucracy: "Administration is everywhere putting its hands to new undertakings."

With all their talk of Darwin and government as a "living thing," the Progressives introduced the concept of the "living Constitution" into our politics. But as Justice Antonin Scalia observed, a "living Constitution" is worthless because it keeps changing—it's really "dead." Those of us who venerate the charter prefer an "enduring Constitution."

Unfortunately, the Progressives' new administrative state very much endures today, even though its performance is a far cry from their vision of a highly competent, efficient, public-spirited bureaucracy. Who thinks, for instance, that the Centers for Disease Control distinguished itself during the coronavirus pandemic? Not the American people: the number who say they don't trust the CDC tripled in the two years since the pandemic began. For that matter, who thinks Lois Lerner, the IRS bureaucrat who harassed Tea Party groups, represents a higher ethical class of selfless public servants? Or Peter Strzok and Lisa Page, the former FBI deep-staters who were pushed out for their role in the Russia collusion hoax? Such examples of bureaucratic incompetence, abuse, and crimes could fill a book.

Yet the entrenched bureaucracy keeps growing, albeit with new euphemisms. No one, not even Democrats, speaks favorably of "bureaucracy" anymore. Bureaucrats hate being called bureaucrats. Instead, they aspire to be a "czar"—a repulsive title unfit for republican government, yet oddly appropriate for the unconstrained power claimed by the administrative state. During the pandemic, progressives told us to "listen to the experts" and to "follow the science." What they meant is that the people and their elected representatives should cede power to unelected bureaucrats to mandate, dictate, and control their lives.

Indeed, Tony Fauci embodies the Progressives' vision of government today. Armed with credentials and a lifetime in government, he claimed that he "only cares about science." He bristles that his critics are "really criticizing science because I represent science." He dodged accountability for funding the Wuhan labs and misleads the public about it. He rebuked elected officials who don't follow his shifting, contradictory directives, as if his narrow expertise in infectious diseases entitled him to pronounce on childhood development, macroeconomics, or supply chains. No one elected him to do all this, yet progressives celebrated him, featured him on glossy magazine covers, and put up yard signs with his name.

These sentiments rest on the pillars of progressive thought: a deep faith in the progress of History, an idealistic belief in the perfectibility of human nature, and a rejection of the Declaration and the Constitution. And just as the Progressives reshaped our domestic institutions, so too did their thought reshape our foreign policy.

PROGRESSIVISM MEETS THE WORLD

As we've seen, the Founders formed our government on the basis of our moral equality and to protect our natural rights, while accounting for our fallen nature. They approached foreign policy with the same sober, clear-eyed views. By contrast, the Progressives, imagining themselves more enlightened by the march of History, pursued a utopian foreign policy, dedicated to unachievable abstractions and detached from America's national interest.

As with domestic politics, the Founders' thinking about foreign policy started with human nature. And if men are not angels at home, they may be worse in the anarchic world of international politics. In *Federalist* 6, Alexander Hamilton dismissed "utopian speculations" about permanent peace because "men are ambitious, vindictive, and rapacious." He had in mind the cruel kings and violent mobs from his own day and the annals of history, but these words could just as easily describe modern dictators like Vladimir Putin and Xi Jinping. Hamilton continued in *Federalist* 34, acknowledging that "the fiery and destructive passions of war reign in the human breast with much more powerful sway than the mild and beneficent sentiments of peace."

In a fallen and dangerous world, foreign policy must prioritize our safety if government is to protect our rights. The Declaration states that "Safety and Happiness" are twin goals of government. Foreign policy is emphatically the province of safety, the prerequisite for the enjoyment of our rights and the pursuit of happiness. John Jay observed in *Federalist* 3 that "among the many objects to which a wise and free people find it necessary to direct their attention, that of providing for their safety seems to be first." I witnessed this maxim firsthand as a soldier in Iraq and Afghanistan, where American policymakers foolishly pursued lofty goals such as economic development and women's rights without establishing a baseline of security. What the Army says to protect its soldiers in training is also true of foreign policy: safety first.

George Washington's Farewell Address sketched a foreign policy based on our safety and our interests. He believed that "our interest, guided by justice," should serve as our North Star. There was nothing wrong, in the Founders' view, with pursuing our national interest; otherwise, we would be slavishly dependent on other nations. But the pursuit of interest must be "guided by justice," understanding other nations pursue their own interests too. Washington therefore counseled "good faith and justice toward all Nations," sought to "cultivate peace and harmony with all," and proposed that a "great rule of conduct for us, in regard to foreign nations, is, in extending our commercial relations, to have with them as little political connection as possible." Such a policy, Washington contended, would "gain time" for our country to grow, our economy to expand, and our strength to gather until America had "command of its own fortunes."

The Founders, in other words, put America first. Who would if we didn't?

Not so with the Progressives, though. In 1915, at a naturalization ceremony, of all places, Wilson admonished the new citizens "not only always to think first of America, but always, also, to think first of humanity." What a rousing welcome! But "humanity first" is what you would expect from Progressives. As History advanced and human nature improved, they believed that nations could and should retire primitive concerns about safety and the selfish pursuit of national interests. Foreign policy could become selfless and altruistic. American power, they believed, should be deployed not to advance America's interests, but rather to improve the social, economic, and political conditions of other nations and the world at large.

The Progressives' approach to foreign policy is best seen in Wilson's response to World War I. When the war broke out in 1914, he committed to a policy of neutrality, not unlike Washington's policy during the French Revolution. But neutrality turned into passivity when the Germans announced a campaign of unrestricted submarine warfare to choke off supplies to the British home front. In May 1915, a German submarine torpedoed the British passenger ship *Lusitania*, killing nearly 1,200 people, including 128 American citizens. The nation was shocked and outraged, much as it would be after Pearl Harbor and 9/11. Yet Wilson reacted with a professor's detachment. He didn't declare war on Germany, or even demand negotiations and redress under threat of war to avenge the deaths. Instead, he sent sternly worded letters to the German government expressing his "concern, distress, and amazement."

At that naturalization ceremony, Wilson explained his timidity in what has become known as, amazingly, the "Too Proud to Fight" speech. Even more amazingly, this speech occurred just three days after the sinking of the *Lusitania*. He cautioned against the nation having "the narrowness and prejudice of a family," lamenting that "family gets centered on itself if it is not careful and is less interested in the neighbors than it is in its own members."

Stop for a moment to consider how astonishing that metaphor is. Who doesn't care more about one's own family than about the neighbors? The Founders certainly did. You surely do. And your neighbors do too! Now, we can and should be good neighbors, but our own family has to come first. To Wilson, though, that's just "narrowness and prejudice." We must care just as much, maybe more, about the neighbors. By extension, we must care as much or more about other nations as we care about America.

"There is such a thing as a man being too proud to fight," Wilson continued. "There is such a thing as a nation being so right that it does not need to convince others by force that it is right." America was "so right" in Wilson's view because he refused to elevate our interests over any other nation. By contrast, the Founders would've demanded redress in some fashion and might well have gone to war, as former president Teddy Roosevelt advocated. Yet Wilson hewed to neutrality for nearly two more years.

As late as January 1917, Wilson still hoped that American mediation could deliver "peace without victory" to Europe, but events soon forced him off the sidelines. First, Germany resumed its campaign of unrestricted submarine warfare, which immediately disrupted American shipping and led to shortages. Second, the Zimmermann Telegram from Germany's foreign minister to the Mexican government proposed a military alliance in return for which Germany would assist Mexico in reclaiming Texas, New Mexico, and Arizona. This was a shocking violation of the principles of the Monroe Doctrine and a direct threat to America's safety and territorial integrity.

The Founders would've considered these affronts to America's interest and honor more than enough to justify war against Germany, yet Wilson cast the war in purely selfless, idealistic terms divorced from our safety and interests. His War Message to Congress is perhaps the most remarkable statement of a wartime president in American history. "We have no selfish ends to serve," Wilson declared, as if protecting our borders, defending our commerce, and avenging dead Americans were unseemly motives. Wilson instead proclaimed that "our motive will not be revenge or the victorious assertion of the physical might of the nation, but only the vindication of right, of human right." Notice he didn't say anything about America's rights.

Wilson sold the war in bloodless, abstract terms. He could barely bring himself to name our enemies. Germany didn't so much wage war against the United States; instead it waged "a war against all nations" and "warfare against mankind." By the same token, Wilson imagined that America fought less against Germany and more against "autocracy" or, what was probably worse in his mind, "selfish and autocratic power." "Our object," Wilson insisted, was only "to vindicate the principles of peace and justice in the life of the world." And America would be just "a single champion" and "but one of the champions of the rights of mankind."

Wilson concluded his War Message with four abstractions America would fight for:

> for democracy, for the right of those who submit to authority to have a voice in their own governments, for the rights and liberties of small nations, for a universal dominion of right by such a concert of free peoples as shall bring peace and safety to all nations and make the world itself at last free.

Nothing wrong with these aspirations, to be sure, but none directly affected America's safety and vital interests. The families of the nearly 117,000 Americans killed in the war probably thought they died to protect America's "rights and liberties," not those of "small nations," and surely not to establish "a universal dominion of right." Nor did they likely imagine that Wilson would try to establish the League of Nations, "a concert of free peoples" designed to bring "safety to all nations." They probably would've settled for protecting America's safety. Indeed, most would probably join Hamilton from *Federalist* 6 in rejecting—as the Senate did reject—the League of Nations as "utopian speculations" from "visionary or designing men who stand ready to advocate the paradox of perpetual peace." I'll discuss the downfall of the League of Nations at greater length in Chapter Three.

In the end, the absence of a single word illustrates the difference between the foreign policy of the Founders and the Progressives. "The world must be made safe for democracy," Wilson famously declared in his War Message. The Founders would've countered that the world must be made safe for *America's* democracy. That task alone is hard enough, without the Progressives' grand utopian schemes.

THE PROGRESSIVES BROKE decisively with the moral and political foundation of our republic. They also changed our long-standing approach to foreign policy away from our national interests and toward the selfless pursuit of abstract ideals, a view that still holds great sway.

This isn't to say liberals won't employ American power—far from it. They're more than happy to use military force, as long as it's on behalf of foreigners or abstract ideas. During the early, bloody phases of the Balkan Wars in the 1990s, United Nations ambassador Madeleine Albright wanted to launch air strikes against the Serbs and even deploy American troops as UN peacekeepers to protect civilians in the former Yugoslavia. General Colin Powell opposed her and she infamously countered, "What's the point of having this superb military that you're always talking about if we can't use it?" Just don't ask liberals to use the military to protect America's interests.

What's worse, this kind of liberal internationalism doesn't merely ignore our interests; it usually undermines them. For example, Barack Obama justified his disastrous intervention in Libya by alluding to a United Nations–inspired academic theory called "R2P"—the supposed "responsibility to protect" other peoples from war and oppression. America, of course, had no such responsibility, while the chaos unleashed in Libya has threatened us for more than a decade (as I'll explain in Chapter Six).

Yet the Progressives didn't just expand the size and power of government and reorient our foreign policy. By rejecting the founding principles, they also laid the groundwork for a new generation of leftist radicals who would curse our nation as a force for evil in the world and actively side with our enemies—the Blame America First Democrats.

CHAPTER 2

The Blame America First Democrats

I T WAS A tale of two conventions in 1984.

The Democratic Party held its convention in San Francisco at the Moscone Convention Center. It might as well have been Moscow.

Their convention reeked of despair. The Democrats' far-left nominee, former vice president Walter Mondale, trailed President Ronald Reagan by fourteen points. Carter-era "stagflation" was over; the Reagan economy was booming. Even young people were abandoning Mondale for Reagan—although a *New York Times* headline celebrated that an "Ivy League Poll Gives Mondale a Clear Lead." Some things never change.

Desperate to shake up the race, Mondale picked the relatively unknown Representative Geraldine Ferraro as his running mate. As usual, the Democrats seemed more interested in the boxes she checked than her readiness for the job. "She's a woman, she's ethnic, she's Catholic," one Mondale adviser told reporters. "We have broken the barrier."

But the Democrats' problem wasn't only their messengers—it was their message. The Democratic agenda was tax-and-spend socialism at home and cut and run from communists abroad.

Reagan had lowered taxes upon taking office; Mondale vowed to raise them, in one of the strangest boasts ever heard at a political convention. "Mr. Reagan will raise taxes, and so will I," he said in his acceptance speech. "He won't tell you. I just did."

The Democrats' foreign-policy message was that Reagan had brought the world to the brink of nuclear war by standing strong against communism. The party platform read like an issue of the Soviet propaganda outlet *Pravda*, denouncing Reagan's "easy and abusive anti-Soviet rhetoric" and "inflammatory nuclear rhetoric and policies." The Democrats pledged to reach arms-control agreements with Soviet Russia, end support for anti-communist forces overseas, and "reassess" defense spending—liberal code for cutting to the bone.

One signature policy was a "nuclear freeze," or a promise by the United States to stop making new nuclear weapons as long as Russia did the same. Yet Russia had thousands more nuclear warheads and launchers than we did, so a "nuclear freeze" would freeze in place the Soviet advantage. Little wonder that Soviet intelligence funneled hundreds of millions of dollars to anti-nuclear activists in the West, which liberals denied then, just as they deny today that Russian intelligence funds many "green" activists to undermine our oil-and-gas industry.

A month later, the Republican convention in Dallas couldn't have been more different than the sad spectacle in San Francisco. Dallas was booming—a great symbol of Reagan's patriotic and dynamic policies. When a small band of communists, anarchists, and other Democrats burned an American flag outside the convention, Dallas police promptly arrested the flag burner. President Reagan could barely get through his speech for all the spontaneous chants of "USA! USA! USA!"

But his speech wasn't the most memorable. That honor went to another former Democrat, Jeane Kirkpatrick, the ambassador to the United Nations. Kirkpatrick was a fierce anti-communist and Cold

Warrior. She noted that the "San Francisco Democrats" sounded very different from past Democrats, who "were not afraid to be resolute nor ashamed to speak of America as a great nation." Whether it was communist revolutionaries taking over Latin America, Muslim terrorists blowing up our Marine barracks in the Middle East, or Soviet diplomats negotiating in bad faith, the Democrats cowered before our enemies. "They always blame America first," Kirkpatrick hammered over and over.

Kirkpatrick electrified the crowd simply by telling the truth about the anti-American turn that the Democrats had taken. Thankfully, as she noted in her speech, "the American people know better."

She was right. Reagan won in a historic landslide. The American people rejected the "Blame America First Democrats."

IN THE PREVIOUS chapter, we learned how Progressives rejected our founding principles to push for utopian internationalism. Now, let's see how the left developed a virulent strain of anti-American isolationism. The Democrats became the Blame America First party in the Vietnam era and remain so today. The Progressives, for all their hopeful talk about History with a capital *H* and "the rational state," set the stage for this dark turn. For three-quarters of a century, the progressive left weakened America by rejecting our founding principles. Without a timeless moral standard to guide them in tough times—as Lincoln had used the Declaration throughout the Civil War—the Democrats were unmoored when the far left raged during Vietnam. In fact, they mostly followed the radicals over the cliff.

The radicals raged about the Vietnam War, but their real target was America. The radicals went beyond contending that the war was unwise or poorly waged; they argued that America itself was corrupt and evil. They dodged the draft, trashed college campuses in violent riots, and bombed government buildings to prove their point. For the first time since the Civil War, sizable numbers of Democrats rooted against our country in a time of war.

Vietnam was a decisive turning point because the Democrats' Blame America First attitude lasted long after the final helicopter took off from our embassy in Saigon. For the rest of the Cold War, prominent Democrats were conspiratorially skeptical of American power and shamefully soft toward our communist adversaries. From the halls of Congress to the liberal media, they did their best to defund and disarm the United States, while promoting the lie that America, not communism, was spreading misery around the world.

The Blame America First Democrats are still alive and well, so we need to examine their mindset to understand why Democrats act as they do today. While the Progressives stood for a liberal *internationalism* that would use American power only to help other countries or to promote abstract ideals, the Blame America First Democrats stood for liberal *isolationism*, which opposes the use of American power at all. Both tendencies are at work today in the Democratic Party. Both are dangerous.

Vietnam: The Democrats Turn on Their Country

Democrats often claim that the Vietnam War shattered Americans' faith in their country, but they're projecting. Vietnam was the moment when liberals turned their backs on America.

Most Americans viewed Vietnam as they had past wars. Between 1955 and 1974, millions of young men went to war in Vietnam, just as their fathers and grandfathers had done from the Revolutionary War to Korea. Two-thirds were volunteers like my dad, who enlisted in 1968, long after the liberal media had turned against the war. Like

many others, he volunteered to fight despite having a valid draft deferment. Within a year, he was in the jungle walking "point," the most
dangerous position in an infantry formation. He never questioned his
duty, nor regretted his service to our country. Ronald Reagan spoke
to millions of patriotic veterans like my dad in 1980 when he called
the Vietnam War "a noble cause." That view may be unfashionable on
the left, but it's still true.

Americans on the "home front" also supported our troops and
rooted for victory. Into Richard Nixon's first year in office, opinion
polling showed that more Americans thought we should escalate the
conflict to win rather than withdraw. One American summed up this
traditional view to Gallup in 1966: "We need to have a showdown,
so that we can bring all our boys home. If we have to fight at all we
might as well win and win it big." Liberals may cringe and roll their
eyes at that sentiment, but it expressed the American people's long-
held attitude about war and peace: go big or don't fight at all.

I'll have more to say in Chapter Five about how Democratic leaders
badly mismanaged the Vietnam War through timidity and "expert"
tinkering in classic progressive fashion. For now, it's worth taking a
closer look at the motley crew of left-wing activists, Hollywood celebrities, journalists, and anti-war Democrats who undermined the war
effort in the streets and in the halls of Congress. These radicals, the
so-called New Left, warrant our attention because they completed the
Progressives' rejection of America. Whereas Progressives like Wilson
rejected the use of American power to defend our interests, the New
Left rejected America itself.

Bringing the War Home

The New Left launched a full revolt against America. The media worked
hard—and still does—to portray the anti-war demonstrators of the

'60s and '70s as idealistic youth—patriotic, even. But they weren't. These radicals railed against "The System," which included classic left-wing villains like capitalism, the family, and the military, plus things that liberals had once supported, like organized labor. As one radical put it, "we're against everything that's 'good and decent' in honky America."

Never mind that "The System" had raised these ingrates in unprecedented prosperity and safety. Much like the left today, they charged that America was spiritually stifling, racist, and oppressive, offering little besides soulless corporate jobs, Jim Crow, and the atom bomb. The New Left believed that America was little better than the fascist regimes their fathers had defeated two decades before. Many contemptuously invoked the German spelling, *Amerika*, to highlight the comparison.

Vietnam was the perfect opportunity for the New Left to act on its hatred of America. These cowards refused to fight, of course, but they did more than that. They condemned their brave fellow Americans who would fight, sided with the enemy, and unleashed violence across our country.

Many pampered radicals avoided the war by dodging the draft. While it's nothing new in wartime for cowards to evade service, the scale at which it occurred during Vietnam was unprecedented. By some estimates, 570,000 young men dodged the draft by abusing the deferment system, starving themselves to fail physical examinations, burning their draft cards, and even fleeing the country.

Students at elite colleges were especially eager to evade the draft and adept at it. In 1969, the student-body presidents of 253 universities wrote a letter to the White House saying they would refuse to show up if drafted. James Fallows's experience is typical. Now a renowned writer at *The Atlantic*, back then he was a Harvard senior and Rhodes scholar. In an infamous essay, he explained how he and other Harvard students avoided the draft so they wouldn't be "complicit in the immoral war effort." Getting a "physical deferment," was akin, he wrote, to "securing my salvation." They scoured the Army's medical regulations with liberal med-school students and attended seminars with "draft counselors" in a "desperate search for disqualifying conditions." On examination day, they rode a bus to the draft station wearing "red armbands" and chanting for Ho Chi Minh. Almost all the students from Harvard and MIT succeeded that day, if cowardice and betrayal is one's definition of success.

But other buses showed up that day, too, full of "the white proles from Boston." Fallows observed that "it had clearly never occurred to them that there might be a way around the draft." He stared at them "like so many cattle off to slaughter." Another word for them might be, simply, patriots—young Americans who perhaps didn't look forward to or even support the war, but who did their duty when their country called. Published in late 1975, the essay didn't stop Fallows from becoming President Jimmy Carter's chief speechwriter barely a year later.

At least Fallows felt "a sense of shame," which is more than can be said for the anti-war radicals who didn't just dodge the draft, but then smeared our troops as ruthless killers and war criminals. Front groups like Vietnam Veterans Against the War paraded real and fake veterans before the cameras to expose the evil deeds they had supposedly committed or witnessed. One veteran was a young Navy officer named John Kerry. In 1971, Kerry testified to Congress that American war crimes were "not isolated incidents" but rather happened every day "with the full awareness of officers at all levels of command." America, he asserted, had created "a monster in the form of millions of men who have been taught to deal and to trade in violence, and who are given the chance to die for the biggest nothing in history."

After this shameful testimony, Kerry held a staged media event where he and other veterans threw their medals over a fence of the Capitol.

John Kerry on his way to throw away someone else's Vietnam War medals.
George Butler/Contact Press Images.

Just one problem: it was all a lie. The Senate investigated these veterans' accusations. Many alleged witnesses refused to cooperate or gave testimony so vague as to be unprovable. Worse, some were fake veterans who had stolen the identities of real heroes. Others had outright lied; one soldier admitted to being coached by a member of the Nation of Islam, Louis Farrakhan's anti-American hate group. Kerry and his fellow travelers hadn't just criticized rare and isolated crimes like the My Lai massacre, probably because our military-justice system handled these tragic cases. Instead, they had asserted a campaign of organized and systematic war crimes. This was a lie and another massive smear against our troops.

Even the medal-throwing ceremony was a fraud: the future Democratic nominee for president threw away someone else's medals! When Kerry first ran for office, he rediscovered his pride in a military that he had accused of savagery, and his medals mysteriously reappeared. John Kerry was—and remains—as phony as his false accusations of war crimes.

The New Left specialized in smearing our troops, but the worst radicals went even further and sided with the enemy.

Hundreds of airhead celebrities and Marxist intellectuals, from Jane Fonda to Noam Chomsky, made pilgrimages to Hanoi, the enemy capital. Fonda infamously took glamour shots with an antiaircraft gun used to shoot American pilots out of the sky. Not to be left out, Kerry traveled to Paris twice to meet with North Vietnamese and Viet Cong officials. One of the visits seems to have occurred during Kerry's honeymoon with his first wife. I guess meeting with communists is what passes for a romantic getaway for some liberals.

Still others took their hatred of America to its logical conclusion by literally "bringing the war home." The '60s and '70s saw a plague of riots and domestic bombings. Student radicals turned college campuses into roiling cauldrons of selfish rage and protest. Drugged-out rioters brawled with National Guardsmen outside the Pentagon and the Democratic National Convention in Chicago, waving the North Vietnamese flag and taunting law enforcement with obscene chants.

At the furthest extreme, left-wing terrorist groups like the Weather Underground, which expressly advocated for violent overthrow of the government, carried out a series of bombings against the U.S. Capitol, Pentagon, police stations, and other government buildings. Weathermen hated law enforcement so much that they destroyed a police-memorial statue in Chicago on three separate occasions, much like the radical who during the Black Lives Matter riots of 2020 defaced the Little Rock Police Department Fallen Officer Memorial by spray-painting "Defund the Police" over the names of fallen officers.

Some of these left-wing terrorists burned fast and bright. Three Weathermen blew themselves up in Greenwich Village making a bomb intended for Army officers and their wives at Fort Dix. Others lived long enough to participate in the Black Liberation Army's infamous 1981 robbery of a Brinks armed car, which killed two heroic police officers and a security guard. Two of these terrorists had a kid, Chesa Boudin, who went on to a brief career in left-wing politics, as we'll see shortly.

The New Left unleashed a torrent of violence and lies out of their hatred for America. This was an actual left-wing insurrection against America, but you won't hear the media use that term, because they egged on the chaos back then, just like they do today.

The War in the Media

Though the media wasn't openly flying the North Vietnamese flag or bombing the Capitol, it played a big role in undermining the American war effort.

At first, major newspapers ran interference for the Kennedy and Johnson administrations, portraying their timidity and bumbling ineptitude as a well-intentioned progressive crusade, but the media turned early against the war. While most Americans still wanted victory, most journalists abandoned the fight. Some even questioned whether Vietnam wouldn't be better off under communist rule. As Arthur "Punch" Sulzberger, the publisher of the *New York Times*, wrote privately in 1966, "I am not sure that what we offer the Vietnamese peasant or what their own leaders offer them is any better than what the Communists offer." The fight had gone out of the press completely.

Soon, the media was portraying even clear victories as catastrophic defeats to prove the war couldn't be won. In 1968, CBS News anchor Walter Cronkite infamously declared North Vietnam's massive Tet Offensive a "draw" that proved the war would end in "stalemate." In fact, we had repulsed the enemy from its key objectives while suffering a tiny fraction of its casualties. But thanks to Cronkite's influence and the news monopoly held by the liberal media, his broadcast misrepresented an American triumph as a demoralizing defeat. Public opinion began to move slowly toward withdrawal instead of escalation and victory.

Like their friends in the New Left, the media eagerly publicized the American military's rare mistakes or abuses while ignoring the commonplace atrocities of the Viet Cong. The media also breathlessly reported American crimes that turned out to be fake.

Not content to lie from home, the *New York Times* even deployed the anti-war leftist Harrison Salisbury in 1966 to lie from behind enemy lines. Salisbury lobbied Hanoi for a visa, compiling letters of recommendation from American communists and Soviet officials. The North Vietnamese preferred openly communist correspondents, but they let in Salisbury. He published a series of reports claiming that our bombing was both so ineffectual that it wasn't harming the North Vietnamese war effort, yet so heavy it was wantonly massacring the North Vietnamese people. It was later revealed that Salisbury stole many of the "damning" details of his reports from a communist propaganda pamphlet.

Patriotic war correspondents of bygone eras such as Ernie Pyle in World War II were probably rolling over in their graves. Then again, the *New York Times* had published Walter Duranty's lies from Moscow in defense of Stalin throughout the 1920s and 1930s and welcomed his Pulitzer Prize in 1932. The *Times* can always be counted on to excuse left-wing radicalism.

Which is exactly what it did again in 1971 by publishing the infamous Pentagon Papers. It began when Daniel Ellsberg, a Pentagon contractor who moonlighted as a radical anti-war activist, stole a top-secret government study on the history of America's involvement in Vietnam and gave it to the *Times*. No paper had published state secrets of this kind before, and with good reason. The paper's longtime lawyer, an Army veteran named Louis Loeb, argued passionately that publishing the report would violate journalistic ethics, not to mention the Espionage Act. The *Times* published it anyway—and fired Loeb. Liberal politics came first, America last.

The Pentagon Papers stories caused a sensation, although they contained little news. The *Times*'s coverage highlighted apparent differences between what the study said secretly and what the government said publicly. The media spun those differences as a deliberate conspiracy, to lie to the country and lead it into war, rather than a bureaucratic miscommunication or disagreement. The stories had the intended effect of harming the war effort. More important, the Pentagon Papers taught the media that they could publish state secrets with impunity.

The *Times* is still at it today, as I learned during my military service. In December 2005, the first news I read after six weeks in the woods at Ranger School was the paper's exposure of a highly classified terrorist-surveillance program, which tracked where terrorists got the money to build bombs and kill American soldiers. The *Times* did it again in June 2006, by which time I was a platoon leader in Iraq. I fired off a letter in response, arguing that the disclosure endangered the lives of our troops and federal law. "By the time we return home," I concluded, "maybe you will be in your rightful place: not at the Pulitzer announcements, but behind bars." The *Times* didn't run the letter, of course, but the conservative news site *Power Line* did. Left-wingers exploded online, some even denying I was a real person. Fortunately, General Pete Schoomaker, the Army chief of staff and legendary Delta Force commander, stood up for me: he forwarded my letter widely within the Army and encouraged commanders to reinforce the need for operational security. But the *Times* can't be bothered with such concerns—it will put our troops' lives in danger for the sake of left-wing advocacy "journalism."

"Begging Is Better Than Bombing"

Democratic politicians either planted or believed the media's spin about Vietnam. By 1968, nearly all of them had thrown in the towel.

Even Johnson, who had staked his legacy on the war, decided that quitting was the only option when he watched Cronkite's misleading broadcast about the Tet Offensive. "If I've lost Cronkite, I've lost Middle America," he reportedly said. In fact, as we've seen, Middle America still wanted victory. What Johnson had really lost was his party. And once Johnson departed in defeat, the radicals seized control.

Consider Senator George McGovern of South Dakota. Though a highly decorated World War II pilot, he spent his political career blaming America first, criticizing our "fixation" on communism, and voting to slash defense spending. McGovern opposed the war from the start, seeking to defund it and withdraw troops recklessly. In 1970, when his defunding amendment finally got a vote, he condemned other senators in hysterical terms. "This chamber reeks of blood," he shrieked. "Every Senator here is partly responsible for that human wreckage at Walter Reed and Bethesda Naval and all across our land." Though he had attacked his colleagues and insulted our veterans as "human wreckage," in a sign of the times thirty-nine senators still voted for his amendment.

Naturally, the Democrats then made McGovern their nominee for president. McGovern's 1972 campaign put the New Left on the ballot. Left-wing terrorists knew an ally when they saw one: despite the Weather Underground's previous rejection of democratic politics, its members worked secretly to elect McGovern. The Nixon campaign dubbed McGovern the candidate of "Acid, Amnesty, and Abortion," a label that stuck because it was true.

But most of all, McGovern ran against the Vietnam War. Nixon's strategy for "peace with honor" through gradual withdrawal wasn't good enough for the Democrats. McGovern's motto was "Come Home, America." The party platform called for "an immediate and complete withdrawal of all U.S. forces in Indo-China"—a position even more radical than McGovern's "human wreckage" amendment. When a fellow Democrat asked McGovern how he planned to bring home American prisoners of war if military force was off the table, McGovern's response was stunning: "Begging is better than bombing."

That's Democratic foreign policy in a nutshell.

The 1972 election was a clash between patriots who had sacrificed for the war and the liberals who had sabotaged it. As Nixon put it, "the country will find out whether what the media has been standing for during these last five years really represents the majority thinking." It didn't, to say the least; the American people rejected McGovern in one of the biggest landslides ever.

But the Blame America First Democrats marched forward with McGovern's surrender plans. Over the next three years, Democrats in Congress worked tirelessly to accelerate the withdrawals and weaken our allies. Even after our troops had left Vietnam, the Democrats banned our military from providing air support and arms to our allies in South Vietnam, Laos, and Cambodia, who were still fighting communist adversaries. As Chris Dodd, then a congressman and later a senator from Connecticut, said, "The greatest gift our country can give to the Cambodian people is not guns but peace. And the best way to accomplish that goal is by ending military aid now." Peace without guns—a Democratic fantasy then as today, and a dangerous gift to our enemies with guns.

Joe Biden, then a voluble freshman senator, was especially eager to wash America's hands of Southeast Asia. As North Vietnamese tanks rumbled toward Saigon in 1975, Biden voted multiple times to deny additional military and humanitarian aid to the South Vietnamese. In a rich irony, Biden even criticized President Gerald Ford for evacuating Americans too slowly—yet he opposed eleventh-hour attempts to stall the North Vietnamese advance and accelerate the evacuation.

Within days, Saigon fell to the communists, forcing Americans to flee our embassy by helicopter. It was the most humiliating moment for America until Biden's retreat from Afghanistan half a century later.

America's headlong retreat had terrible consequences for the region. Hundreds of thousands of South Vietnamese disappeared into communist "reeducation camps." Even more of them desperately fled the country by boat. Next door, the Khmer Rouge, or "Red Cambodians," seized power. In just a few years, Pol Pot's genocidal regime killed two million people out of a population of only seven million.

After years of undermining the war effort and calling for a hasty retreat, the Democrats got what they wanted. The result was disaster.

CODDLING THE COMMUNISTS

As America retreated from Vietnam, our enemies advanced. Communism spread like wildfire across the Third World. In Africa, Soviet arms and Cuban "advisers" helped Marxists exploit the bloody chaos that followed decolonization. In Latin America, the same combination of arms and advisers helped Marxist guerillas in their wars against anti-communist governments. In the Middle East, Soviet Russia invaded Afghanistan.

Moscow couldn't believe its luck. The map was turning communist red, with hardly any resistance from the Free World. As Yuri Andropov, who was then the KGB chief, reportedly said, "now all we have to do is to keep the Vietnam-era anti-Americanism alive."

He didn't have to worry. The Blame America First Democrats did most of the work, first through Jimmy Carter's disastrous policies, and then through hysterical opposition to Ronald Reagan's winning strategy. Until the Soviet Union collapsed, liberals appeased the communists and blamed America at nearly every turn.

Getting Over "Inordinate Fear"

Jimmy Carter hardly came across as a New Left radical, which is partly why he was the only Democrat to win the White House over a span of six elections in the last half of the Cold War. But his failed administration shows what happens when our government is staffed with liberals motivated by the Blame America First impulse.

Take his very first act in office. Claiming he wanted to "heal our country after the Vietnam War," Carter issued a blanket amnesty for Vietnam draft dodgers, implying that these cowards and radicals were all moral heroes on par with the Americans who answered their country's call to duty, whatever they thought of the war. Yet the New Left complained he didn't go far enough! Soon after, Carter created a process to upgrade the undesirable discharges of deserters, trouble-makers, and other shirkers, allowing them to improve their military-discharge status and avoid consequences for their actions.

Of course, veterans' groups reacted with outrage, justifiably so. Imagine how the amnesty and upgrades felt to men like my dad, who had done their duty, risked their lives, and served honorably. Now the Democratic Party treated them little different from draft dodgers and deserters. How could we blame these young men, Democrats suggested, when the blame really lay with America? Needless to say, the Soviet Union agreed. *Pravda* hailed Carter's amnesty as an American admission of guilt for the war.

This kind of moral equivalence, relentless negativity, and guilty conscience about Vietnam hobbled Carter's administration from the start. In his first major foreign-policy speech, he claimed that Vietnam had "produced a profound moral crisis" and he lamented our "inordinate fear of communism." Most Americans, observing the killing fields and the boat people, probably thought fear of communism was pretty reasonable, but Carter argued otherwise. Indeed, in his infamous malaise speech, in the midst of runaway inflation and global chaos, Carter scolded the nation for a "crisis of confidence" and "a crisis of the spirit." He laid the blame not on his policies, but on the American people.

Carter's cabinet officials reflected his attitude. UN Ambassador Andrew Young denounced American foreign policy as an "apparatus of repression" and "imperialism, neo-colonialism, capitalism, and what have you." On another occasion, he said America was part of a "vast network of oppression" that ground down "oppressed peoples everywhere."

But curiously, Young lost his righteous anger when talking about our enemies. The Soviets persecuted dissidents, he conceded, but "now prisons, too, there are hundreds, perhaps even thousands of people whom I would call political prisoners." Cuban troops aided Marxist governments and revolutionaries across Africa and Latin America, but Young praised their "stabilizing" presence. As reelection approached, Young became too embarrassing even for Carter, who asked Young to resign after lying about unauthorized meetings with the Palestinian Liberation Organization.

Bad as this rhetoric was, though, Carter's policies were worse. He consistently abandoned our allies, courted our enemies, and weakened our defenses. As we'll see in Chapter Three, Carter surrendered the Panama Canal for no good reason beyond, in his mind, clearing America's conscience. In Iran, he stood by while Islamic theocrats deposed the pro-American monarch, raided our embassy, and took fifty-two Americans hostage for more than a year. At the negotiating table, Carter struck arms-control deals that preserved the Soviet edge in nuclear weaponry. During the energy crisis, he pleaded with Americans to turn down their thermostats, wear more sweaters, drive smaller cars, and live smaller lives.

And then there was Nicaragua, where Carter actively helped Marxist revolutionaries take over a country, perhaps the best example of the Blame America First mindset.

Carter blamed America for most of Latin America's problems. He criticized past presidents for working with pro-American strongmen while crushing left-wing insurgencies at the first hint of Soviet involvement. Of course, this strategy was consistent with our Founders' approach. They would've never tolerated meddling with our New World allies by our chief European enemy. But Carter thought that we should stop worrying so much about communism and take a "more detached attitude toward world revolutionary processes," as his national-security adviser put it. Nicaragua was the awful test case for the Democrats' new "detached" foreign policy.

Since 1935, the country had been ruled by the Somozas, a corrupt but shrewd family engaged in on-again, off-again warfare with its opponents, including the Cuban-backed Marxist guerillas known as the Sandinistas. The Somozas were no one's idea of good liberal democrats, but they fought communists such as the Sandinistas who struggled to recruit for years because few of the country's small farmers had any interest in revolution. By Latin American standards, Nicaragua was stable and quiet.

As important, Nicaragua was a strong ally of the United States. During World War II, Nicaragua seized Axis property. During the Cold War, it fought the spread of communism in Latin America. As President Franklin Roosevelt reportedly said of one of the Somoza clan, "he's a sonofabitch, but he's ours."

In 1978, when the Sandinistas launched another round of guerrilla warfare, Carter decided it was the perfect time to betray our decades-long ally. He soon cut off military aid, imposed sanctions, isolated the government diplomatically, and legitimized the Marxist guerrillas by calling for them to be included in a unity government. For once, the Carter team proved ruthlessly effective—in undermining a loyal American ally. As Jeane Kirkpatrick wrote, "for the second time in a decade an American ally ran out of gas and ammunition while confronting an opponent well-armed by the Soviet bloc."

For Carter's team, this was all part of the naive plan. They seemed to think that democracy would magically flower if America threw the Somoza government overboard. What happened instead was the fall of a flawed but pro-American government and the rise of a much worse and virulently anti-American dictatorship. Shortly after the Sandinistas seized the capital of Managua, they welcomed a Cuban delegation and pledged to help Cuba resist "Yankee imperialism." Amazingly, Carter responded to this catastrophe by resuming economic aid to Nicaragua to curry favor with the new Marxist regime.

Fidel Castro rejoiced at this turn of events. A communist government had just seized power in Grenada months earlier; Nicaragua was an even bigger prize. "Now there are three of us," he crowed. He had Jimmy Carter's guilty conscience to thank for his new friends.

Excusing the "Evil Empire"

Jimmy Carter blamed the American people for our nation's problems; Ronald Reagan blamed Jimmy Carter. And, as you might expect, Reagan won a landslide victory in 1980. Americans want and deserve a president who has confidence in them and in our country, not a president who blames them for a "crisis of confidence." The election proved yet again that weakness and self-loathing aren't attractive qualities to the American people. Instead of lectures and reversals, they demonstrated their preference for Reagan's straightforward strategy toward dangerous enemies: "We win, they lose."

Reagan based his foreign policy on the conviction that America could and—this is key—*should* prevail over our enemies. Americans agreed, and they saw an immediate return on their decision. On Reagan's first day in office, Iran released the hostages it had held for the final 444 days of Carter's presidency.

But instead of learning from yet another humiliating defeat, the Blame America First Democrats doubled down on radicalism and revenge. They spent the rest of the Cold War warning that American strength and confidence would lead to nuclear war, or at least a second Vietnam (as they wrongly viewed that war).

In 1983, Reagan stunned his critics by calling Soviet Russia an "evil empire" and urging against the temptation "to label both sides equally at fault." The Cold War, according to Reagan, was a "struggle between right and wrong and good and evil." On one side, the Soviets murdered and imprisoned millions of their enemies, starved millions more, and exported violent revolution and tyranny around the globe in the name of a heartless, godless ideology. On the other, we stood and fought for peace, freedom, and the dignity of every soul.

Reagan's critics didn't quite see it this way. The Democratic Speaker of the House, Tip O'Neill, accused Reagan of "Red-baiting." The *Washington Post* quoted a "distinguished historian" who called Reagan's speech "the worst presidential speech in American history." Anthony Lewis, a columnist at the *New York Times*, sniffed that the speech was "primitive," "offensive," "terribly dangerous," and even "not funny." Official Soviet news agencies agreed, denouncing Reagan's "bellicose, lunatic anti-Communism." Birds of a feather flock together, I suppose.

Joe Biden, a reliable weathervane of liberal opinion, denied we were in a Cold War at all. "We're not in a Cold War," Biden asserted, "but we're a whole heck of a lot closer than we were two years ago" due to Reagan's "escalation of rhetoric." Nearly forty years later, Biden says the same thing about Communist China. He hasn't learned a basic lesson: you can't wish away a war if your enemy is determined to fight. Your only choice is to win or lose.

As with Vietnam, some liberals opposed Reagan's agenda so ferociously that they supported our enemies. Take Bernie Sanders, who was to the 1980s what Jane Fonda was to the 1970s.

Most Americans today know Sanders as an angry old man who wants to bring socialism to America; back then, he was an angry young man who wanted to bring socialism to America. As the mayor of ultra-liberal Burlington, Vermont, he routinely denounced America and praised our communist enemies. Sanders was so cozy with the communists he even honeymooned in Soviet Russia. Maybe he and John Kerry used the same travel agent.

Sanders especially despised Reagan's policy toward Nicaragua. Reagan had immediately reversed Carter's policy, cutting off the Sandinista regime and directing covert aid to the anti-communist guerrillas known as the Contras. Many of the Contras were poor farmers who had been pushed off their land by the Sandinistas, but the left invariably portrayed them as CIA puppets and brutal killers. Congressional Democrats opposed Reagan's policy, but Sanders outdid them. In 1985, he went to Nicaragua to meet Daniel Ortega, the country's communist dictator. During the trip, he attacked American reporters, calling them "worms" for not telling "the truth" about Ortega. He even attended a massive Sandinista rally where the crowd chanted "here, there, everywhere, the Yankee will die."

Sanders's radical communist sympathies haven't hurt his political career on the left—far from it. Decades later, Nicaragua is still run by Ortega and Sanders is a senator who twice nearly became the Democrats' nominee for president. He hasn't apologized for his past support of communist regimes. On the contrary, his main foreign-policy priority these days is stopping a "New Cold War" with China. He doesn't understand—along with Biden—that China is already waging a cold war against us.

THE NEW SAN FRANCISCO DEMOCRATS

Jeane Kirkpatrick's 1984 convention speech remains as relevant today as it was back then. Kirkpatrick criticized Jimmy Carter and Walter Mondale, but she could've just as easily been describing Joe Biden and Kamala Harris today. The Democrats haven't changed: "they always blame America first."

In a perfect turn of fate, an actual San Francisco Democrat, Nancy Pelosi, has sat at the head of the party for twenty years. San Francisco itself has declined into shameful squalor thanks to decades of Democratic misrule.

Like the New Left of the Vietnam era, radicals today condemn America as rotten to its core. It's hardly surprising since many of the students who dodged the draft, wore red armbands, and occupied college campuses back then now hold endowed chairs at those very colleges.

In some cases, the Democrats are *literally* the heirs of the New Left. Chesa Boudin, the former Democratic district attorney of (naturally) San Francisco was raised by not one but *two* pairs of left-wing terrorist parents. His biological parents are the Weather Underground terrorists responsible for the 1981 Brinks armored car robbery, during which two police officers were killed. When his parents went to prison, fellow Weathermen, Bill Ayers and Bernardine Dohrn, adopted Boudin. (Those names may sound familiar; Ayers and Dohrn were early fundraisers and supporters of a young Chicago politician named Barack Obama.)

Normally, I wouldn't criticize someone for their parents, not even a red-diaper baby, since we don't get to choose our parents. But Boudin carried on the family legacy by working for the former Venezuelan dictator Hugo Chávez and later unleashing dangerous criminals onto San Francisco's streets. In one infamous case, Boudin cut a plea deal with a career criminal named Troy McAlister, even though he was eligible for a life sentence based on prior convictions for carjacking and robbery. McAlister was arrested multiple times while on parole, but Boudin still refused to bring new charges. Finally, McAlister held up yet another store, stole yet another car, and ran over and killed two women. Boudin shrugged that "hindsight is 20/20," a cold comfort to the victims' families. Ultimately, crime got so bad on his watch that the voters recalled him in the summer of 2022. This former darling of the party elite proved too liberal even for literal San Francisco Democrats!

But even Democrats who aren't descended from Weathermen have embraced their hateful critique of our country. It's now routine for Democrats, from Joe Biden down, to slander our country as "systemically racist." Vice President Kamala Harris said that the United States is only "pretending" to value equality under the law, and that "some form of reparations" is necessary to atone for our country's "dark history." Ilhan Omar, a member of the socialist "Squad" of Democratic House members, accused the United States of committing "unspeakable atrocities" in the Middle East on a par with Hamas, a terrorist group that uses children as human shields.

Because of their doubts about America, the Democrats engage in the same moral equivalence with the evil empire of our day, Communist China, as they did with Soviet Russia. When Biden first addressed the United Nations early in his presidency, he offered only the faintest rebuke of China's crimes and couldn't even bring himself to single out China by name. John Kerry, always quick to side with a communist regime against America, has refused to criticize China's human-rights abuses lest it imperil his climate-change negotiations with the Chinese government.

And just like the Soviets before them, our enemies use the Democrats' anti-American rhetoric against us. In 2021, Chinese Communist Party officials launched into a fifteen-minute diatribe during a diplomatic summit about America's "suppression" of foreign countries and "deep-seated" human rights problems, citing BLM as an example. Instead of striking back or walking out, Secretary of State Antony Blinken immediately went on the defensive: "we're not perfect, we make mistakes, we have reversals, we take steps back." Instead of batting away the disingenuous attack by genocidal communists and going on offense, he sheepishly accepted their premise.

But the most troubling parallel between today's anti-American radicals and yesterday's is what they do when they're angry. The anti-police riots of 2020 followed the same hateful playbook as the riots of the Vietnam era. Rioters clashed with the police, arsonists burned down entire city blocks, and vandals smashed small businesses to pieces. Left-wing street militias laid siege to the Portland federal courthouse for months. Radicals defaced statues not just of dead Confederates but of American heroes like George Washington, Thomas Jefferson, Ulysses S. Grant, and Abraham Lincoln. Anarchists in Seattle briefly tried to secede from the United States, creating a lawless "autonomous zone" run by a warlord.

Did Democratic politicians condemn the anarchy? Hardly. Democrats and their media allies at first pretended the deadly riots didn't happen, calling them "mostly peaceful protests." Pelosi scoffed that "people will do what they do," which must be easy to say when you live behind a phalanx of bodyguards. When the riots could no longer be ignored, they justified them as legitimate protests against, of course, our "systemically racist" country. "There needs to be unrest in the streets for as long as there's unrest in our lives," said Representative Ayanna Pressley, another Squad member. Kamala Harris even encouraged her supporters to bail rioters out of jail.

They're still blaming America first.

THERE'S A DIRECT line from the Progressives to the Blame America First Democrats. Now, no one would mistake a prim, bespectacled professor like Woodrow Wilson for a Weatherman or leftist radical. Indeed, BLM would justifiably condemn the virulently racist Wilson. But the Progressives, the New Left, and today's liberals share common premises. They reject the moral basis of the American founding principles. They believe America is sinful and therefore deny that American power should be used in pursuit of America's interests, as the Founders and Reagan believed. They differ only on how we should atone for America's supposed sins. The progressive tradition aims to redeem America by using our power on behalf of other nations or abstract ideals. The Blame America First Democrats believe our sins are irredeemable; nothing good can come from this country, so American power—and perhaps America itself—should be dismantled.

But they agree again on the need to constrain American power and to prevent its use for our "selfish" interests. That's why the Democrats surrender our sovereignty to globalist institutions like the United Nations and reflexively favor harmful, one-sided treaties, as we'll see in the next chapter. Whatever their small differences here and there, the Democrats agree that America shouldn't have freedom of action in the world—especially if the American people keep electing "cowboy" presidents like Ronald Reagan.

CHAPTER 3

The Globalist Surrender of Sovereignty

As 1919 dawned, Americans felt pride and hope for the new year. Our troops had decisively won the Great War, ending four years of bloodshed in Europe and restoring the peace. But the first progressive president, Woodrow Wilson, squandered our victory with the ill-conceived Treaty of Versailles. At times both punitive and utopian, the treaty humiliated Germany, infuriated our allies, and sparked national animosities that contributed to the outbreak of World War II.

Not surprisingly with Wilson as one of its authors, the treaty also launched a century-long assault by the progressive left on American sovereignty. Wilson candidly declared that "some of our sovereignty would be surrendered for the good of the world."

That was putting it mildly, for the treaty would have undercut our sovereignty in several ways. Most dangerously, the treaty created a League of Nations, which makes the United Nations seem restrained and sensible by contrast. The League would have bound the United States to go to war to defend any nation in a vast, globe-spanning alliance of countries with few shared interests and radically different cultures and political systems. This commitment would have ended a central hallmark of any nation's sovereignty, namely, the power to decide when, where, and with whom we go to war.

The treaty would also have created an "equitable" free-trade system, with rules rigged against the United States and in favor of war-torn European nations. And the treaty would have created a court to give foreign judges power over Americans.

Thankfully, some Americans fought back against this assault on our sovereignty with Republican senators leading the charge. The legendary Henry Cabot Lodge, chairman of the Foreign Relations Committee, suggested the compromise of removing the League's power to order American troops into war. But Wilson would have none of it. According to Wilson, America had to surrender our power over matters of war and peace to international bureaucrats.

Though a New England patrician and accomplished historian with four Harvard degrees, Lodge nonetheless sounded like an America First populist in his answer to Wilson. He proudly declared during the Senate debate:

> You may call me selfish if you will, conservative or reactionary, or use any other harsh adjective you see fit to apply, but an American I was born, an American I have remained all my life. I can never be anything else but an American, and I must think of the United States first, and when I think of the United States first in an arrangement like this, I am thinking of what is best for the world, for if the United States fails, the best hopes of mankind fail with it. I have never had but one allegiance—I cannot divide it now. I have loved but one flag and I cannot share that devotion and give affection to the mongrel banner invented for a league.

In another speech, Lodge bluntly laid out the stakes of the treaty for Americans: "you are being asked to exchange the government of

Abraham Lincoln, of the people, for the people, by the people, for a government of, for, and by *other* people."

Lodge appealed to our first Republican president because Lincoln defined a nation as "a political community without a political superior." Wilson attacked this core principle by trying to make the League of Nations superior to our nation.

Wilson embarked on a nationwide tour, rare in those days, to rally support for the treaty. Perhaps he believed that the Senate—one of those outdated institutions of the "Newtonian" Constitution he so despised, as we learned in Chapter One—didn't reflect the public opinion. But plenty of Americans joined Lodge in thinking of the "United States first," just as many normal Americans do today. Wilson ended the unsuccessful tour after a debilitating stroke, after which Lodge and the Senate thankfully defeated the League of Nations and preserved Lincoln's vision of sovereignty.

Although the League died, the globalist ideology behind it lives on and has only gained strength in the modern Democratic Party. We remain today in a struggle between Lincoln and Lodge's vision of sovereignty and Wilson's plot to surrender it.

To UNDERSTAND HOW liberals have worked to undermine our sovereignty, let's start at the beginning. The progressive left has always harbored doubts about America. Wilson explicitly repudiated the Founders and our Constitution. Leaders of the Blame America First Democrats appeased communists and condemned America's actions around the world. Nor is this only an elite view. Each year, Gallup asks Americans "how proud they are to be an American" and Democrats consistently poll from 15 to 50 percentage points less proud than do Republicans.

It's natural, then, that progressives want to surrender our sovereignty.

It starts at home with wide-open borders and markets, which may be good for other countries, but which are bad for America. Liberals today oppose not just border security, but the very idea of borders. Americans bear the brunt of lost jobs, lower wages, gang violence, and the drug epidemic. Liberals also want to open our markets without taking into account America's interests, leading to bad, one-sided trade deals that hurt Americans but benefit China.

Progressives also want to constrain American power and erode our freedom of action abroad. John Kerry infamously voiced this sentiment in a presidential debate in 2004 when he said that the use of the American military must pass "the global test." Barack Obama claimed to believe in American exceptionalism, "just as I suspect that the Brits believe in British exceptionalism and the Greeks believe in Greek exceptionalism"—which is to say, exceptionalism is just a kind of quaint prejudice for one's own country. Why, after all, if America is not a special place—and particularly if it's a bad place—should we put America first?

Progressives don't just apply a "global test" to decide what we can do; they also want to constrain America permanently with globalist institutions and laws. The great Jeane Kirkpatrick, whom we met in Chapter Two, put it well: "foreign governments and their leaders, *and more than a few activists here at home,* seek to constrain and control American power by means of elaborate multilateral processes, global arrangements, and UN treaties that limit both our capacity to govern ourselves and act abroad."

Beyond open borders, open markets, and deference to globalist bureaucracies, the progressive left also tries to bind America to flawed, one-sided agreements. In many cases, such as the Iran nuclear deal, these agreements also undermine our Constitution by evading the Senate's power to ratify treaties, in addition to eroding our sovereignty.

Of course, the Progressives never cared much for the Constitution anyway.

Although it may seem like an abstract concept, the progressives' surrender of sovereignty can harm you in concrete ways. Open borders and open markets have already devastated the American working class. Had the Senate ratified Bill Clinton's Kyoto Protocol on global warming, you would be paying much more to gas up your car and to heat your home. That's what we'll get from the Paris Climate Accords, which Joe Biden rejoined on his first day in office. If we ever join the International Criminal Court, American troops could face trial and imprisonment by foreign bureaucrats. If we ratified the UN Arms Trade Treaty, foreign bureaucrats could decide whether you have the right to own a gun.

Sovereignty matters, to you and to America. We must preserve our freedom of action to preserve our freedom.

A BORDERLESS AMERICA

The surrender of sovereignty starts at home. For decades, progressives have sought to erase two vital hallmarks of a free country: a secure border and strong domestic markets. Progressives prefer a borderless world instead of sovereign peoples looking after their own interests. Global elites live in such a world, after all, so why shouldn't we all? The simple answer is that well-regulated borders with clear rules about whom and what can cross them are essential to sovereignty and to protect America's interests.

Open Borders

The most basic attribute of a nation is its borders, and the most basic element of a sovereign country is to control who and what crosses those borders. Yet, the Democratic Party has tried to surrender this sovereign right by opening our 2,000-mile border with Mexico. The consequences for our workers and communities have been devastating.

The open-borders ideology is the de facto position of today's Democrats. In a presidential debate in 2020, eight out of ten Democratic candidates, including future vice president Kamala Harris, raised their hands when asked if they would decriminalize crossing the border illegally. A confused Joe Biden half-raised his hand, but later retreated from the position in rambling, incoherent remarks.

He should've raised his hand enthusiastically, because he put open-borders radicals in charge once he took office. He halted deportations for one hundred days, ended the state of emergency at the border, and stopped construction of the border wall. He also stopped the Trump administration's highly effective Remain in Mexico Policy, which required migrants seeking asylum to wait in Mexico. While America has always welcomed those facing genuine risk of persecution, almost every border-crosser today is an economic migrant, not a targeted minority. On a trip to the border early in the Biden administration, I spoke to dozens of migrants huddled under a bridge at night. Not a single one said they came because of persecution. The explanations were along the lines of "a better job," "because I can get in now," and, of course, "Biden." Little wonder that migrant caravans wore T-shirts that say "Biden, please let us in!" Biden happily obliged their request.

The results are shocking, but not surprising. In Biden's first year in office, more than two million illegal aliens crossed our southern border. In his second year, Biden is on track to shatter his own record. Because of the Biden administration's lax enforcement against employers for hiring illegals and laughably permissive standards for asylum, the large majority of those illegal aliens released into the country will never be sent home, joining the more than twenty million illegal aliens already here. Yet progressives welcome and even celebrate this uncontrolled influx of millions of foreigners into our sovereign nation.

Uncontrolled migration hurts working-class Americans the most by adding competition for their jobs and undercutting their wages and benefits. This is especially true in immigrant communities where illegal aliens are most likely to settle. I've heard from so many naturalized Americans who feel betrayed by open-borders politicians. They played by our rules and came here the right way, only to have their livelihoods put at risk by migrant labor. They notice, of course, that illegals never seem to settle in Silicon Valley or Washington as green-energy lobbyists or diversity consultants. I bet liberals might sing a different tune if they did.

Criminals, gangs, and drug cartels also take advantage of our open border, importing violence from abroad. Mexican cartels are fighting an insurgency against the Mexican government that has made our southern neighbor one of the most dangerous countries on Earth outside of war zones. Mexico had more than 100,000 murders in just the past three years—a rate more the five times higher than ours. The five most dangerous cities in the world are all in Mexico; two, Juarez and Tijuana, are on the border. Residents of El Paso can see tracer fire from cartel machine guns lighting up the night sky near their homes. Cartel gunmen have executed American citizens and law-enforcement officers inside Mexico.

This violence inevitably spills across our border. Between 2015 and 2020, the Border Patrol apprehended over 4,000 foreign gang members, including nearly 1,800 members of the sadistically violent MS-13, a Central American street gang whose unofficial motto is, "kill, rape, control." Once in our country, these gangs fight bloody turf wars; MS-13 has terrorized communities from New York to Virginia to

California with rape, torture, dismemberment, beheadings, and mass murders.

Much of this violence results, of course, from the drug trade, a third tragic consequence of our open border. The vast majority of heroin, fentanyl, cocaine, and meth is smuggled into America from Mexico, with these criminal gangs and drug cartels acting in concert to move the drugs into and around our country. Aside from violent crime, these drugs have inflicted unspeakable carnage and heartbreak in communities across America. In the last year on record, drug overdoses killed more than 100,000 Americans, a sad milestone. The trends aren't getting better. In 2021, the Border Patrol seized enough fentanyl to kill every single American man, woman, and child several times over. And that's just the overdose deaths. Millions of Americans struggle with addiction or live the daily anguish of helping loved ones fight this demon.

Despite these deadly consequences, Democrats would make the situation even worse. For instance, along with the police, progressives have also sought to defund Immigration and Customs Enforcement, the agency primarily tasked with removing illegal-alien criminals. They've smeared ICE for supposed cruelty—Squad member Representative Rashida Tlaib accused ICE of trying to "terrorize migrant communities"—when in reality ICE typically protects lawful immigrants from illegal-alien violence that falls disproportionately on fellow immigrants. In 2019, ICE removed over 150,000 convicted criminal aliens and over 5,000 gang members from our country. These foreign criminals were collectively responsible for hundreds of thousands of crimes, including nearly 2,000 murders. By contrast, in Joe Biden's first year in office, removals of convicted criminal aliens fell to just 39,000 and removals of gang members fell by half. Of course, rich and powerful progressives like Nancy Pelosi have insulated themselves from these consequences. When you have a security detail and live behind guarded walls, it's easy to virtue signal.

A country without borders isn't a country. This is not an assertion or an opinion, but a simple fact, no different than saying two plus two equals four or a square is a figure with four equal sides and four right angles. But it gives progressives the vapors, sparking cries of xenophobia, nativism, and racism. That's because progressives know that the surrender of sovereignty starts at home. If they can open our borders and silence their critics, they can change the meaning of nationhood and citizenship, making it all the easier to change America's role in the world.

Open Markets

The Democrats are also the party of wide-open markets. Much like Woodrow Wilson's approach to military power, Democrats today will promote trade agreements and practices as long as they don't serve Americans' interests. Instead of pursuing hard-nosed trade deals that enrich our nation and open foreign markets, Democrats have exported our jobs, our factories, and our prosperity to other nations. No nation has benefited more from this globalist trade policy than Communist China, and no trading relationship has undermined our sovereignty more.

Bill Clinton, more than any other politician, is responsible for China's exploitation of our market. Having fought us in Korea and Vietnam, China became our de facto ally against Soviet Russia for the last twenty years of the Cold War. But once the Soviet Union crumbled, we should've shifted our strategic focus to China, the next serious threat to America—just as we had confronted the Soviets after allying with them to defeat. George H. W. Bush made a mistake not to do so, and Clinton justifiably hammered Bush on the campaign trail for it. Clinton promised to link trade to human rights. It would've been better if he had insisted on fair trade practices for Americans in addition to more human-rights protections for the Chinese. Nevertheless, it was good that Clinton proposed at least some brakes on China's trade ambitions.

But Clinton caved entirely once he took office. In 1994, he extended China's most-favored-nation status—giving China special trading privileges—despite its continued economic and human-rights abuses and, worse still, he pledged not to link the trading status to China's human-rights record anymore. In the following years, the annual votes in Congress to override Clinton's grants of most-favored-nation status to China became increasingly contentious as China's abuses continued. To be fair, the blind spot on China wasn't just a problem on the left. Congressional Republicans typically provided the majority of the votes to uphold Clinton's decisions, though a sizable number of Democrats also supported the misguided policy. Yet the Clinton administration was the driving force all along, lobbying Congress and negotiating with China to give away permanent most-favored-nation status and to facilitate its entrance into the World Trade Organization. In late 2000, Clinton signed into law a bill to do both. China entered the WTO and received permanent most-favored-nation status a year later.

It's hard to overstate the importance of the annual votes on China's trade status. Although Clinton won each vote, the very fact of the votes discouraged nervous CEOs from sending jobs to China. They feared a Chinese crackdown and shifting political winds might cost China its trading status, which would cost them their investment. But once the trading status was permanent and China entered the WTO, CEOs could safely outsource entire factories to China.

The results of China's permanent trading status with America and its entry into the WTO are now known as the China Shock. Clinton had assured his fellow Americans that these actions were the economic "equivalent of a one-way street." He was right, just wrong about the direction: the benefits of Clinton's "one-way street" flowed to China. America lost three million manufacturing jobs and over sixty thousand factories. The mighty industrial states of Michigan, Ohio, and Pennsylvania alone lost six hundred thousand manufacturing jobs. My home state of Arkansas lost over a quarter of our manufacturing jobs. And these numbers only scratch the surface since one manufacturing job can support several more jobs in other sectors. When the factories closed, so did the shops, diners, bars, and convenience stores as main streets across the country were hollowed out and boarded up. The China Shock ripped the heart out of many of our small towns and working-class communities.

The China Shock would've been bad enough if China had followed the WTO rules, which of course it hasn't. Instead, China has pursued a malignant economic model based on three key principles: lying, cheating, and stealing. China has manipulated its currency and its regulations to protect its (often state-owned or state-subsidized) companies from foreign competition. These companies then engage in widespread product dumping to hurt our businesses. China also has forced many companies to transfer their most sensitive technologies as a condition of gaining access to Chinese markets. When that fails, China simply engages in economic espionage, stealing the intellectual property of America's inventors and entrepreneurs.

The China Shock and China's crimes against America's workers and businesses have transferred a staggering amount of wealth to the Chinese Communists. In 1992, we traded only $33 billion in goods with China. By the end of Clinton's term, it was $116 billion. By the end of Obama's term, it had grown to $578 billion. America has funded the economic and military rise of our most dangerous enemy, one of the worst strategic errors in our history.

Not only that, we've enabled China's meddling in our domestic politics, a grave threat to our sovereignty. Such enormous sums of money inevitably lead to political influence peddling. This is one reason that we didn't have much of a trading relationship with Soviet Russia: we didn't want to give our enemy a say in our domestic political debates. But that's exactly what China now has. I call it the "China Lobby," a network of American institutions deeply invested in China and thus dedicated to preserving the dangerous status quo.

The China Lobby is present in every state and often in surprising ways; it's not just big multinational corporations. My governor, Asa Hutchinson, urged me to meet with China's consul general from Houston early in the Trump administration. I refused, saying I might meet with the ambassador in Washington. But he persisted because the Houston consulate managed Chinese investment in Arkansas, which he was courting. That gave me even stronger reason to refuse: I didn't want Chinese officials to think I would temper my criticism or alter my views for an illusory promise of Chinese money. I would also add that our government shuttered China's Houston consulate in 2020 because it was a den of spies. And Arkansas isn't alone: China attempts to exert its influence through state and local officials in every state.

Another surprising example of the China Lobby is Hollywood. Have you noticed that there hasn't been a movie with a Chinese villain in more than a decade? That's because the studios are desperate for access to the Chinese market. China banned Brad Pitt for two decades because he played the Dalai Lama's tutor in *Seven Years in Tibet*. China also banned Harrison Ford, Richard Gere, and Sharon Stone for speaking out for Tibet. Hollywood studios quickly got the picture. In *Mulan*, Disney even gave special thanks to the authorities in China's Xinjiang province, who are committing genocide against ethnic and religious minorities.

But powerful multinational companies are the heart of the China Lobby. During tense moments in trade negotiations with the Trump administration, China's leaders asked American CEOs to lobby on China's behalf. In 2021, blue-chip American corporations like Coca-Cola, Apple, and Nike lobbied Congress against legislation to crack down on Chinese slave labor. At a committee hearing that year, I grilled executives from Coca-Cola, Visa, Procter & Gamble, and Airbnb for refusing to condemn China's genocide against the Uighur people. Delta, United, and American airlines have agreed to remove Taiwan from their drop-down menu list of country destinations under pressure from Beijing. At the same time, some of these companies, like Coca-Cola and Delta, eagerly criticized Republican state legislatures even as they shilled for Chinese Communists.

To appreciate the pervasive cultural and political influence of the China Lobby, let's return to show business. Aside from Fox, every major news network in America is owned by or affiliated with a major Hollywood studio: NBC and Universal, ABC and Disney, CBS and Paramount, CNN and Warner Brothers. Do you really think those news networks report objectively on China's crimes against America? I sure don't. Or consider the NBA's kowtowing to Beijing. When a Houston Rockets executive tweeted his support for democratic protests in Hong Kong, Beijing came down on him like a ton of bricks, and so did much of the league, LeBron James in particular. Like the movie studios, the NBA is desperate to broadcast its games into China. For that matter, James also wanted his new movie, *Space Jam 2*, released in China.

These are just a few examples of the China Lobby's power. And while the lobby obviously targets politicians of both parties, it's more insidious with the progressive left. Most of these institutions—the media, Hollywood, corporate America, colleges—are run by progressives. Further, many Democrats view China through the lens of identity politics, contending it's racist and xenophobic to rebuke Chinese Communists. Some liberals called me racist in early 2020 for pointing out that the coronavirus very likely emerged from the Wuhan labs. When their ideological friends, donors, and voters all favor a softer line on China, we shouldn't be surprised to see progressive politicians follow.

The China Lobby's influence is simply another reason we should've never opened our markets to the Chinese Communists. A veritable fifth column now works on China's behalf in Washington and our state capitals. The China Lobby wants to sell out our workers, outsource our prosperity, and globalize our supply chains, making us reliant on others for the essentials of civilization and human life. We're a nation with an economy, not an economy with a nation. And a nation that cannot feed itself, fuel itself, heal itself, and defend itself isn't a sovereign nation.

THE IVORY TOWERS OF INTERNATIONALISM

Ever since Wilson, progressives have been enamored of international organizations. These organizations sit outside and above their member nations, take on lives of their own, and embody the left's grandest dreams for unelected, global, bureaucratic government—all virtues to the progressive mind. International organizations vary in size and power, but all infringe on American sovereignty. We can see how the progressive left uses these organizations by examining a couple of illustrative cases. The United Nations is the epicenter of the liberal internationalist system and the source of a sprawling web of new international organizations. The International Criminal Court is the logical and extreme outgrowth of the left's globalist ambitions.

United Nations

Founded in the aftermath of World War II, the UN resembled the failed League of Nations, with less power but equally grand ambitions: securing world peace and ending poverty and hunger. From the beginning, the UN's reach has exceeded its grasp. Now, the UN seems to specialize in corruption, coddling dictators, and sticking its nose in America's business, with the help of Democratic politicians.

The UN doesn't merely fail at conflict resolution and peacekeeping, but usually makes matters worse. The notorious Oil-for-Food program, which allowed Saddam Hussein to evade international sanctions while enriching his cronies and UN officials, is only one of the worst examples of the UN's endemic corruption and mismanagement. Meanwhile, brutal dictatorships like China, Cuba, and Venezuela sit on its human-rights council and North Korea has chaired the UN's disarmament conference. Also, pervasive anti-Semitism plagues the UN, which has adopted more resolutions about Israel than every other nation combined.

Nevertheless, the UN continues to expand, demanding ever larger budgets. As hundreds of billions of dollars have poured in over the decades, the UN has metastasized into a vast bureaucracy and an alphabet soup of bureaus, agencies, and committees pursuing a globalist agenda. American taxpayers spend more than $11 billion a year on the UN network, far more than any other country—and more than what we spend combined on the Border Patrol and our national parks.

What do we get in return for all that money? A hostile, left-wing, international bureaucracy that undercuts America at every turn. Our adversaries use the UN to constrain America, while confident the UN would never target them. UN agencies like the World Health Organization cover up for dictatorships like China, while UN secretaries-general criticize America and draw false moral equivalences with our enemies. To add insult to injury, UN employees don't even pay their parking tickets in New York City—a sum of millions of dollars—sticking our taxpayers with the bill while illegally taking their parking spots.

Even worse than the UN's attempts to constrain America abroad is its meddling in our domestic affairs. During the riots in the summer of 2020, for example, the UN Human Rights Council called for an "urgent" meeting to focus on America's supposed "systemic racism, police brutality, and violence against peaceful protests," only the fifth such call in its history. In 2019, the UN high commissioner for human rights claimed to be "appalled" and "deeply shocked" by the Trump administration's border policies, while the deputy high commissioner declared that pro-life policies are "torture" and a form of "extremist hate."

A particularly offensive intrusion into our sovereignty is the UN's "special rapporteur," which might as well be French for "anti-American busybody." These so-called investigators arrive on our shores, meet with their fellow liberals, and lecture us about our supposed failures, usually racism and sexism—all on expense accounts you paid for. In 2017, a special rapporteur condemned Republican tax cuts and welfare reforms, asserting that "the American dream is rapidly becoming the American illusion" and "the equality of opportunity, which is so prized in theory, is in practice a myth, especially for minorities and women."

If this rant sounds a lot like what Democrats say, that's because progressives around the world use the same playbook and work toward the same goals. Indeed, Democratic presidents like to invite special rapporteurs to our country to advance their policies. In 1994, for instance, Bill Clinton welcomed one to investigate supposed human-rights offenses. The result was an unhinged report condemning Ronald Reagan's economic policies and accusing America of "structural and insidious racism and racial discrimination." The report was so crazed that the Clinton administration felt compelled to repudiate it as "distorted and misleading."

Yet Democrats continue to welcome these unhinged leftists to judge America. In 2021, Joe Biden invited a special rapporteur to investigate—once again, you'll be shocked to hear—racism in America. For the progressive left, the intrusion on our sovereignty is the point; they have more faith in globalist bureaucrats than they do in the American people.

Another tool for the progressive left to erode our sovereignty is the UN's many misbegotten conventions and treaties. These agreements come with politically appealing names used by liberals to hide their deeply unpopular implications for our sovereignty and domestic policy. For instance, every Democratic president since Jimmy Carter has supported the UN Convention on Elimination of All Forms of Discrimination against Women. Sounds nice—no one wants discrimination. But what does it actually do? The convention would create a right to abortion and a wide-ranging system of affirmative action, all monitored and enforced by a meddlesome body of international bureaucrats.

Likewise, Democrats also support the UN Convention on the Rights of the Child. Again, it sounds nice. But this convention would allow foreigners to interfere with American parents' right to raise our kids as we see fit, dictate curriculum at American schools, and crode religious liberty. The UN Arms Trade Treaty may sound like a noble effort to stop warlords from getting military weapons, but it would imperil your Second Amendment rights by creating a de facto national gun registry leading to gun bans and regulations—which was exactly the point of a UN agreement negotiated by Barack Obama and supported by Joe Biden.

Democratic administrations signed up the United States for each of these UN conventions—and many more, which would limit our freedom to make the laws we live by. But as with the League of Nations, these globalist ambitions crashed upon the good sense of the Senate. Indeed, these conventions are often so unpopular that Democratic presidents don't even bother to submit them to the Senate for debate and ratification. Yet they nonetheless reveal the progressive dream of surrendering our sovereignty to unelected and unaccountable foreign bureaucrats.

International Criminal Court

The International Criminal Court is a chief example of the menacing powers that progressives will seize for international organizations with seemingly modest ambitions. This kangaroo court threatens the freedom of every American who wears our country's uniform.

In 1998, a conference of UN bureaucrats and anti-American globalists created the ICC through a treaty called the Rome Statute. The ICC includes both a court of international judges and an independent prosecutor's office; neither is accountable to a democratically elected legislature or head of state, nor subject to meaningful checks and balances. The court has jurisdiction over war crimes, crimes against humanity, and vaguely defined "crimes of aggression." But the ICC lacks the basic due process afforded to all Americans such as the right to trial by jury, high evidentiary standards, and protection against double jeopardy. Most alarming, the ICC has asserted jurisdiction to prosecute American troops, even though we haven't ratified the treaty.

Nevertheless, Democrats have coddled the ICC from the start, looking for ways to cooperate with it and holding out hope to join it one day. Even though his administration opposed many key provisions and voted against the Rome Statute, Bill Clinton still signed it in 2000, while refusing to submit it to the Senate—a classic Clintonian move. The signature reflected, in his view, a desire to continue negotiations and improve the court. Yet no amount of negotiation could salvage a court so antithetical to our Constitution.

Clinton's waffling reflected the deep unpopularity of exposing our troops to an unaccountable international court. After the Rome Statute took effect in 2002, George W. Bush revoked our signature and Congress passed the American Servicemembers' Protection Act with large, bipartisan majorities. The law restricts intelligence sharing with the ICC, bans funding for it, and encourages our military partners to agree not to turn over U.S. personnel to the ICC. The law also authorizes the president to "use all means necessary" to free Americans in ICC custody at its headquarters in the Hague, a provision that inspired the law's humorous nickname, "the Hague Invasion Act." Two years later, Congress strengthened the law by blocking economic aid to countries that didn't agree to protect our troops from arrest. As a result, dozens of countries signed immunity agreements to give our troops the protection they deserved.

But Democrats continued to bolster the ICC, probably torn between their desire to surrender our sovereignty and their justified sense of political peril. Democratic Congresses soon weakened the law, allowing aid to flow once again to ICC member nations. When Barack Obama took office, he expanded American cooperation with the court, even though the ICC's rogue prosecutor announced early in Obama's first term that he was investigating American soldiers for alleged war crimes in Afghanistan.

When the ICC prosecutor renewed the investigation in 2019, the Trump administration lowered the boom. The United States revoked the prosecutor's U.S. visa, sanctioned several other ICC leaders, and labeled the court a "threat" to the United States. Unfortunately, Democratic support for the ICC resumed when Joe Biden restored the prosecutor's visa and revoked the sanctions shortly after taking office.

Our military wages war with the highest ethical standards and goes over and above the demands of the laws of war. During my service, I trained soldiers on these standards and I led them in combat as they displayed remarkable bravery and morality. I cannot imagine having them second-guessed by a bunch of globalist lawyers sitting remotely in Europe.

The ICC isn't and can't ever be compatible with American sovereignty and the constitutional rights of our citizens, whatever the ambitions of the progressive left. We shouldn't cooperate with this wholly illegitimate "court." National courts are usually capable of investigating and prosecuting crimes committed during war, as Ukrainian courts have done since Russia invaded in early 2022. When they're not, temporary and specialized tribunals with democratic legitimacy and oversight are another option. But the ICC should be treated with scorn and met with force if it ever comes to that.

SIGNING AWAY AMERICAN POWER

Progressives also use international agreements to achieve their ideological goals. For most of our history, these agreements took the form of treaties to be ratified—or rejected—by the Senate. In recent decades, though, liberal presidents have bypassed the Senate with executive agreements, usually because they knew ratification was unlikely. These agreements rarely serve our interests, regularly undermine our constitutional system of checks and balances, and usually undercut our sovereignty.

Treaties

Democratic presidents rarely enter treaty negotiations from a position of strength and they usually give away the store. Again, this isn't an accident but rather by design since they come from a progressive tradition bashful of American power and hostile to American sovereignty. And once America joins a treaty, progressives act as if it were holy writ handed down on stone tablets, never to be abrogated, even when it's obsolete and other treaty partners are cheating.

The Panama Canal Treaties of 1978 showcase the progressive theory of treaties. Under the Hay–Bunau-Varilla Treaty of 1903, the United States had recognized Panama's independence from Colombia and in return we got the right to build the canal and exercise sovereignty over a Canal Zone—a straightforward deal and diplomatic success. The canal, an engineering wonder of the world, became a key artery for world trade and a source of American pride.

Yet Jimmy Carter surrendered both the canal and the Canal Zone in return for nothing—treaties so one-sided you might've concluded that Panama had defeated us in a war. He celebrated that the canal would remain "neutral" and open to U.S. vessels, but of course we already had these rights. What's worse, Carter conducted these negotiations under ongoing threats of sabotage and guerilla war.

In the end, progressives assuaged their guilty conscience about accusations of "imperialism," and America lost a vital strategic asset. Regrettably, the Senate ratified the treaties, though only with one vote to spare. A majority of Republican senators and more than a few conservative Democrats voted no, heeding Ronald Reagan's argument: "we bought it, we paid for it, it's ours, and we're going to keep it."

Fortunately, the Senate preemptively killed another example of the progressive approach to treaties, the Kyoto Protocol on climate change. Negotiated by Al Gore on behalf of the Clinton administration, this punitive treaty would have destroyed nearly five million American jobs, crippled our coal industry, and significantly increased the cost of gassing up your car, heating your home, or running your business. Meanwhile, the protocol exempted 80 percent of the world from carbon-emission reductions, most notably China, which became the world's worst polluter as it stole millions of our manufacturing jobs.

As is so often the case with progressives, the Kyoto Protocol traded concrete, massive costs for vague, intangible benefits. So one-sided was the protocol that the Senate voted 95–0 to oppose such a deal. Yet Bill Clinton signed it anyway. The protocol died when George W. Bush withdrew American support.

But progressives don't just negotiate bad treaties; they defend old treaties that have outlived their usefulness, even when our treaty partners are cheating. The Intermediate-Range Nuclear Forces Treaty and the Open Skies Treaty are two battles that I've fought in the Senate.

When Ronald Reagan signed the INF Treaty in 1987, it was a triumph of hard-nosed diplomacy. The treaty banned ground-launched, intermediate-range (500–5,500 kilometer) missiles, which could carry either nuclear or conventional warheads. Reagan started the negotiations with a strategic advantage: our missiles in Europe threatened Russia, but Russia couldn't deploy missiles close enough to our territory to threaten us. But we still had hundreds of thousands of troops at risk in Europe, as well as our NATO allies. Plus, when compared to intercontinental missiles, these missiles' shorter flight times yield less warning time and their smaller size makes them easier to move and hide. The treaty therefore promoted stability, while also working in our favor; Russia had to dismantle more than 1,800 missiles, while we only had to destroy around 850.

By the time I joined the Senate in 2015, though, Russia had violated the INF Treaty for years by developing missiles in the banned ranges. Even the Obama administration had finally acknowledged these violations. Moreover, China had rapidly built up its arsenal, leaving Taiwan and our troops in the Western Pacific dangerously exposed. I urged the Obama administration to gain leverage over Russia by designing new missiles of our own and withholding support for other arms-control treaties. To no avail, because Obama and John Kerry were only willing to plead with Vladimir Putin to come back into compliance. Of course, he did not.

After the Trump administration negotiated with Russia for two years, we smartly withdrew from this treaty that no longer provided any benefit and imposed severe risks. Yet progressives still got the vapors. Nancy Pelosi accused Trump of "undermining international security and stability" and Bernie Sanders called the withdrawal "dangerous and irresponsible." Strangely, the very same progressives who had hysterically accused Trump of being in Vladimir Putin's pocket now criticized him for being too tough on Putin. I suppose their deep-seated ideological commitments overcame their short-term political cynicism.

The Open Skies Treaty followed a similar trajectory. George H. W. Bush signed the treaty with Russia and many European nations in 1992, shortly after the Soviet Union collapsed. The treaty permitted flights of specialized reconnaissance aircraft over each nation's territory to allow for photography of military bases, troop movements, and other areas of interest. These overflights were intended to promote transparency and build trust.

As with the INF Treaty, by the time I entered the Senate, Russia was violating the Open Skies Treaty by refusing overflights of sensitive areas such as Russian-occupied Georgia and its European exclave, Kaliningrad. We were getting the costs of this treaty, but none of the benefits. Again, I pushed the Obama administration to take action, at a minimum to retaliate by restricting Russian flights over U.S. territory. Again, Obama and Kerry refused.

When Donald Trump took office, I encouraged him to scrap the treaty altogether. Not only was Russia cheating, but they needed the treaty more than we did because American satellite technology is superior to Russia's. We could easily replace Open Skies imagery with satellite imagery; not so for Russia. Moreover, our Open Skies aircraft needed more than a quarter-billion dollars in upgrades, a needless expense to support an outdated treaty. When the Trump administration finally withdrew from the treaty, Joe Biden condemned Trump for "abandoning American leadership" and called for yet more open-ended negotiations with Putin, with no plan to compel Russia's compliance.

Executive Agreements

As we've seen, the Senate has often defended America's sovereignty and dashed progressive dreams for globalist government. In response, Democratic presidents in recent years have begun using executive agreements to evade the Senate and surrender our sovereignty.

There's nothing inherently wrong with executive agreements; what matters is how they're used. Presidents have always used executive agreements for administrative matters—for instance, the delivery of international mail, military-basing arrangements abroad, or the legal status of U.S. forces in foreign countries—that, while important, don't touch upon the highest questions of war, peace, and prosperity. Thus, in a tacit political understanding with the Senate, presidents didn't submit them to the Senate for ratification. But Democratic presidents now abuse executive agreements to commit America to one-sided deals in pursuit of their ideological goals.

A turning point in the abuse of executive agreements was the Agreed Framework—Bill Clinton's failed nuclear deal with North Korea in 1994. When he announced the deal, Clinton remarkably claimed that the agreement was "a crucial step toward drawing North Korea into the global community" and would help "ease North Korea's isolation." Clinton committed the United States to provide hundreds of millions of dollars of economic relief to North Korea and to build two proliferation-resistant nuclear reactors for them. In return, North Korea offered a mere promise to close a reactor used to create plutonium for nuclear weapons. But North Korea had another path to the bomb, a secret uranium-enrichment program. When the Bush administration exposed this program, North Korea broke its promise, restarted its reactor, and detonated its first nuclear device just twelve years after the deal.

Never before had a president attempted to commit our nation to a major nuclear-arms-control agreement with a mere executive agreement. Yet it provided a helpful precedent for Barack Obama to pursue an even worse deal with Iran.

By the time I entered the Senate in 2015, the broad outlines of Obama's deal were reasonably clear. America would provide sanctions relief of $100 billion or more to Iran, while the ayatollahs offered only modest, temporary, and easily reversible limits on their nuclear program. And things got worse as negotiations proceeded. But one thing that never changed was Obama's insistence that this sweeping deal wasn't a treaty and he wouldn't submit it to the Senate.

So I took matters into my own hands. I wrote an open letter to the ayatollahs, joined by forty-six other Republican senators. We explained two basic points about our Constitution. First, a legally binding treaty requires a two-thirds vote in the Senate, while an executive agreement is a mere understanding with our current president. Second, we as senators have six-year terms without term limits, whereas the president is limited to two four-year terms. The upshot, of course, was that the next president and any Congress could modify or withdraw from Obama's flawed deal.

Democrats attacked furiously. Hillary Clinton called a press conference to address her inappropriate use of a private email server as secretary of state, but she kicked it off by condemning our letter and accusing us of "trying to be helpful to the Iranians." I'm still confused by what she meant, but it previewed her tactic of accusing political opponents of being in league with foreign adversaries. Joe Biden, in a typically long-winded statement, complained that the letter was "beneath the dignity of an institution I revere." I would've thought that purposely evading the Senate to conclude an arms-control treaty with a mortal enemy was more offensive to the Senate as an institution, but what did I know? I had only been around for a couple months, not forty-two years like Biden. However, Clinton, Obama, Biden, nor any other Democrat ever refuted the content of the letter. Nor could they, since we only stated the constitutional facts.

Nevertheless, the Obama administration and the ayatollahs reached a dangerous deal. It was even worse than we had feared. Obama and Kerry even agreed to end the arms embargo on Iran and to pay $1.7 billion in ransom for four hostages, while ignoring Iran's support for terrorism, ballistic-missile program, and proxy wars against Israel and other countries. As I'll explain in Chapter Six, it was all part of Obama's ideological plan to make amends to Iran for what he viewed as America's sins.

Obama wasn't done. In 2016, he signed the Paris Climate Accords, a complicated, globe-spanning treaty to regulate carbon emissions. Recalling the fate of the Kyoto Protocol, Obama again refused to submit this agreement to the Senate. And he planned to use the vast regulatory powers of the administrative state to comply with the accords, no matter the cost to American jobs and growth.

A common thread runs through these accords and the failed nuclear deals with Iran and North Korea: progressive presidents weakened America with one-sided international agreements. Our adversaries benefited, while we got little in return. Mindful, though, that most Americans want a strong and sovereign nation, they refused to submit these agreements to the Senate, traditionally a more jealous guardian of our national interests and sovereignty.

Put differently, this abuse of executive agreements embodies Wilson's vision of progressive government: Rule by supposed neutral experts, in this case foreign-policy elites. Abstract internationalism over concrete national interests. Disrespect for the Constitution and its system of checks and balances. Ironically, the outdated "Newtonian" Senate that Wilson despised could've been a potent tool for these presidents in negotiations, giving them leverage to strike a better deal for America. But they don't want the leverage, or a better deal. They want to achieve their ideological goals.

Thus, they ignore the Constitution as inconvenient. When asked why the Iran deal wasn't submitted as a treaty, John Kerry said "it has become physically impossible" to ratify a treaty. Yet he had guided a major (and badly one-sided) nuclear-arms-control treaty with Russia through the Senate just a few years earlier when he chaired the Foreign Relations Committee. Just two years later, we voted to ratify another treaty that Kerry himself had literally signed, the accession of Montenegro into NATO. Three years after that, the Senate ratified the North Macedonia accession treaty. So while it may be hard to ratify a treaty, it's far from impossible. Besides, hard is exactly what our Founders wisely wanted it to be, for our nation should only enter international agreements that protect our interests and enjoy broad popular support.

FOR MORE THAN one hundred years, the progressive left has weakened America and surrendered our sovereignty through open borders, bad trade deals, a web of international organizations, and one-sided agreements. They've done so intentionally, because of their doubts about America's founding and suspicion of American power. As usual, Wilson put it first and best: "some of our sovereignty would be surrendered for the good of the world."

Democratic presidents still preach this globalist gospel. As he campaigned against Brexit—the progressive hostility to sovereignty extends to all nations—Barack Obama asserted that "the nations who wield their influence most effectively are the nations that do it through the collective action." The last thing Democrats want is a strong, confident America with freedom of action in a dangerous world.

But there's one institution above all that reflects our strength and preserves our freedom of action: the American military. Liberals try to hamper our military with bad arms-control deals and international bureaucracies like the International Criminal Court. Yet the military remains the single strongest tool of American power, ready to be used by presidents to protect our nation, advance our interests, and defend our sovereignty. Naturally, therefore, the left takes aim at our military, trying to weaken it from within and tie the hands of our leaders. Let's take a look at how liberals aim to neuter the military.

CHAPTER 4

Neutering the Military

T HE PRESIDENT IS calling for you," said the message that popped up on my phone early in Donald Trump's tenure. I left a committee hearing and returned to my office. Though we had talked during the campaign and transition, this was our first conversation since he took office. It would turn out to be a memorable one.

I called his assistant, who patched me through. After some small talk, we got to the point of his call, a question about a potential nominee, a common topic in those early days. When we wrapped that up, I asked how he was settling into the White House and the job.

"You know, Tom, it's good, but stuff was really screwed up around here," Trump answered. I asked him what he meant.

"Just how Obama did things. The other night, they called me and asked for approval to kill some terrorist. I never heard of the guy."

"Well, did you approve?" I asked.

Trump replied, "Oh yeah, but I asked why they'd called me in the first place. Didn't they have some captain or major or someone who knew more about this guy? I mean, I'd never heard of him. 'Sir, your guidance was to keep the last administration's protocols in place until further direction,' the guy said. 'And this is the way they did it?' 'Yes, sir,' he said."

"What did you say to that?" I interjected. None of this surprised me. Having spent my first two years in the Senate on the Intelligence and Armed Services Committee, I was pretty familiar with the Obama administration's procedures for counterterrorism strikes. But I was curious what Trump thought about it all.

"I approved it! And I told them not to call me back again, to find someone else way lower down next time. What do you think about that, Tom?"

I answered, "I think that's exactly right, Mr. President. These decisions should be made by commanders in the field, not by politicians and bureaucrats back here in Washington." He was pleased and we signed off.

Trump's instincts were correct. The Obama administration had imposed needless layers of bureaucratic and legal review on these strikes as a way to micromanage our military on the other side of the world. In the Army, we used to call it the "5,000-mile screwdriver." It's one thing to require presidential approval for highly sensitive operations, such as the raid to kill Osama bin Laden in Pakistan. But it's another thing altogether for routine strikes against ISIS or al-Qaeda terrorists in places like Syria, Iraq, Yemen, and Somalia. Soon enough, the Trump administration formalized the president's instincts.

Beyond the risk of a missed target, though, these rules revealed the liberal mindset about the military. The Obama administration didn't trust the military to make such decisions. They still don't; the Biden administration has reinstated a lot of these Obama-era policies. What's behind it all is an unease with the military itself and doubts about the use of American power. This mindset runs through Democratic thinking about the military, whether it's defense budgets, the civil-military relationship, or how to organize and train our forces. And it's not just insulting to our men and women in uniform; it's dangerous to our nation.

THE ARMED FORCES of the United States have two simple missions: prepare for war and win war. It's just that simple.

A military second to none is the surest way to prevent or win wars. In his famous Iron Curtain speech, Winston Churchill, fresh off victory in World War II, observed of Russia that "there is nothing they admire so much as strength, and there is nothing for which they have less respect than for weakness, especially military weakness." So it is with most adversaries. Churchill thus warned against the understandable desire after years of war to "work on narrow margins, offering temptations to a trial of strength." Mere strength is not enough; overwhelming strength is necessary to keep the peace.

Yet progressives are deeply skeptical of military strength. They understand that the military is the foundation of American power, but they harbor doubts about American power, especially when used to defend America's interests. As we've seen, they prefer to use power on behalf of abstract ideals—if they will use it at all—and even then only in concert with others or through multilateral organizations. But the military remains out there, cocked like a loaded gun, ready and able to smash our enemies when called upon by strong, confident leaders. To the progressive mind, nothing could be more dangerous.

Their answer is to constrain the military. Democrats habitually slash funding for the military, setting back vital efforts to train and equip our troops. Democrats also feel unease about the military and its customs and cultures, leading them to subject our troops to misguided policies and priorities. And they engage in social engineering in the military to advance politically correct goals.

As a result, Democrats invariably leave the military in a weaker position than they found it, which is just fine with them. But a weaker military endangers our troops and our country by "offering temptations to a trial of strength."

THE "HOLLOW FORCE" DEMOCRATS

It's practically an iron law of politics that a vote for a Democrat is a vote for a smaller, weaker military. Like birds migrating south for the winter, Democrats instinctively cut defense spending when they take control in Washington. These budget cuts shrink the force, hamper its readiness, and delay or cancel new weapons, especially nuclear weapons. As a result, our enemies are tempted and our troops face greater danger when war comes.

Downsizing Defense

Our defense budget is a special, even unique, part of the government's total budget. I've long argued in the Senate that we can't set our strategy based on our budget, but rather must establish the budget based on our strategy. And our strategy depends on the threats, which we can't ignore or wish away except at our grave peril. These facts make the defense budget different in kind from other parts of the budget, where revenues have more influence on which priorities we can afford to address.

Ronald Reagan outlined "the simple truth of how a defense budget is arrived at" in an Oval Office address in 1983. "It isn't done by deciding to spend a certain number of dollars," he began. Instead, he explained:

> We start by considering what must be done to maintain peace and review all the possible threats against our security. Then a strategy for strengthening peace and defending against those threats must be agreed upon. And, finally, our defense establishment must be evaluated to see what is necessary to protect against any or all of the potential threats. The cost of achieving these ends is totaled up, and the result is the budget for national defense.

Reagan countered the Democrats who proposed arbitrary budget cuts: "There is no logical way that you can say, let's spend X billion dollars less. You can only say, which part of our defense measures do we believe we can do without and still have security against all contingencies?"

Democrats, suffice it to say, don't see things this way—and never have. They view the military as just another government program, a budgetary kitty to fund their domestic schemes.

This pattern of neglect goes back to the start of the Progressive era, when liberal ambitions for big-government domestic programs took off. There's the conventional wisdom that Woodrow Wilson, Franklin Roosevelt, Harry Truman, John Kennedy, and Lyndon Johnson were "tough" Democrats and strong on the military. Each took the country to war, after all. But on the core question of the defense budget, especially relative to the threats we faced and the commitments we made, these Democrats didn't measure up.

Wilson and Roosevelt both underfunded the military as war clouds gathered in Europe and had to scramble to arm the country. When Wilson declared war, our Army had only 130,000 soldiers; by that point, Germany had millions of men under arms. The legendary General John "Black Jack" Pershing, commander of American forces in the war, observed that "we had no organized units, even approximating a division, that could be sent overseas prepared to take the field." The story was the same with Roosevelt and World War II. When Nazi Germany and Soviet Russia invaded Poland in 1939, our Army ranked nineteenth in size—smaller than Portugal's. General George Marshall, who became Army chief of staff in 1939, observed that budget cuts and neglect "had reduced the Army virtually to the status of that of a third-rate power."

The story was the same as the Cold War began. Truman approached the defense budget exactly as Reagan said we shouldn't: he funded his domestic priorities first, then gave the military what was left over. Truman slashed defense spending to just one-tenth of its wartime peak even as tensions grew with Soviet Russia. Just one month before the outbreak of the Korean War, Truman was still advocating further defense cuts, despite warnings from General Omar Bradley. Our troops fought the opening battles of the war with obsolete weapons and insufficient munitions, which bounced off North Korea's Soviet-made tanks "like ping-pong balls," in one observer's words. A contrast to Dwight Eisenhower's defense budgets is instructive: Ike never let defense spending fall below 9 percent of the economy, while it collapsed at one point to 3.5 percent under Truman.

Similarly, Kennedy and Johnson underfunded our military while dramatically expanding our role in the Vietnam War. Defense spending as a share of the economy fell throughout Kennedy's presidency, in part because he wanted to keep federal spending under the symbolic level of $100 billion—a prime example of letting the budget drive the strategy instead of the other way around. Johnson initially continued the downward trend, ignoring the dark clouds gathering over Vietnam and hoping to plow money into his domestic agenda. Johnson's first, paltry defense budget was totally inadequate for wartime, leading to yet another mad scramble to fund an adequate force. Despite their tough anti-communist rhetoric, these Democrats didn't put their money where their mouths were.

But things got much, much worse after Vietnam, as the Blame America First Democrats took hold of their party. As we saw in Chapter Two, the New Left turned not only against the war but against American power itself. And what better way to constrain American power than to gut our military, the most basic source of American power?

Jimmy Carter entered office during a low point for America's military—and he kept digging. Watergate had weakened Richard Nixon and Gerald Ford, while emboldening liberal Democrats in Congress who targeted the military. By 1976, the defense budget had declined to its lowest level as a share of the economy since Truman's last budget before the Korean War. A strong president would've recognized the danger and ordered a buildup to match the Soviet threat, but Carter wasn't a strong president. He had campaigned on slashing defense spending; by contrast, Reagan advocated a boost in military spending when he had challenged Ford in the 1976 Republican primary.

Though Carter thankfully never made good on his pledge, he still let the military sink into disrepair during his first three years in office. Defense spending remained near thirty-year lows. Pay for our troops fell to such shameful levels that some military families had to go on welfare. Senior military leaders began to warn that the United States would lose a conventional war against Russia. The Army rated six of its ten U.S.-based divisions and one front-line division in Europe as "not combat-ready." General Edward Meyer, the Army chief of staff, famously warned that the force was becoming a "hollow Army," one that appeared mission-ready on paper, but was so poorly manned, trained, and equipped that it couldn't win a war in reality.

By late 1979, with reelection looming, a revolution in Iran, and Soviet Russia's invasion of Afghanistan, Carter was mugged by reality. In a tacit admission of his earlier mistakes, he sought and received a modest increase in defense spending. Voters weren't fooled by this sudden U-turn, however, and they turned to Reagan to rebuild our military in the 1980s.

Democrats justly spent twelve years in the political wilderness; the voters wouldn't trust them with the White House again until the Soviet Union no longer existed. We won the Cold War thanks partly to Reagan's large increases to the defense budget, which the Soviets couldn't match. During those twelve years, our strengthened and revitalized military also crushed Saddam Hussein's army, then the fourth-largest in the world, in addition to lightning victories in Grenada and Panama. America's military might was unchallenged. And then Bill Clinton became president.

Under Clinton, the defense budget fell every year as a share of the economy, reaching levels not seen since before World War II. Clinton claimed a "peace dividend" after the Cold War ended, a phrase first invoked by George H. W. Bush, but seized by Clinton. Some decline was probably inevitable, as had happened after earlier, hot wars. Yet Clinton, like Truman, went much further. His devastating cuts slashed the Army from eighteen divisions to ten and the Navy from 567 ships to about 300. Pay for the troops fell to Carter-era poverty levels. The Pentagon canceled or delayed new weapons programs, which it spun as a "procurement holiday." Of course, Osama bin Laden, China, and other enemies weren't taking a holiday while Democrats slept, and the post–Cold War peace ended tragically on 9/11.

Clinton's destructive budget harmed the military for years. Unlike, say, a tax cut, which takes effect quickly, it takes time to build a ship or develop a seasoned, well-trained soldier. By the time I joined the Army, years after Clinton had left office, the service was still too small. Soldiers faced repeated and extended deployments, stressing the force and their families. The Army also lost many dynamic young leaders in the Clinton era. I recall a conversation about Army leadership with my regimental commander while I had overnight duty in the command post. I remarked that many junior officers like myself found our senior commanders somewhat tentative and risk-averse. He conceded as much, while recounting what it was like to be a junior officer in the Clinton era. The president had cut so quickly and deeply, he explained, that the military developed a "zero-defect mentality." But zero defects means zero risks, and wars aren't won without risk. With rapid downsizing, talented leaders willing to take risks found themselves passed over for promotion, which went increasingly to cautious officers who played it safe and had no mistakes. When the next war came, it sure would've helped to have more of those bold, aggressive officers still in uniform.

After seven years of war, Barack Obama inherited a larger defense budget and increased it slightly during his mini-surge in Afghanistan, but then slashed it by almost as much as Clinton had. In some ways, Obama's cuts were even more dangerous. Much of the increased spending since 9/11 had gone to wartime operations, not investments in weapons for the future. By 2009, China's rapid military buildup was plain for anyone to see and there was no mystery which nation it aimed to challenge. If anything, Obama should've maintained Bush-era defense budgets, while shifting wartime spending to advanced weaponry to counter the People's Liberation Army.

But Obama had the typical Democratic mindset of seeing the military as just another budgetary line item, as revealed by an incident early in his tenure. He and Secretary of Defense Bob Gates agreed on major defense reforms. Gates would find hundreds of billions of dollars in savings from outdated programs, bureaucratic bloat, and other efficiencies—on the condition that the military could then reinvest the savings in future weaponry. But Obama broke his word and used the savings for other government programs. The reason was entirely political; Gates recalled Obama saying that "he couldn't slash domestic spending and leave Defense untouched." Gates was irate, concluding that "agreements with the Obama White House were good for only as long as they were politically convenient."

Following that double-cross, things only got worse. A new

Republican House of Representatives wanted to get deficit spending under control, but Obama insisted that the cuts come equally from domestic and defense spending. He "felt that defense could and should be cut on its merits," as Gates put it. But this approach was misguided for two reasons. First, as I've discussed, our military is different from other parts of the government's budget. It must be based on the threats we face and the strategy to counter those threats. The defense budget can't be set by arbitrary spending decisions—not safely, anyway. Second, defense spending accounted for less than one-fifth of federal spending in 2011 and following years, yet it absorbed half of the spending cuts. As a result, real defense spending shrank by more than 15 percent during Obama's second term, and defense spending fell to its lowest level as a share of the federal budget since the Great Depression. When Obama left office, America had our smallest Army since World War II, our smallest Navy since World War I, and our smallest Air Force ever.

Vice President Biden shared his boss's mindset and he hasn't turned over a new leaf as president. Biden's first budget proposed to blow out spending on everything except the military, which would've received the smallest increase of any federal department—and an actual cut of 6 percent after accounting for runaway inflation. Meanwhile, he proposed to increase domestic spending by an astounding 16 percent. Other Republican lawmakers and I strongly opposed this inadequate budget, and not even the liberals in charge of Congress could stomach it. In the end, we added another $25 billion to Biden's defense budget, still not enough but better than the alternative.

Like Carter, Biden was mugged by reality when Russia invaded Ukraine; unlike Carter, he refused to press charges. Despite the worst war in Europe in seventy-seven years and China's continued military buildup, Biden's second budget proposal still didn't increase defense spending when accounting for inflation. What's worse, Biden's budget office expects defense spending as a share of the economy to shrink almost every year of Biden's term, after rising every year during the Trump administration. It remains to be seen whether the gathering storm of threats will shock Biden out of his stupor. But since Biden prioritized sending stimulus checks to criminals like the Boston Marathon bomber over increasing defense spending, I wouldn't bet on it.

Nuclear Negligence

Democrats reserve their deepest antipathy for the most essential weapons in our military arsenal: our nuclear forces. It's no exaggeration to say our survival as a free nation depends on our nuclear weapons. The Democrats' reflexive hostility to nuclear weapons is therefore among their most dangerous and irresponsible views.

Nuclear weapons are elemental to our survival because they deter Russia, China, and North Korea (and perhaps soon, Iran) from launching a nuclear attack against our country. For years at the Armed Services Committee, however, I've heard objections from liberal senators and witnesses that boil down to a simple question: Why do we spend so much on weapons we never use? The question is wrong on both of its premises. We don't spend all that much on our nuclear forces, only around 3 to 6 percent of the annual defense budget. More important, we use our nuclear weapons every single day and we have for seventy-seven years because their mere existence deters our enemies. America's nuclear arsenal is a powerful force for world peace and goes a long way to explaining why there's been no general war between great powers since World War II.

For sixty years, we have maintained a nuclear "triad" of land-based intercontinental ballistic missiles, ballistic-missile submarines, and heavy bomber aircraft. Each leg has unique and complementary features. With more than four hundred silos spread across the Great Plains, the missiles are most responsive, ready to launch in minutes, and almost impossible to target effectively. The bombers are most flexible, providing many options in a crisis and signaling our intent and resolve. The submarines are most survivable, ensuring a second-strike capability against our enemies. This triad structure has proven strategically sound; not surprisingly, Russia also has a nuclear triad. China probably does too.

Yet anti-nuclear liberals have worked for decades to weaken America's nuclear arsenal, which would only increase the risk of nuclear war. (In many cases, these ideologues were dupes of Russian intelligence, which has a long history of covertly funding anti-war and anti-nuclear movements in the West.) America held a position of nuclear superiority over Soviet Russia until the 1960s, when the Kennedy and Johnson administrations decided instead to settle for "strategic stability," a euphemism for allowing the Soviets to match our arsenal. Acting on this impulse, they foolishly froze our missile forces and dismantled our defenses against Soviet bombers.

By the mid-1970s, the Soviets had gained the nuclear upper hand through a combination of new weapon systems and flagrant cheating on arms-control agreements, yet Democrats took further steps to weaken our arsenal. Carter campaigned on removing America's nuclear weapons from South Korea, a pledge that he never fulfilled due in part to congressional opposition, but which still rattled our Asian allies. Carter also canceled the B-1 bomber. He foolishly hoped a display of goodwill would convince the Soviets to draw down their arsenal. But his own secretary of defense, Harold Brown, later admitted, "Soviet spending has shown no response to U.S. restraint—when we build, they build; when we cut, they build." Wisdom for the ages.

Reagan campaigned on and took office determined to rebuild our nuclear forces, even as Democrats opposed his efforts. He brought back the B-1 bomber, built the even better B-2 stealth bomber, added new intercontinental and submarine-launched ballistic missiles to our arsenal, and deployed new medium-range ballistic and cruise missiles in Europe. Incredibly, Democrats in Congress complained that these weapons would hand America an unfair advantage over Soviet Russia and upset arms-control negotiations. Joe Biden, then a senator and wrong as usual, lamented that the new missiles would give us "a first-strike capability that far exceeds what the Soviet first-strike capability is now" and put us in a position "to inflict serious damage, overwhelming damage upon the Soviet Union if we struck first." Biden didn't understand peace through strength back then, and he still doesn't.

After the Cold War ended, liberals intensified their efforts to weaken the very weapons that had helped win the war. In 1997, Bill Clinton issued a top-secret order scrapping Ronald Reagan's nuclear doctrine that stated our military should prepare to fight and win a protracted nuclear war. The new doctrine stated that America's nuclear forces existed only to prevent a war, not win a war. Clinton hoped the change would allow the United States to dismantle thousands of warheads held in reserve. One Clinton official admitted that "nuclear weapons now play a smaller role in our nuclear security strategy than at any point during the nuclear era."

In another egregious case, Clinton's secretary of energy, Hazel O'Leary, declassified decades of America's nuclear secrets, in keeping with the administration's mistaken belief that nuclear weapons were a relic of the past. Not for our enemies. The declassified information was a gold mine for North Korea and Libya's nuclear programs. Not long after, a Chinese defector walked into a CIA station with proof that China had top-secret schematics of America's warheads. They'd been learning from the Clinton administration too.

Today's Democrats haven't changed. When the Trump administration proposed a sea-launched nuclear cruise missile and a new low-yield, or "tactical," sea-launched warhead, both meant to counter Russia's massive advantage in such weapons, congressional Democrats moved to block funding. They failed, but the Biden administration canceled the cruise missile. Even that doesn't go far enough for some liberals. Senator Bernie Sanders has proposed to eliminate the new intercontinental ballistic missile needed to replace our current fifty-year-old Minuteman III missiles. The title of his bill is the ICBM Act, which stands for Investing in Cures Before Missiles Act. Sanders wants to take money from our nuclear forces and give it to Tony Fauci and the hapless Centers for Disease Control. You can't make this up.

Following in Bill Clinton's footsteps, Democrats also want to tie our hands in the event of a nuclear crisis. Biden campaigned on a "no first use" policy, which would tell our enemies in advance they don't have to worry about nuclear retaliation no matter how hard they attack us or our allies, even if they use chemical or biological weapons. Biden flip-flopped on the issue, I suspect only because of Russia's invasion of Ukraine. But Senator Elizabeth Warren continues to push her legislation to make "no first use" a matter of law.

These latest Democratic efforts to weaken our nuclear capabilities are especially dangerous because we face more nuclear threats today than at any time since the Carter era. As clueless liberals work to dismantle our arsenal, China and Russia are racing to expand theirs.

China's nuclear buildup is especially worrisome. For decades, China maintained what it called a "minimum deterrent." Not anymore. Unconstrained by any arms-control agreements, China is undertaking a "breathtaking expansion" of its nuclear forces, in the words of the commander of our nuclear forces. In 2022, he testified before my committee that China "likely intends to have at least one thousand warheads by 2030, greatly exceeding previous [Department of Defense] estimates." Satellite imagery indicates that China is building around three hundred missile silos for its new intercontinental missiles. China also has as many as one hundred road-mobile missiles, which are hard to track and monitor. And if China doesn't already have a triad, our military assesses that it's well on the way to establishing one, including nuclear-capable hypersonic glide vehicles, which it successfully tested in 2021.

Russia is also up to no good, as usual. During Vladimir Putin's tenure, Russia has modernized all three legs of its triad: its missiles, submarines, and bombers are now substantially newer than ours. Russia also has around two thousand tactical warheads, about ten times what we have. Russia is even experimenting with cruise missiles and torpedoes with nuclear propulsion systems, which could potentially travel for days before hitting their target, with worldwide range. And Putin is more than willing to rattle the nuclear saber as we saw in the first days of the war in Ukraine.

Given these developments, we face the very real threat of nuclear overmatch against the combined forces of China and Russia. To avert that possibility, we should accelerate the modernization timeline for our nuclear triad and add other, flexible elements to our nuclear forces. Yet Democrats refuse to face these facts, imperiling not merely American power, but our survival as a nation.

DEMOCRATS VERSUS THE MILITARY

The root of liberals' hostility to the defense budget and key weapons is distrust of the military as an institution. The military embodies

American power at its hardest and most lethal edge. The Democratic Party is sometimes called "the mommy party" because of its focus on softer, caring, and nurturing priorities. Few characters in American culture are more distant from "mommy" than the military's iconic drill sergeant. Tensions are bound to arise.

These tensions undermine our military's ability to fight and win wars. Too often, liberals suspect the military of racism, sexism, and extremism lurking just below a highly polished and creased veneer. They distract from training and readiness to rectify these supposed sins, engaging in social engineering that both threatens our security and puts our troops at risk. Liberals seem more comfortable training social-justice warriors than actual warriors trained to kill.

This is all dangerous folly. The military is a fighting force, not a liberal-arts college or Fortune 500 company. Phyllis Schlafly, the famed conservative activist who defeated the Democrats' first attempt to draft women into the military, put it well when she said, "The purpose of the armed forces of the United States is to defend our country. The purpose is not to engage in social experimentation or to give jobs to needy people or to run day-care facilities for people who have babies. The purpose is to defend us." The military operates in a different way and reveres different things than do civilian institutions precisely because the stakes are higher. If the military is mismanaged, protesters don't occupy a campus building and shareholders don't take a loss. Americans die.

"The Military Can't Be Trusted"

Democrats have an uneasy relationship with the military, to say the least. Their unease leads them into mistaken views, bad policies, and misguided priorities.

Bill Clinton, Barack Obama, and Joe Biden all had rocky

relationships with the military. It's probably not a coincidence that none had served in the military, making the institution somewhat alien to them. Nor did it help that they surrounded themselves with far-left aides who also didn't serve and, in some cases, scorned the military.

Clinton was probably destined to a rough relationship with the military. He was the first president in sixty years who hadn't served, plus he dodged the draft during the Vietnam War. Many Vietnam veterans served in the upper ranks of the military during Clinton's presidency. General Colin Powell, Clinton's first chairman of the Joint Chiefs of Staff, wrote in his memoir that he and Clinton personally "had gotten along well and had become close." Still, Powell observed that Clinton "had an academic streak" and national-security meetings tended "to meander like graduate-student bull sessions or the think-tank seminars" where Clinton aides had spent the past decade.

Clinton didn't help matters by getting off to a bad start with the military. He ignored Powell's advice about how to implement his campaign promise to end the ban on gays serving in the military, which the Joint Chiefs had openly opposed. The issue dominated his early days, setting back the rest of his agenda. Behind the scenes, Powell wrote, Clinton was "surrounded by young civilians without a shred of military experience or understanding." In one notorious incident, a general greeted a young female White House staffer "to which she replied with upturned nose, 'We don't talk to soldiers around here.'" Powell reported that "the young woman's comment rocketed back to the Pentagon and whipped through the place like a free electron."

The military was also an alien institution to Obama, who had spent his life as an academic and community organizer. During the 2008 campaign, he gave a commencement address on the theme of service and specifically mentioned community service, the Foreign Service, the Peace Corps, even volunteering to teach about renewable energy. He never mentioned military service. By contrast, when I speak to high school and college students, I always encourage them to join the military. No matter what else they aspire to do with their lives, I assure them the military will make them better at it, and make them a better citizen and person.

Once in office, Obama's relationship with the military was distant. Bob Gates served as defense secretary for both George W. Bush and Obama, so he was well placed to judge the relationship both men had with their senior military leaders. "Bush never (at least to my knowledge) questioned their motives or mistrusted them personally," Gates wrote, but Obama "was deeply suspicious of their actions and recommendations." In addition, "Bush seemed to enjoy the company of the senior military," but he observed, "Obama considered time spent with the generals and admirals an obligation."

Gates recalled one particularly galling moment that reflected just how mistrustful Obama and Biden were of the military. After a long, tortured process to get Obama to settle on a strategy for the Afghanistan War, Biden jumped in and yelped, "the military 'should consider the president's decision as an order.' 'I'm giving an order,' Obama quickly said." Gates described himself as "shocked." He had served eight presidents and never heard a president "frame a decision as a direct order." Same for me: I can't recall saying or hearing it during my service in the Army. "Obama's 'order,' at Biden's urging, demonstrated," Gates wrote, "the complete unfamiliarity of both men with the American military culture. That order was unnecessary and insulting, proof positive of the depth of the Obama White House's distrust of the nation's military."

Gates gave more glimpses of the kind of commander in chief Biden has become. Unlike Clinton and Obama, Biden had spent a lifetime in Washington around senior military leaders, which only seemed to feed his distrust of them. Gates feared that Biden was "poisoning the well" with Obama, "every day saying, 'the military can't be trusted,' 'the strategy can't work,' 'it's all failing,' and 'the military is trying to game you, to screw you.'" Obama confirmed Biden's perspective in his own memoir, writing that Biden told him, "Listen to me, boss. Maybe I've been around this town for too long, but one thing I know is when these generals are trying to box in a new president." Biden concluded with a warning: "Don't let them jam you."

These views are poisonous coming from a vice president, but deadly when held by the president, as demonstrated by the disastrous way Biden executed the withdrawal from Afghanistan against his military advisers' best judgment. During the botched withdrawal, Biden then lied about the advice he had received from the military, saying that "no one" recommended keeping troops in Afghanistan. Multiple senior commanders refuted Biden under oath during a hearing before the Armed Services Committee.

Of course, these three presidents aren't the only Democrats with misgivings about the military. Other Democrats, unburdened by any weight of command, express their opinions about the military with more gusto. John Kerry infamously maligned our troops as poorly educated slackers with no future: "You know, education, if you make the most of it, you study hard, you do your homework and you make an effort to be smart, you can do well. If you don't, you get stuck in Iraq." I was serving in Iraq when he said that; trust me, it wasn't appreciated among the rank and file.

Many Democrats also see racism, sexism, and extremism lurking around every corner of the barracks. Senator Kirsten Gillibrand of New York has long crusaded to upend the entire military-justice system, on the grounds that it's biased against women and minorities. As she put it, "if you are a black or brown servicemember, I'm sorry to say, there may well be biases against you." During a hearing on supposed extremism in the military after the Capitol riot, Senator Dick Blumenthal of Connecticut asserted with zero evidence that up to 10 percent of the force might be white supremacists.

Senator Dick Durbin of Illinois in 2005 compared American troops to "Nazis, Soviets in their gulags, or some mad regime—Pol Pot or others—that had no concern for human beings" because he thought Guantánamo Bay was too harsh for terrorists. After days of hemming and hawing over the controversy, he issued a typical politician's apology: "if anything," he offered, "cast a negative light on our fine men and women in the military." I wonder what kind of light he intended to cast. I remember the episode vividly because I was on a weekend pass from Officer Candidate School at Fort Benning, Georgia. After being largely cut off from the outside world for five months, I checked into a hotel in downtown Columbus, flipped on the TV, and learned of Durbin's comment, which dominated the news all weekend. And it dominated our conversation when we reported back to OCS on Sunday night. Suffice it to say, none of us soon forgot Durbin's slander.

In reality, the Democrats' prejudices about the military are all wrong. Far from being laggards, our troops have higher levels of academic achievement and fewer blemishes on their character than the military-age population as a whole. And far from being "stuck" in Iraq, virtually every soldier I knew wanted to go fight for our country.

Moreover, America's military also has a proud record of racial equality. Truman integrated the military in 1948, just one year after Jackie Robinson broke the color barrier in baseball and six years before *Brown v. Board of Education*. Today, African Americans serve at a higher rate in our military than their share of the population—hardly evidence of a racist institution. Contrary to Dick Durbin, America's military swiftly and severely demands accountability for wrongdoing, unlike brutal regimes that employ terror and torture as official state policy. As we've seen, though, you can count on Democrats to blame America first.

But these mistaken views still lead to badly misguided policies and priorities that impugn the military's culture and alienate our troops. Biden's secretary of defense, Lloyd Austin, for example, spoke at his confirmation hearing about the need to "rid our ranks of racists" and asserted that we can't defend America against our enemies "if some of those enemies lie within our own ranks"—all before he spoke of any foreign enemies, like China.

Hearing his testimony that morning left me disappointed. I felt he must've known better. His own distinguished career as an African American four-star general who has held several of the Army's highest commands refuted such accusations against our military, as had Colin Powell's career thirty years earlier. I knew as well as he did that the military has a strict zero-tolerance policy against all forms of discrimination and harassment. Every unit in which I served had periodic training sessions on all sorts of standards, including equal-opportunity policies and expectations.

More to the point, the soldiers with whom I served always lived up to these high standards. I had African American and Latino instructors, commanders, peers, and subordinates. Not once did I witness racial discrimination or harassment. I suspect Powell and Austin unfortunately did, coming from an earlier generation, but that merely highlights the progress the military has made. What mattered most wasn't our skin color, but the red, white, and blue we had all volunteered to wear on our right shoulder. We were comrades in arms. That was a deeper bond than skin color.

Nevertheless, once confirmed, Austin ordered an extraordinary military-wide, daylong "stand-down" for training on "extremism." By contrast, the most aggressive all-Army training stand-down I can recall came in 2007 for brain injuries and post-traumatic stress. It was needed and useful, given how many soldiers suffered these injuries—and it lasted thirty minutes. Predictably, a lot of these full-day training sessions went off the rails. An Army truism is that if the commanding general wants a division formation at 0600, young privates will have to report at 0400 because each subordinate leader below the commanding general takes it a step further, directing his troops to arrive "five minutes prior" to his own boss's hit time. The same thing happened with this directive from the secretary of defense. Instead of reinforcing the military's zero-tolerance policy and demanding equal opportunity for all, I received hundreds of complaints about training sessions that accused the military of "systemic racism" and "white supremacy," segregated servicemembers by race, presumed that they held "implicit bias," mandated "confessions" of "privilege" and bias, conducted "privilege walks," and other left-wing fads. Some complaints came from minority soldiers, who found the sessions condescending and belittling.

The same is true for the Biden administration's witch hunt for "extremists" in the military. Launched with great fanfare after the Capitol riot, a "Countering Extremist Activity Working Group" bombed embarrassingly for the administration. After a six-month search, it identified fewer than one hundred "extremists" in the ranks—out of a force of more than two million. And many of those cases were criminal street gangs. Again, this shouldn't have surprised Austin or anyone else with military experience. The military rigorously screens its recruits for extremist ties, conducting criminal background checks and even doing full body scans during physical exams for extremist tattoos. Like most veterans, I remember shuffling around in my underwear on exam day, getting poked and prodded for various maladies, and checked out for disqualifying tattoos.

Such distractions and misplaced priorities aren't limited to race, or to the Biden administration. Ray Mabus, Obama's highly political secretary of the Navy, waged an eight-year culture war against the traditions of the Navy and Marine Corps. In his final year, he directed both services to change "gendered" job titles such as "infantryman" to gender-neutral names. I suppose Mabus thought the Obama administration had done so well against ISIS and countering China's naval buildup that it could focus on such matters. His directive was especially disruptive to the Navy, which has a tradition predating America's founding of using job-rating titles such as "yeoman" or "corpsman" instead of ranks such as "petty officer." Besides, even changing the Navy's job titles wouldn't have solved the supposed "problem," since the first three enlisted ranks in the service are "seaman." After months of open rebellion from the enlisted ranks and veterans, and with Mabus on the way out, Navy leadership ditched the insulting plan.

In the summer of 2021, I saw up close another instance of the Democrats' misguided views and resulting bad policies during the Armed Services Committee's debate over the annual defense bill. Normally, we consider many amendments about how we recruit, train, and equip our troops or which weapons, aircraft, and ships to purchase. But not this time, with Democrats back in charge. Over more than twelve hours, we didn't vote on a single amendment about something that would kill a bad guy. What did we vote on? Registering women for the draft. Creating a new bureaucracy to "counter extremism" in the military. Dismantling the military-justice system to combat its supposed racism and sexism. Taking privately owned guns away from troops. The longest debate was on Senator Elizabeth Warren's amendment to rescind Medals of Honor granted at the Battle of Wounded

Knee more than a century ago. Afterward, as I marveled with fellow Republicans about the unseriousness of the session, a senator walked over from the Democratic side. With a bemused smile, he asked, "Isn't it something we spent the whole time on these social and cultural questions and not on military ones?" I answered icily, "Yeah, it's really something, isn't it."

In an ironic turn of fate, we killed most of these bad provisions during negotiations with the House. Because we had also added $25 billion to Biden's anemic defense budget, the Democrats lost votes for the bill from their far left. They had to drop the "social and cultural" amendments from the language to secure enough Republican votes for passage. Democrats were hoisted with their own petard.

But the scene repeated itself in 2022, the second time as farce. What I call the "Draft Our Daughters" amendment stands out in particular. In 2021, I was one of just five senators on the committee to oppose this measure to require women to register for the draft. Some called us out of touch, when in reality the Democrats were out of touch: according to one poll, two-thirds of *women* opposed it. After the amendment got dropped from the final bill, the Democrats gave it another run in 2022. In a telling glimpse into their mindset, several Democratic senators this time gushed about how registering for the draft would improve their daughters' self-esteem. I was the only senator to speak against the amendment and I said simply: "The purpose of the military isn't to help your kids' self-esteem; it's to kill our enemies."

The Democrats still hadn't gotten the message, but I suppose it's hard to overcome decades of unease with the military. But they should, because Democratic misgivings usually end up sowing division in the ranks, undermining morale, and distracting troops from their core mission.

Ideology First, Mission Last

Because liberals don't view the military as a special institution, they're more than willing to put their ideological goals ahead of combat effectiveness and mission accomplishment. The Obama and Biden administrations illustrated this dangerous tendency in their headlong drive to open ground-combat jobs to women, even if it meant lowering standards for all troops, harming unit performance, and hurting the very female troops they wanted to help.

In one of his final official acts, Obama's secretary of defense Leon Panetta announced in January 2013 that he would end the military's rule against women serving in ground-combat roles. But he insisted that "we are not talking about reducing the qualifications for the job." As a new congressman, I opposed this policy change, despite warnings from many not to tackle such a controversial issue in my first month in office. But I suspected the Obama administration would do exactly what Panetta had warned against, reducing standards and putting lives at risk. I also realized for the first time how little many of my colleagues knew about the military. Since military service is a rare thing these days in Congress, most of my peers had never served and didn't understand basic facts about the military, whereas I wasn't even four years removed from Afghanistan.

A case in point is how many liberals celebrated Panetta's decision to allow "women in combat," which reflected their ignorance and also was a little insulting to the thousands of women who had already served bravely and honorably in combat. For decades, women had flown combat missions. In Iraq and Afghanistan, wars without front lines meant that female soldiers on supply convoys and other missions could find themselves "in combat" at any moment. I had many occasions to take female soldiers on my infantry patrols. These women always did their share of the task, and then some.

Liberals didn't understand the specific issue at hand. This debate wasn't about "women in combat." It wasn't even about women in combat units like infantry battalions, which have many jobs open to women, such as medics, mechanics, and intelligence specialists. Rather, the debate was about women in frontline ground-combat jobs, especially the infantry and special forces. These are the most physically demanding jobs in the military and have irreducible requirements of strength, stamina, and durability, whether it's shouldering an eighty-pound load on a twenty-mile foot march, carrying an unwieldy twenty-eight-pound M240B machine gun, or dragging a wounded 250-pound battle buddy to safety.

So many Democrats, and more than a few Republicans, just didn't understand the unique physical demands of these ground-combat jobs. I recall one conversation with a group of representatives in which a Democrat argued that if the Navy could open ships and submarines to women, then the Army and Marines should be able to open infantry to them, as well. I couldn't believe what I was hearing. Most Navy jobs are technical and intellectual. The Navy's challenge mostly dealt with facilities and behaviors—for instance, how to provide berthing and bathrooms for female sailors in extremely limited ship space. Ground-combat jobs, by contrast, are intensely, unforgivingly physical. The challenge for the Army and the Marines was the unavoidable reality of biology and physiology.

Panetta recognized this reality, because he gave the services the opportunity to demonstrate the need for an exception for specific ground-combat jobs. But I believed the fix was already in. The chairman of the Joint Chiefs of Staff, General Martin Dempsey, noted that "if we decide that a particular standard is so high that a woman couldn't make it, the burden is now on the service to come back and explain to the secretary, why is it that high? Does it really have to be that high?" No doubt facing pressure from the administration, Dempsey was signaling that any requests for exceptions would be looked upon unfavorably.

Nevertheless, the Marine Corps did exactly what Panetta proposed, designing a rigorous, data-driven study of the effects of having women serve in ground-combat roles. The Marines compared mixed-sex units against all-male units, testing everything from marksmanship to injury rates to casualty-evacuation times. The results vindicated my and the Marines' concerns: the all-male units outperformed the mixed-sex units in 70 percent of the tests. Perhaps most disturbing for Marine safety, mixed-sex squads took up to 159 percent longer to evacuate casualties, which could often be the difference between life and death in combat. The female Marines also suffered injuries at much higher rates because of the different physiological impacts of heavy load-bearing on male and female bodies. The summary memo of the study dryly concluded, "the bottom line is that the physiological differences between males and females will likely always be evident to some extent." These findings mirror those of similar British and Israeli studies, to say nothing of the commonsense logic of having separate men's and women's sports.

But ideology was in the saddle, not common sense, and Panetta was long gone, replaced by Ash Carter, who rejected the Marine Corps' request for an exception without seriously engaging its findings. Worse, Mabus was still around and as politicized as ever. He accused the Marines of sexism, sneering that the study "started out with a fairly large component of the men thinking this is not a good idea and women will never be able to do this. When you start out with that mindset, you almost presuppose the outcome." He even denigrated the women who volunteered for the study, saying "there should have been a higher bar to cross to get into the experiment."

I still had my doubts that liberal ideologues wouldn't force the military to reduce standards, and I wasn't the only one. General John Kelly, then a four-star Marine and later Donald Trump's secretary of Homeland Security and White House chief of staff, bluntly warned about it in his final days in uniform. "They're saying we are not going to change any standards," he noted, but added, "there will be great pressure, whether it's twelve months from now, four years from now, because the question will be asked whether we've let women into these other roles, why aren't they staying in those other roles?" He suspected the answer: "if we don't change standards, it will be very difficult to have any real numbers coming in the infantry, or the Rangers, or the SEALs." In that case, he predicted future generals would come under immense pressure to lower standards, "because that's the only way I think that people, the agenda-driven people here in the land want it to work."

Those "agenda-driven" ideologues have since done exactly what Kelly and I predicted. In early 2022, the Army buckled under pressure from far-left activists and liberal politicians, announcing it would adopt lower physical-fitness standards for female soldiers after years of promising a gender-neutral standard. In a way, this decision merely continues decades of Army practice of separate scoring scales on its fitness test for male and female soldiers. The key difference, of course, is now ground-combat jobs are open to women. A young female soldier can qualify for the infantry today by doing as few as ten push-ups and "running" two miles in fewer than twenty-three minutes, among other tests.

To be fair, the pathetic standards for male soldiers aren't much better. But the paper standards for male soldiers were never the actual standards. During my service, the Army's minimum score per event on the fitness test was sixty out of one hundred. Every infantry unit in which I served, however, insisted upon ninety points per event; anything less would result in remedial fitness training and limit a soldier's chances for promotion, awards, and advanced schooling.

I've asked my friends still in the Army, many of whom have taken command of infantry battalions, whether they can still set higher fitness standards than the Army minimum. They all say no, and many laugh at the question. The reason is simple: higher standards would exclude most women from the infantry. As a result, we now have not just separate standards for women, but lower standards for men, as well.

The Army has come a long way from its own promises, as well as Panetta's promise that the military wouldn't be "making tests less rigorous merely so that women would have an easier time passing them." While it will please politically correct ideologues, the Army's decision will endanger the lives of both male and female soldiers and put their mission at risk. One Army officer wrote bluntly in opposition:

> While it may be difficult for a 120-pound woman to lift or drag 250 pounds, the Army cannot artificially absolve women of that responsibility; it may still exist on the battlefield. The entire purpose of creating a gender-neutral test was to acknowledge the reality that each job has objective physical standards to which all soldiers should be held, regardless of gender. The intent was not to ensure that women and men will have an equal likelihood of meeting those standards.

She should know: Captain Kristen Griest is the Army's first female infantry officer and one of its first female Ranger School graduates. Griest called it "wholly unethical to allow the standards of the nation's premiere fighting units to degrade so badly." I couldn't agree more and

I've acted to uphold those standards. At the time of publication, Congress is poised to adopt an amendment to the annual defense bill that I offered with Senator Joni Ernst, also an Army veteran, to require gender-neutral fitness standards for ground-combat jobs. We'll see if the ideologues in the Biden administration take the hint and follow Captain Griest's advice.

THE DEMOCRATS' HOSTILITY to military power and strained relationship with the military give them political blind spots, which is one reason why they end up getting rebuked by a trailblazing female leader. But they just can't help themselves from pursuing ideologically appealing but politically unpopular goals.

Nevertheless, Democrats are very sensitive to the perception (based in reality, as we've seen) that they're weak on defense. As a result, Democrats often feel compelled to act tough, even if they can't actually get tough. As we'll see next, when that happens, Americans usually die and our safety is endangered.

CHAPTER 5

When Democrats Act Tough

I N SEPTEMBER 1988, America was in the middle of a presidential campaign between Governor Michael Dukakis and Vice President George H. W. Bush. Dukakis badly needed to turn things around. After having led the polls for most of the summer, Dukakis's popularity collapsed as Bush's campaign highlighted Dukakis's liberal record in Massachusetts. On a crisp fall day, Dukakis traveled to a General Dynamics facility in Michigan to recast his image.

Dukakis, nicknamed "the Duke," was Woodrow Wilson's ideal of a big-government expert. He graduated from Harvard Law, spoke six languages, and reputedly studied Swedish Land Use Planning for fun. For progressives, it was love at first sight. But the American people saw "the Duke" as cold, stiff, robotic, and superior. Newspapers described him as an "enigma" and a "cool technocrat."

Americans thought Dukakis was a milquetoast, too weak to be president—and for good reason. As governor, he was very soft on crime, furloughing violent felons for weekend getaways from prison. Willie Horton, a convicted murderer who was supposed to be locked up for life, didn't return from his weekend furlough, but instead raped a woman and beat her fiancé. The story horrified Americans and turned them against Dukakis. And there was more. For instance,

Dukakis even opposed the recitation of the Pledge of Allegiance in schools, typical for the Blame America First Democrats.

Dukakis was no better on major defense and foreign-policy issues. He had supported the nuclear-freeze movement, opposed major weapons systems including the B-1 bomber, opposed the Reagan administration's rapid expansion of the Navy, and opposed the liberation of Grenada and the retaliatory bombing of Libya. This record of weakness was a major handicap in the waning days of the Cold War. The Bush campaign pressed its advantage on national security, and the Dukakis campaign knew it had to toughen up his image and fast.

That's why Dukakis, master technocrat and pencil pusher, found himself in a massive military garage wearing coveralls. The elfish governor climbed into a sixty-eight-ton, eight-foot-tall M1A1 Abrams tank and donned an oversized tank commander's helmet.

Mike Dukakis rides a tank into electoral oblivion. AP Images.

Once properly situated for his photo op, Dukakis gave the order and the M1A1 roared out of the garage. As the tank emerged, the assembled press corps burst out laughing at what they saw—hardly the intended reaction. The top half of the governor protruded from the open hatch of the massive tank and the would-be president was wearing a giant helmet that made him look like Dark Helmet from *Spaceballs*, the Star Wars parody hit from a year earlier—only this wasn't a parody, at least not an intentional one. The governor then pointed toward the cameras with an aura of command as the tank circled the practice track.

Far from looking strong, Dukakis looked weaker than ever. Dukakis's anxiety about appearing weak caused him to commit one of the worst gaffes in presidential campaign history. The media and Bush campaign skewered his performance. His collapse continued and, two months later, Bush won forty states in yet another electoral blowout for the Republicans.

ALTHOUGH MICHAEL DUKAKIS'S tank ride into electoral oblivion is amusing to recall, it also reflects a deeper truth about Democrats: they understand their national-security weakness can be a political liability. The American people love our country, want it safe and strong, and revere our troops. They put America's interests first, have little time for abstractions, and expect the same from their elected officials. All these instincts run contrary to the progressive mindset, as we've seen. As a result, Democratic politicians have a self-consciousness bordering on paranoia about appearing weak. This truth is reflected in a Bill Clinton aphorism: strong and wrong beats weak and right. But the saying itself reveals the Democrats' dilemma: it doesn't cross their mind that one can be strong and right.

The electoral scoreboard during the Cold War tells the political tale. In the first half of the Cold War (1948–1964), the Democrats won three of five presidential races. But once the Democrats turned not just on the Vietnam War, but on American power itself, the Democrats lost five of six elections from 1968 to 1988, four in historic landslides. Only with the collapse of the Soviet Union did the American people feel safe electing a Democrat again in 1992—perhaps not coincidentally the first person elected president in sixty years without military service.

But what's laughable on the campaign trail is deadly in the White House. Democrats feel compelled to act tough, usually with disastrous consequences. They get us into foolish fights they aren't prepared or willing to win. They fear appearing weak, but they're uncomfortable with the exercise of power to defend our interests. Democratic presidents hedge and trim, capable of starting wars but incapable of winning them, employing hesitant half measures at every turn. The end result, tragically, is usually the same: defeat, dishonor, and dead Americans.

While the examples of Democrats acting tough sadly abound, three cases in particular illustrate the dangers of what happens when Democrats act tough: the Bay of Pigs, Vietnam, and Somalia.

THE BAY OF PIGS: "KENNEDY VACILLATED"

The Bay of Pigs was a disaster and a betrayal that Democrats would like to forget, but one that Cuban Americans and anti-communists never will. The operation failed because of John Kennedy's desire to look tough in the 1960 presidential campaign and early in his presidency, but his fear of actually being tough in a crisis. As a result, Kennedy weakened our security, emboldened Soviet Russia, and condemned Cubans to six decades and counting of communist hell.

Kennedy campaigned in 1960 as a new, stronger Democrat. After witnessing World War II hero Dwight Eisenhower deride Adlai Stevenson as a weak "egghead" and win landsides in both 1952 and 1956, Kennedy had no appetite for a repeat against Richard Nixon in 1960. Kennedy carried the burden of his father's legacy too. Joe Kennedy had served as Franklin Roosevelt's ambassador to the United Kingdom when World War II broke out. He had supported Neville Chamberlain's appeasement policy, opposed American economic and military aid to the British, and repeatedly sought unauthorized meetings with Hitler. In the war's early days, he was ready to concede defeat.

But the younger Kennedy had the benefit of decorated Navy service during the war. Kennedy also burnished his hawkish reputation by criticizing Eisenhower and Nixon for allowing a supposed "missile gap" to develop with the Soviets and for losing Cuba to Fidel Castro's communist insurgency. On Cuba, in particular, Kennedy sounded the trumpet of strident Cold Warrior. He campaigned to strengthen "democratic anti-Castro forces in exile, and in Cuba itself, who offer eventual hope of overthrowing Castro," while seething that "these fighters for freedom have had virtually no support from our Government."

So it was on January 20, 1961, that Kennedy took his Cold War rhetoric to new heights. He famously promised that "we shall pay any price, bear any burden, meet any hardship, support any friend, oppose any foe, to assure the survival and the success of liberty." Less famous but more to the point, he offered a "special pledge" to Latin America "to assist free men and free governments in casting off their chains," and specifically "to oppose aggression or subversion." These words surely filled Cuban exiles with hope—vainly, it would prove.

Even if he hadn't campaigned on freedom for Cuba, Kennedy could hardly avoid the growing communist threat just ninety miles off the Florida coast. Because Cuba controls sea-lanes into the Gulf of Mexico and the Caribbean Sea, American statesmen since colonial times had worried about it falling into enemy control. With modern technology, the island also amounts to an unsinkable aircraft carrier and missile pad. Now, the far-left Castro had moved Cuba into Soviet Russia's strategic orbit, surrounding himself with communist hardliners and importing Soviet weapons. He also had established himself as one of the world's most vehement America bashers and posed a clear threat to stability in the Western Hemisphere. Put simply, it was in America's interest to remove Castro. The Eisenhower administration thus had begun planning to support a rebel invasion of the island and had started training Cuban dissidents in Guatemala.

The CIA briefed Kennedy on the plan in his first days in office. The plan called for air strikes to destroy Castro's air force, followed by a daytime amphibious landing by the Cuban exiles. The CIA expected that the landing forces could join the ongoing guerilla campaign against the new, fragile Castro regime and inspire a large-scale revolution. If the operation went awry, the planners had selected a landing beach near the Escambray Mountains, the heart of the insurgency, where the rebels could escape and safely join the guerillas.

This plan was well intentioned, but also had its flaws. From the outset, the plan was covert, which limited the nature and amount of military support available for the rebels to achieve the military objectives. The plan also relied on the element of surprise, but rampant media speculation surrounded the operation. Ten days before Kennedy's inauguration, a *New York Times* headline read, "U.S. Helps Train an Anti-Castro Force at Secret Guatemalan Air-Ground Base"—not a good omen of operational security. The Joint Chiefs of Staff also expressed doubts about the plan and only gave it a "fair chance of ultimate success." The Joint Chiefs preferred stronger military action to topple Castro.

But Kennedy did the opposite, weakening the plan even further. Despite his tough talk on the campaign trail and in his inaugural, Kennedy complained that the plan "looks too much like a military operation" and worried it would "fix a malevolent image of the new Administration" in the words of Arthur Schlesinger Jr., his close friend and Harvard professor who became his White House adviser. To meet Kennedy's demands, the CIA moved the landing site from a tactically sound location to beaches near Bahía de Cochinos—the Bay of Pigs—where coral reefs threatened the landing craft and eighty miles of swampland awaited the exiles. He also insisted the amphibious landing occur at night and sought to minimize or eliminate plans for air strikes.

Kennedy's nervous tinkering undercut the needed conditions for victory. The plan always depended for success on a popular revolt, which was less likely to occur after a nighttime landing in secluded swamplands far removed from the ongoing insurgency. Also, his insistence on more deniability seemed increasingly foolish with, for instance, *U.S. News & World Reports* running the headline, "The Big Buildup to Overthrow Castro." The whole world knew what Kennedy was up to, yet he continued to hamstring the mission's tactical planning. And he feared that congressional Republicans would savage him if he backed down. Given this fear and his own words, he felt compelled to act tough in Cuba, but he defaulted to half measures.

What's worse, Kennedy blinked when the chips were down during the operation. At the insistence of the Joint Chiefs, Kennedy initially approved plans for a series of air strikes against Castro's air force in the lead-up to the invasion. Strikes were planned for the two days before the landing and for the day of the invasion. Kennedy got cold feet a few days out, though, and ordered the CIA to make the strikes "minimal." The CIA cut in half the number of aircraft for the first strikes, then Kennedy called off the remaining strikes. Out of forty planned sorties to destroy Castro's air force, Kennedy allowed only eight. His secretary of state, Dean Rusk, told flabbergasted planners that "political considerations were taking over." After Kennedy canceled the air strikes, one disgusted general shouted, "there goes the whole fuckin' war!" Kennedy's indecision was sabotaging his already inadequate plan.

Things got even worse as the operation unfolded. In the early hours of April 17, the freedom fighters of Brigade 2506 navigated jagged coral reefs and returned to their native Cuban soil. Back in Washington, Kennedy betrayed them by refusing multiple requests for air cover. Soon after first light, Castro's still-operational air force devastated the rebels, strafing them on the beaches, shooting down two of their only aircraft, and bombing their supply ships. One rebel leader radioed for help to American destroyers on the horizon, only to receive the American commander's response, "my heart is with you, but I cannot help you. My orders are not to become engaged in any way."

Abandoned by Kennedy, Brigade 2506 courageously faced the full might of Castro's communist army. Thanks to media reporting and foreign spies, Castro had cracked down and imprisoned 100,000 known and suspected dissidents. He also had readied his 32,000-man regular army and 300,000-man militia, and he threw them into the battle. But this lone brigade "fought like tigers," as one CIA officer attested. They weathered a four-hour, 2,000-shell artillery barrage and then repulsed multiple waves of tanks and infantry. After two days of intense fighting, however, the vastly outnumbered brigade was exhausted, low on ammunition, and desperate for American support. The brigade commander begged for air support, pleading in one message, "please don't desert us."

But that's exactly what Kennedy did. When Admiral Arleigh Burke, the Chief of Naval Operations, urged him to send air support to help resupply the rebels on the beach, Kennedy whined, "we just can't get involved." Burke, a legend of World War II and Korea, snapped back at his callow commander in chief: "goddammit, Mr. President, we are involved, and there is no way to hide it." Involved, but not committed to victory.

Even in retreat, the rebels suffered thanks to Kennedy's ineptitude. Rather than vanish into forbidding mountains to link up with friendly guerrilla forces, they had to flee into the hellish swampland that Kennedy had foolishly selected for the landing. After several days, the one thousand surviving fighters surrendered to the communist forces on whom they had inflicted so many casualties. For nearly two years, these men faced brutal imprisonment, show trials, and in some cases execution. The surviving members of Brigade 2506 were finally released in late December 1962, when they received a well-deserved hero's welcome in Miami.

When asked why the rebels lost at the Bay of Pigs, Fidel Castro answered simply, "lack of air cover." His brother Raul expanded:

> Kennedy vacillated. If at that moment he had decided to invade us, he could have suffocated the island in a sea of blood, but he would have destroyed the revolution. Luckily for us, he vacillated. If instead of Kennedy we had had any of the later presidents, they would have intervened and destroyed the revolution.

"He vacillated." That's a pretty succinct summary of what happens when Democrats act tough, even more damning for coming from a mortal enemy. Kennedy abandoned the brave warriors of Brigade 2506 on that beach, and he condemned the Cuban people to decades of communist misery.

Kennedy's indecision also endangered America's safety by emboldening our enemies, who soon took advantage of the disaster. Castro benefited directly from Kennedy's violation of Napoleon's famous maxim: when you set out to take Vienna, take Vienna. Castro consolidated his brutal rule on the island, lionizing himself as the great revolutionary who had defeated the impotent giant. Soviet premier Nikita

Khrushchev also capitalized on America's humiliation, welcoming Castro's Cuba fully into the communist camp. Speaking of Vienna, it was just six weeks after the debacle when Khrushchev berated and humiliated Kennedy at their first summit there. "He just beat the hell out of me," Kennedy later reflected, "he savaged me." Khrushchev, for his part, observed of Kennedy, "this man is very inexperienced, even immature."

The insults to our honor and threats to our security continued. Just two months after Khrushchev took Kennedy's measure at Vienna, he ordered the construction of the Berlin Wall. Kennedy stood meekly by. And less than a year later, Khrushchev and Castro secretly agreed to place nuclear-capable missiles in Cuba. Though the Cuban Missile Crisis in October 1962 is often portrayed as a great victory for Kennedy, it was in reality a major strategic defeat. Khrushchev had precipitated the crisis with the incredible provocation of deploying ballistic missiles and bombers just ninety miles from our shores. Yet Kennedy granted three massive concessions to end the manufactured crisis: the removal of our nuclear missiles from Turkey, a promise not to invade Cuba and depose Castro, and the tacit acceptance of all non-nuclear Soviet arms in Cuba.

The Bay of Pigs is a classic example of what happens when Democrats act tough: half measures that end up worse than nothing at all. Kennedy wanted to sound tough on Cuba during the 1960 campaign, then he feared the political backlash if he didn't follow through. But he and the progressives around him, bashful of how their fellow liberals and the "international community" might react, refused to use sufficient force to protect our vital interests in Cuba. America has paid the price ever since. Soviet Russia turned Cuba into a massive arms depot in our backyard, while Castro aided the Soviets in sponsoring left-wing insurgencies throughout Latin America and as far away as Africa. Even after the Soviet Union collapsed, Cuba continued to support anti-American movements and governments throughout the hemisphere, as it still does today.

Democrats may want to forget the Bay of Pigs and reconcile with communist Cuba, but Cuba won't unclench its fist. And why would the Cuban regime? They just need to wait for a progressive president like Barack Obama to grant unilateral concessions and even visit Havana to pal around with Raul Castro at a baseball game, as he did in 2016. I believe one day Cubans will live in freedom, but I mourn the suffering inflicted upon them ever since "Kennedy vacillated."

VIETNAM: A DEMOCRATIC TRAGEDY

Not one, but two Democratic presidents turned the Vietnam War into America's worst military debacle. Kennedy transformed Vietnam into an American war. And Lyndon Johnson, desperate to be loved by both hawks and doves, forced our military to fight the war with one hand tied behind its back. Instead, both sides grew to hate him, tens of thousands of American troops died in the jungles and rice paddies, and America was forced into strategic retreat in the Cold War.

Kennedy's Folly

Kennedy inherited a volatile Southeast Asia, but the situation deteriorated because of his foolish mistakes. By ceding Laos—a strategically vital neighboring country—to the communists and then overthrowing the pro-American strongman running South Vietnam, Kennedy created the conditions that turned a Vietnamese war into an American war and ultimately led to the fall of South Vietnam to the communists.

Southeast Asia had suffered fifteen years of violence and instability by the time Kennedy took office. France had lost control of its long-time colonies in French Indochina—Vietnam, Laos, and Cambodia—during World War II and fought communist insurgencies to reclaim them after the war. In Vietnam, in particular, France faced off against Ho Chi Minh, a merciless butcher and a doctrinaire acolyte of Joseph Stalin. Soviet Russia and Communist China supported Ho's forces. America under Dwight Eisenhower in turn supported France until its final defeat in 1954. As in Korea a year earlier, Vietnam was partitioned between a communist North under Ho and an American-aligned South Vietnam under Ngo Dinh Diem.

But unlike Korea, the fighting in Vietnam ground on. With the continued support of the Russians and the Chinese, the North Vietnamese Army waged war directly against the South, while Ho's government also underwrote communist rebels throughout the south. Eisenhower transferred our support to Diem, a heavy-handed ruler who was far from perfect, but who was preferable to any viable alternative and was strongly pro-American. Diem's government didn't make much headway in the north, but with American support it kept the insurgents at bay and consolidated control in the south. Critical to this effort, the Diem government had destroyed the first Ho Chi Minh Trail, a logistics network connecting North and South Vietnam that the North and its allies used to arm and supply communist rebels against the South. The communists began to establish a new Ho Chi Minh Trail in neighboring Laos, which the Eisenhower administration opposed through its support for the anti-communist government in Laos. A proxy war in Laos escalated quickly and brought us to the brink of open conflict with the Soviets by the time Kennedy took office.

As with the Bay of Pigs, Kennedy dithered in Laos. The Joint Chiefs of Staff proposed an overwhelming force of 60,000 troops if Kennedy wanted to intervene, but he could only stomach 10,000 Marines, which might have looked tough, but likely would only have gotten us into a shooting war without a prospect of victory. But Kennedy shifted course, pursuing a cease-fire and neutrality for the small nation that Eisenhower had called "the cork in the bottle" holding back communism in Southeast Asia. The Laotian communists agreed six weeks later—only after the North Vietnamese Army had seized the key terrain in eastern Laos for a new Ho Chi Minh Trail. One month later, at the disastrous Vienna summit, Kennedy and Khrushchev agreed to a cease-fire, while punting the final political agreement to an international conference. Both sides ultimately agreed to leave Laos, but the communists never did, and continued using supposedly neutral Laos to supply their forces in South Vietnam.

Kennedy's misstep on Laos was also his first grave mistake in the Vietnam War. He foolishly trusted assurances from Khrushchev, Ho, and the Laotian communists, effectively ceding control of the eastern half of Laos to them. This was precisely the territory needed for the new trail, and the North Vietnamese stayed in Laos and kept constructing it. In the years to come, thousands of American troops would be maimed and killed by weapons smuggled down that trail. More immediately, though, this outcome further destabilized South Vietnam and the rest of Southeast Asia.

After a brutal first year in office—the Bay of Pigs, the Vienna summit, the Berlin Wall, and Laos—Kennedy acknowledged that "now we have a problem in making our power credible, and Vietnam is the place." In 1962, he increased our troop presence from 3,000 to 11,000. These troops continued to work mostly as advisers to the South Vietnamese Army, not in combat roles.

But Kennedy soon undercut our troops' efforts to stabilize South

Vietnam with a second and much worse mistake: he permitted a coup against Diem, South Vietnam's pro-American ruler. In 1963, amid continued success against the communist guerrillas, Diem confronted a communist-influenced Buddhist uprising. Diem cracked down on dissent in response. Buddhist priests set themselves on fire in protest and the images soon appeared in American newspapers, horrifying Americans. Diem's critics in our government seized the opportunity to plot his removal.

Foremost among those critics, and a chief supporter of the coup, was our ambassador to South Vietnam, Henry Cabot Lodge Jr. Like Kennedy, Lodge was the scion of a Massachusetts political dynasty; in fact, he had been a senator until Kennedy beat him in 1952. He also had been Nixon's vice presidential nominee in 1960. Kennedy asked his old rival to serve as ambassador partly because he wanted Republican "cover" in case he lost Vietnam to communism. Lodge arrived in Vietnam in the midst of the crisis. But Kennedy had backed himself, not Lodge, into a corner. Now that Lodge aligned with State Department officials against Diem, Kennedy feared that he couldn't oppose the coup without appearing weak, perhaps even giving Lodge a campaign issue should he run for president the next year, as was rumored. Once again, Kennedy vacillated and then concluded he would only "discourage" the coup, as if it wasn't his decision as president.

Kennedy's urge to look tough for political reasons again led to a fiasco. With Kennedy's tacit approval, South Vietnamese generals removed Diem from office and had him executed. With fewer than 20,000 troops in a country fighting a communist insurgency, Kennedy had acquiesced to the decapitation of a friendly government, without any viable successor. No doubt Diem was a flawed ally, but he was the best horse we had in Vietnam, as subsequent events proved.

After the coup, the South Vietnamese government descended into chaos, the new leadership purged Diem's efficient bureaucracy, and military factions engaged in one coup after another, hamstringing the war effort. North Vietnam seized the initiative over the next two years.

Worst of all, Kennedy transformed a Vietnamese war into an American war. We could've preserved, at low cost, a pro-American and anti-communist government in Saigon. Instead, by foolishly toppling Diem, we had assumed the responsibility for the fight against the advancing communists. Only an overwhelming use of American power could forestall the communist takeover.

The Joint Chiefs of Staff aptly called the Diem coup "the Asian Bay of Pigs." Kennedy tragically died from an assassin's bullet just three weeks after Diem, so he never witnessed the full scale of his folly. His successor, Lyndon Johnson, would inherit the debacle.

Johnson's Defeat

President Johnson only turned this inherited mess into a bigger, bloodier conflict. For five years, he showed what happens when Democrats act tough but don't follow through. He feared the political consequences of losing South Vietnam to the communists, yet he couldn't bring himself to use enough force to win the war. The result was a battlefield stalemate with more than 36,000 Americans killed in action on Johnson's watch.

Johnson elevated the Democratic political imperative to act tough without being tough to a national war doctrine. He feared suffering the fate of Harry Truman, who was criticized as weak on communism after the fall of China, and asserted, "I am not going to be the president who saw Southeast Asia go the way China went." But he didn't just fear hawkish Cold Warriors; he also feared the "sob sisters and peace societies," as he called them—and he vainly tried to placate both. His guidance to the Joint Chiefs regarding the North Vietnamese was to "upset them a little bit without getting another Korea operation started." Johnson wanted to show strength to fend off political criticism while also pulling punches to avoid an all-out war. He feared victory as much as he feared defeat.

Johnson turned to Secretary of Defense Robert McNamara for intellectual justification and bureaucratic support for his political desire to act tough on the cheap. McNamara was another Wilsonian ideal of a scientific expert; he had spent World War II as a statistician for the Army Air Forces and then became the CEO of the Ford Motor Company. A good progressive, McNamara believed that scientific management and computer spreadsheets had replaced the eternal lessons of war learned from generals like Thucydides and George Washington. Instead of principles like overwhelming force and speed, war could now be conducted with "pinprick operations" and based on principles like "graduated pressure" and "measured response."

Of course, these concepts worked perfectly to excuse the weaknesses and half measures of his two bosses. H. R. McMaster, who wrote the landmark Vietnam history *Dereliction of Duty* as a young Army officer and later served as Donald Trump's national security adviser, explained McNamara's theory of graduated pressure: "the aim of force was not to impose one's will on the enemy but to *communicate* with him. Gradually intensifying military action would convey American resolve and thereby convince an adversary to alter his behavior." The advantages were thoroughly political, allowing Johnson to demonstrate "resolve" with only the minimum of force and resources. National Security Adviser McGeorge Bundy recognized that this policy had only a 25 percent chance of success, but he claimed that "even if it fails, the policy will be worth it" because it will "damp down the charge that we did not do all that we could have done." Victory came second to looking tough and avoiding criticism.

These theories weren't—and aren't—suited to winning a war, to say the least, as military men knew. The Joint Chiefs strongly opposed McNamara's policy of "slowly walking up the [escalatory] ladder" and "communicating" with the enemy, and instead called for a "sudden sharp blow." But they were thwarted at every turn. A war game in the early days of the Johnson administration showed that McNamara's strategy of "graduated pressure" would result in painful defeat. The Joint Chiefs urged him either to end the war or to go for the jugular. But the bureaucratically talented McNamara suppressed many of these findings and criticism. One haughty McNamara aide lectured a seasoned admiral: "I know you military fellows have always been taught to get in there with both feet and get it over with, but this is a different kind of war." Indeed, our military was accustomed to winning wars, whereas Johnson and McNamara only wanted to avoid losing one.

But in war, when you're not winning, you're losing—and that's doubly true for a superpower. Time and again, Johnson forced the military to pull its punches out of fear that he would "communicate" the wrong message. He scaled back retaliatory strikes after the North Vietnamese attacked our ships in international waters in the Gulf of Tonkin and after the guerrillas in the south bombed a barracks and bombarded an American air base. He refused to bomb Hanoi, to mine the Haiphong harbor—a critical port through which most of North Vietnam's supplies flowed—or to destroy communist supply routes in Laos. McNamara even refused to allow the military to bomb a North Vietnamese airfield hosting Russian-supplied jets and surface-to-air missile sites. But he sent our pilots into that contested airspace, putting them at risk.

126

Even when he initiated bombing campaigns and surged troops into Vietnam, Johnson remained tentative and reactive. He often waited until after a major enemy attack or until South Vietnamese forces were on the verge of collapse to authorize more aggressive action. Amazingly, he micromanaged targeting decisions from the White House, saving critical Vietnamese military targets from destruction for potential future "messages." Ho Chi Minh, who had no such scruples, was no doubt appreciative. Johnson also authorized several bombing pauses with no strategic reason, though often with political reasons, such as the pause the week before the 1968 election. These pauses merely gave the North Vietnamese time to regroup and plot new attacks.

Johnson failed in Vietnam because he didn't understand that the goal of war is to destroy the enemy's will and ability to resist—not to look tough politically or to "communicate messages" to the enemy. Despite increasing troop numbers every year while he was president—from 16,000 in 1963 to 530,000 in 1968—he nevertheless restrained those troops from fighting to win. They were never allowed to fight Ulysses S. Grant's way of war: "the art of war is simple enough. Find out where your enemy is. Get at him as soon as you can. Strike as hard as you can and as often as you can, and keep moving on."

A Democratic Tragedy

Vietnam didn't have to turn out the way it did. America could have won in Vietnam early and at very low cost if Kennedy hadn't given the communists a supply route in Laos and decapitated the South Vietnam government. America still could've won early, albeit at somewhat higher cost, if Johnson had used overwhelming force against North Vietnam early in his administration. Instead, Democrats sacrificed victory, satisfied with merely looking tough in the short run.

When Richard Nixon became president, our military was finally allowed to fight without one hand tied behind its back and it achieved our objectives. We pressed our advantage against the communist guerrillas in the south, who had suffered severe losses during their Tet Offensive in 1968, and essentially destroyed them as a fighting force. And facing ever greater pressure on the battlefield, North Vietnam began peace talks, which concluded in early 1973. All this occurred during the period of Vietnamization of the war, with our troop levels declining from 475,000 in 1969 to 24,000 in 1972. Nixon secured the peace in part with his personal assurances to the South—and threats to the North—that America would return if the North renewed its attacks. For a while, the South seemed to maintain the upper hand militarily, but Watergate badly damaged Nixon politically and the liberal Democratic Congress refused further military aid to South Vietnam. Abandoned by the party that had gotten America into the war, Saigon fell in April 1975.

These glimpses of what might have been underscore why Vietnam was a tragedy: not because we fought, but because we didn't fight earlier, smarter, and harder. Ronald Reagan called the Vietnam War "a noble cause." Reagan was right: Vietnam was a noble cause and a necessary war to protect America's vital national-security interests.

First, Eisenhower was right about the domino theory. Laos and Cambodia fell to communists alongside South Vietnam. These communists then committed genocide on a horrific scale. And while no other dominoes fell in the region, no less a statesman than Lee Kuan Yew of Singapore explained that the main reason the rest of Southeast Asia didn't fall to communism was because America had fought in Vietnam. America's humiliation in Saigon did, however, embolden the Soviets and their Cuban proxies across the globe in the second half of the 1970s. War and communist revolution in Afghanistan,

Angola, Nicaragua, Grenada, and elsewhere occurred in the shadow of an American helicopter fleeing Saigon.

Second, Vietnam is and always will be invaluable strategic territory in Asia. This is a simple geographic fact. South Vietnam holds a commanding position on the South China Sea and just above the Strait of Malacca, two of the most critical waterways in the world. Vietnam is also the gateway to the rest of Southeast Asia—the Philippines, Malaysia, Singapore, Indonesia, and Australia—which is why the Japanese prioritized it in World War II. Just imagine how different our struggle with China would look today if South Vietnam was, in effect, another South Korea: a dynamic capitalist economy offering ready access to American ships, aircraft, and troops.

The Democrats tragically squandered these potential strategic advantages, emboldened worldwide communism through their criminal mismanagement of the Vietnam War, and condemned millions to the darkness of communist tyranny. If only Kennedy and Johnson had fought to win instead of wanting to look tough, none of this might have happened. And that truly is a tragedy.

SOMALIA: "PAPER TIGER" DEMOCRATS

The instinct to act tough for political reasons runs deep in the Democratic psyche; it's not just an artifact of the Cold War. Democrats are often torn between, on the one hand, their progressive instincts to pursue grandiose plans abstracted from our vital interests and, on the other hand, their hostility to the exercise of American power. As a result of these incoherent tendencies, Democrats get our troops killed, imperil our interests, and stain our honor. The first post–Cold War president, Bill Clinton, did exactly that in the 1993 debacle in Somalia.

In late 1992, during the final days of President George H. W. Bush's tenure, a famine gripped the war-torn African nation of Somalia, killing an estimated 350,000 Somalis. Warlords had caused the famine by disrupting local agriculture and using food as a weapon to starve rival clans. The reliably incompetent United Nations couldn't prevent the warlords from stealing its food shipments, making matters worse. The UN once again sought America's help, not only to secure the food shipments but also to disarm the warlords.

Bush wisely rejected the expansive security mission, though he agreed to the food-aid mission. Even that mission was questioned by some of his key aides. Bob Gates, the CIA director and later secretary of defense to both George W. Bush and Barack Obama, pointed out that the famine resulted from the civil war, not a natural disaster. As long as the warlords kept fighting each other, food aid would only treat the symptom, not the cause. No one in the Bush administration thought America could or should resolve Somalia's civil war.

In any event, Bush insisted on a strategy of overwhelming force with a strictly defined and limited mission. With President-elect Clinton's support, he sent more than 25,000 troops to Mogadishu. Faced with such overwhelming power, the warlords stood down and allowed the food aid to flow into Mogadishu. General Colin Powell, who served as chairman of the Joint Chiefs of Staff under both Bush and Clinton, later reflected that "within weeks, we were so successful that we had upset the economics of the marketplace. So much free food came pouring into Somalia that it became tough to make a living by farming."

Clinton inherited a successful mission nearing its end, which he immediately botched by acting on his worst liberal impulses. In March 1993, he turned over responsibility for the peacekeeping operation to the inept UN. He also slashed our troop presence to 4,000, reflecting the usual Democratic reluctance to use overwhelming force. But at the same time, he indulged progressive fantasies by supporting the UN's vastly expanded mission to end the civil war and redeem Somalia—something Bush had purposefully avoided, even with far more troops. UN Ambassador Madeleine Albright celebrated the "unprecedented enterprise aimed at nothing less than the restoration of an entire country." Gates later called this plan "a pipe dream" and "hopelessly unrealistic." Powell scoffed at the notion that "since the catastrophe had been provoked by feuding fourteenth-century-style warlords, the solution was a dose of twentieth-century-style democracy."

The situation on the ground rapidly—and predictably—spiraled out of control. The Somali warlords and clans, no longer afraid of America's shrunken force, started attacking one another and UN personnel. In June, the militia of one powerful warlord, Mohammad Farah Aydid, massacred two dozen Pakistani UN peacekeepers. Two months later, Aydid's forces killed four Americans in one attack and wounded seven more in another.

Faced with American casualties in a foolhardy mission, Clinton felt compelled to respond, but in typical Democratic fashion he resorted to half measures. He deployed 450 Army Rangers, Delta Force operators, and Night Stalker helicopter crews. Their mission was to capture Aydid and destroy his command structure. These soldiers are some of our nation's best, but Clinton asked too much of such a small force. Mogadishu was a dense city of more than one million residents, including thousands of Aydid's clansmen and fanatical supporters, some of whom probably received training from al-Qaeda operatives in how to shoot down our helicopters. Our commander responsible for Somalia gave the operation only a 25 percent chance of capturing Aydid. But Clinton went ahead anyway.

Then, as worrying signs mounted during the task force's first month on the ground, Clinton's liberal secretary of defense, the rumpled and hapless Les Aspin, blithely rejected a request for four M1 Abrams tanks and fourteen armored Bradley Fighting Vehicles to transport American troops safely and punch through Somali roadblocks if needed. The request ran counter to Clinton's desire for a minimal American footprint in Mogadishu, despite his maximalist goals. The conditions were now set for disaster.

It's hard to overstate the ferocity of the Battle of Mogadishu on the night of October 3–4, 1993. *Black Hawk Down*, the intense movie based on Mark Bowden's best-selling book, gives some sense of our troops' incredible bravery and skill. Jeff Struecker was a young Ranger who received the Silver Star for his actions. He explained, "what you see in the movie *Black Hawk Down* basically happened. It's about as accurate as you're going to get." Struecker had seen combat before Mogadishu and many times since. He said of that night, "nothing came close to Mogadishu. I mean not even close." I heard the same from General Scott Miller at his retirement ceremony in 2021. A legend of the special-operations world and our last commanding general in Afghanistan, back then he was a young Delta captain on the ground. "I've seen a lot of firefights these last twenty years," he observed, "but nothing close to Mogadishu."

The mission was straightforward for these seasoned warriors. Intelligence had pinpointed key Aydid lieutenants inside the city. Rangers would fly on Blackhawk helicopters and fast-rope to the streets around the target building to establish a perimeter, while Delta operators would fly on Little Bird helicopters to the roof, secure the building, and capture the targets. Meanwhile, a ground convoy would stage nearby to exfiltrate the troops and detainees back to the American base.

Despite intense fire from Somali mobs and enemy militiamen, the operation went largely according to plan until disaster struck: one Blackhawk was shot down, then a second. The Rangers and Delta operators were able to secure the first crash site and worked to recover the bodies of the flight crew, but the small force couldn't reach the second crash site before Somalis overwhelmed it. In another indica tion of the intensity of the battle, two Delta operators, Gary Gordon and Randy Shughart, received posthumous Medals of Honor—the only two medals between Vietnam and Afghanistan—for volunteering to insert from their helicopter to the second site to try to save the downed crew. The ground convoy also took heavy casualties, in part because our troops didn't have those armored vehicles that Aspin had denied them.

The task force, trapped in the city, consolidated its position and overnight fought off wave after wave of Somali attacks, aided by heroic helicopter flight crews providing close air support from above. Meanwhile, American commanders had to cobble together another convoy using Malaysian and Pakistani armored vehicles to evacuate the pinned down Rangers and Delta operators. But the nervous and poorly trained Malaysian drivers sped away too quickly, leaving behind several Americans. Exhausted and with little ammunition, they ran what has come to be known as the Mogadishu Mile to the rally point through intense gunfire as the sun rose over the city.

Back at home, Americans were shocked at the images of the desecrated bodies of American soldiers dragged through the streets of Mogadishu. I remember well the anger I felt even as a sixteen-year-old boy. My anger only grew a few days later when Clinton announced our withdrawal from Somalia. Not understanding much about how our mission had expanded over the last ten months, I simply wanted to avenge the deaths of our troops and the dishonor of our nation. Either the mission was worth it and we should stay the course, or we never should've been there in the first place. Suffice it to say, Mogadishu was a formative experience for me.

It turns out I wasn't the only one who felt this way. I've had the privilege, first as a soldier and now as a senator, to meet several veterans of Mogadishu. They share many views in common. As their commanding general put it in a handwritten letter to Clinton the day after the battle: "The mission was a success. Targeted individuals were captured and extracted from the target." And while eighteen Americans died in the battle and seventy-three were wounded, our troops inflicted far, far more casualties on Aydid's men; even conservative estimates put enemy deaths over 500 and casualties over 1,000. Even in the moments after the battle, one Delta operator knew, as Bowden put it, "they'd just fought one of the most one-sided battles in American history." As one wounded Ranger colorfully responded to a medic's expression of sympathy, "you should feel sorry for *them*, 'cause we whipped ass."

These heroes also understood the strategic situation and implications of Somalia better than Clinton did. Some believe Bush erred by undertaking even the food-aid mission, but almost all agree that Clinton never should've expanded the mission. After the battle, though, most wanted to stay and complete the mission of capturing or killing Aydid. Some of that was the noble desire for vengeance, but much of it was strategic. We must show the world, their thinking went, that we won't abandon a mission as soon as it gets hard, and we especially must teach our enemies what happens when they commit atrocities like desecrating the bodies of American soldiers. Tragically, this is the kind of hard choice Democrats often create when they act tough: escalate a conflict, to avoid dangerous lessons, even if it wasn't originally in our vital interests, or cut our losses.

Of course, Clinton tucked tail and ran. His decision shocked many members of the task force: if those eighteen lives were worth the mission, they should've continued the mission. Moreover, their fears about teaching our enemies dangerous lessons were proved out. In particular, Osama bin Laden cited Mogadishu repeatedly in his many fatwas. He claimed that "the American soldier was a paper tiger and after a few blows ran in defeat." He was badly wrong about "the American soldier," but bin Laden was sadly right about Democratic politicians. His belief that America was a "paper tiger" emboldened him to attack our nation repeatedly leading up to 9/11.

Clinton later wrote, "the battle of Mogadishu haunted me. I knew how President Kennedy felt after the Bay of Pigs." For once, I believe we can take Clinton at his word. Like so many of his weak Democratic predecessors, he knew exactly what it felt like to bring humiliation and shame to a great and proud nation.

DEMOCRATS, INCLUDING KENNEDY himself, have made a mockery of the thirty-fifth president's famous declaration to "pay any price, bear any burden, meet any hardship, support any friend, oppose any foe, in order to assure the survival and the success of liberty." Instead, Democrats have time and again proven that they will only pay a modest price, bear a minimum burden, and meet only limited hardship in the defense of America. But they will betray any friend and appease any foe to advance their political objectives.

The Democrats may act tough from time to time, but they will never actually be tough. Their party habitually blames America first and is embarrassed by American power. They prefer to subordinate our interests, outsource our sovereignty, and hamstring our military. At their best, the Democrats can muster limited strength; at their worst, they're comfortable with unlimited weakness.

No two men have exposed this enduring truth more than Barack Obama and Joe Biden.

CHAPTER 6

Obama Apologizes

D URING HIS 2008 campaign, Barack Obama traveled to Berlin and, strangely for a man who sought to lead the United States, declared himself "a citizen of the world." Once he became president, Obama took the show back on the road in what's become known as the Apology Tour. And what a tour it was.

Our globe-trotting Citizen of the World president confessed America's sins, sought forgiveness, and promised to atone. In London, Obama blamed America for the 2008 financial crisis, though of course adding, "I wasn't even president at the time." In France, he apologized for what he said was America's "dismissive, even derisive" attitude toward Europeans. He also belittled the concept of American exceptionalism that so many of his actual fellow citizens held dear: "I believe in American exceptionalism, just as I suspect that the Brits believe in British exceptionalism and the Greeks believe in Greek exceptionalism." He may as well just have said "no." In Turkey, Obama lamented that "the United States is still working through some of our own darker periods in our history.... Our country still struggles with the legacies of slavery and segregation, the past treatment of Native Americans."

The Apology Tour reached its zenith—or rather its nadir—in Cairo with Obama's "New Beginning" speech, a mishmash of self-loathing, apologies, moral equivalence, and historical ignorance unbecoming of a president of the United States, though fitting from a Citizen of the World. Obama blamed "tension between the United States and Muslims around the world" on "colonialism" and the "Cold War," not on Muslim terrorists who had massacred Americans and were still at it. He regretted that 9/11 had provoked "fear and anger" that "led us to act contrary to our ideals." Obama minimized Iran's decades of aggression against America on the specious premise that we once engineered a coup there. He gently chastised the lack of religious freedom and women's rights in much of the Middle East, while claiming that we still fell short as well—as if restrictions on taxpayer funding of abortion were no different from the wholesale denial of rights to religious minorities and women.

Worst of all, Obama repudiated the very idea of American power, preeminence, and leadership: "any world order that elevates one nation or group of people over another will inevitably fail."

At least that's what I thought watching from our command post in Afghanistan. I had grimaced many times at the new commander in chief's early actions and rhetoric. But now he aspired for an international order in which America would be just one country among many, nothing exceptional about it, and certainly not "the last best hope of earth," in Abraham Lincoln's phrase. Several other soldiers shared my disappointment over a meal in the chow hall. This really was a "new beginning," but not one that we wanted.

BARACK OBAMA WAS a committed ideologue, the most ideological man to become president since Woodrow Wilson. He marinated in Blame America First politics throughout his life. Among his friends and early political patrons were Weathermen Bill Ayers and Bernardine

Dohrn, whom we met in Chapter Two. Obama sought out as his pastor and wedding officiant the infamous Jeremiah Wright, who said of 9/11 that "America's chickens are coming home to roost" and who thundered, "not God bless America, God damn America!" In the final days before the Iowa caucuses in the 2008 campaign, Obama traveled to the hometown of former vice president Henry Wallace and celebrated the progressive icon—a man so far to the left and so soft on communism that Franklin Roosevelt dropped him from the ticket in 1944.

Don't believe for a minute that Obama was a naive bumbler when it came to the world; he had an ideological plan from the beginning that reflected his Blame America First politics. In one of his major foreign-policy campaign speeches, he condemned "the conventional thinking that has turned against the war, but not against the habits that got us into the war in the first place." What he meant were the habits of singular American strength, assertiveness, and confidence. He planned to overcome those bad "habits," once and for all. During his presidency, he may have miscalculated here and bowed to political reality there, but he worked steadily for eight years to diminish American power and leadership.

Obama's tenure was the logical conclusion of the left-wing impulses and approaches we've seen so far: the denial of America's special role in the world, the neglect of our vital interests, sympathy for our enemies, the surrender of our sovereignty, the hollowing out of our military, and the instinct toward passivity and half measures. The results weren't pretty. Virulent anti-American regimes in Iran and Cuba were rewarded and emboldened. The Middle East went up in flames as Obama toppled friendly regimes while hostile regimes thrived. Meanwhile, China and Russia stole a march while America slept.

But make no mistake: what we and our allies around the world see as the smoking ruins of Barack Obama's foreign policy, he smugly sees as the smashing success of America pulling in its horns and ending a "world order that elevates one nation."

OBAMA THE IDEOLOGUE

The two clearest cases of Obama's ideological approach are Cuba and Iran. Both regimes are deeply hostile to America, but Obama believed that America had wronged them for decades and wanted to atone for our sins through new diplomatic openings with them. He negotiated in secret for years with Cuba and Iran before reaching shockingly one-sided deals with both nations. I was often asked why Obama didn't drive a harder bargain, or why he didn't use congressional critics like myself as leverage in the negotiations. The simple answer is, he didn't want better deals; he wanted to cleanse America's soul of what he considered its sins against Cuba and Iran, while empowering our adversaries for the future.

Cuba

Cuba has threatened America's interests and destabilized Latin America since Fidel Castro seized power in 1959; for just as long, Cuba's communist revolution has thrilled American leftists. When I arrived on Harvard's campus in 1995, I noticed several students wearing T-shirts with a beret-wearing, scraggly man's face. Communist chic wasn't a big thing on the farm in Arkansas, so I didn't think much of it. After a while, though, I learned the image was Che Guevara, a brutal Marxist revolutionary and Castro's right-hand man. I found this cult of personality repugnant. Would any of these left-wing students, I wondered, wear T-shirts bearing the image of Hitler, Stalin, or Pol Pot? But it speaks to the enduring attraction to the far left of the Castro regime, which America spurned for fifty-five years under presidents of both parties. And then came Obama.

Castro antagonized America from the very beginning, as we saw in Chapter Five. In return for military, economic, and political support from Moscow, Castro provided the shock troops to foment communist revolutions across Latin America and Africa. He turned his island nation into a Soviet arms depot. And the communist regime in Havana today still runs one of the world's most brutal police states, denying freedom of speech and assembly and imprisoning political opponents, if not torturing and executing them.

America has responded with an embargo against the island for more than half a century. The embargo isn't some Cold War relic, as critics claim; many of the laws governing the embargo were passed after the Cold War ended. The embargo has had several rationales, some of which haven't yet succeeded—for instance, regime change or political liberalization—but there's little question its effect has been to keep pressure on the Castro regime and prevent it from causing even more problems. Despite criticizing it, Obama largely kept the embargo in place during his first term, probably so as not to alienate the large Cuban American community in Florida and risk losing that state in his reelection.

By early in Obama's second term, the Castro regime was on the ropes. After losing its Soviet patron in 1991, the Castros struggled to maintain power until the socialist Hugo Chávez took power in oil-rich Venezuela in 1999 and started to prop up Castro. But Chávez died in early 2013, Venezuela fell into turmoil, and the price of oil collapsed by the end of 2014. Obama's response was naturally to throw the Castro regime a lifeline.

Obama initiated secret negotiations to reverse five decades of bipartisan Cuba policy. He assigned the task to one of his closest political aides in the White House—not diplomats at the State Department—a revealing detail about the personal and ideological premium that Obama placed on a deal. Over eighteen months, Obama's amateur team tolerated trademark Castro rants about America, apologized for our supposed sins, and granted concessions until the Castro regime finally accepted our surrender. But Obama himself first had to endure his own ranting, forty-five-minute phone call with Raul Castro, the first substantive contact between a president and a Cuban dictator in more than fifty years.

In December 2014, Obama shocked the world by repudiating America's bipartisan consensus on Cuba. He regretted our "complicated history" with Cuba and how "an ideological and economic barrier hardened" between our nations, as if these barriers just sort of happened and both nations were to blame. He ridiculed our "outdated approach" and noted that "no other nation joins us in imposing these sanctions," like that's the measure of America's interests.

Worse, Obama's deal was so one-sided that—much like the Panama Canal Treaties, as we saw in Chapter Three—one might have thought Cuba had defeated us in a war. Aside from an ancillary (and unjust) prisoner swap, the Castro regime granted no concessions whatsoever. Obama had simply tired of our Cuba policy and threw in the towel. He promised to restore diplomatic relations and open an embassy in Havana, to remove Cuba from the State Sponsors of Terrorism list, and to open more avenues for trade, commerce, and travel with Cuba. Obama secured nothing in return from Cuba—no political reform, no respect for the rights of the Cuban people, no pull-back from its destabilizing activities across Latin America. In fact, his only demand was to Congress: repeal the embargo.

Obama continued to apologize to Cuba over the last two years of his presidency. He met with Raul Castro in 2015 in Panama, where he noted that "the Cold War has been over for a long time" and "those controversies date back to before I was born"—as if Cuba had changed its behavior since the Cold War, or history began when Obama was born. A year later, Obama became the first president since Calvin Coolidge to travel to Cuba. He declared that "I have come here to bury the last remnant of the cold war in the Americas." But the communist fervor of the cold war was alive and well within the Castro regime, which has only increased its deadly support for Venezuela. Likewise, Obama also said he wanted "to extend the hand of friendship to the Cuban people," while the regime has only cracked down harder on its people.

Obama may have wanted the image of him and Raul laughing at a baseball game to capture the moment for history, but I think two other images do a better job. In one, Obama attended a ceremony in Havana's "Revolutionary Square" with a giant mural of Che Guevara looming in the background—the exact same image that I once saw on those T-shirts. In the second, Raul Castro raised Obama's arm in friendship, but Obama passively resisted by letting his arm go limp. Castro held up Obama's wrist anyway, illustrating America's humiliation.

Obama stands in front of the image of Che Guevara, which he probably once wore on a T-shirt. Getty Images.

Raul Castro celebrates Obama's limp foreign policy. Getty Images.

Iran

As bad as the Cuba deal was, Obama's nuclear deal with Iran was worse. Ever since the Islamic Revolution succeeded there in 1979, Iran has threatened, kidnapped, tortured, murdered, and terrorized Americans. For decades, the ayatollahs and their followers have chanted "Death to America." At some point, even liberals should believe them. Perhaps Obama did, but he didn't really care. He wanted to reach a grand bargain with Iran, justified by America's own offenses against Iran. And if such a bargain paved Iran's path to the nuclear bomb, gave them billions in cash, and emboldened their terrorist aggression—well, that was just the price of achieving his ideological goals and rebalancing power in the Middle East in Iran's favor.

Iran was probably Obama's most urgent foreign-policy challenge when he took office. Since 2002, details had emerged about Iran's secret and growing nuclear program. The Bush administration had formed a strong international coalition to pressure Iran with sanctions and other measures, but the ayatollahs hadn't backed down. Meanwhile, Iran was killing American troops in Iraq; ultimately, Iran was responsible for killing more than 600 Americans in Iraq. One weapon was the explosively formed penetrator, or EFP, an especially dangerous kind of roadside bomb that could penetrate the armor on almost any American vehicle. As a platoon leader, I briefed two new soldiers in 2006 to trust their armor—it had protected us so far and it would protect them too. One of the young soldiers asked me, "But what if it's an EFP?" I paused and studied their anxious faces. "Let's hope it's not our day to die," I finally answered.

But Obama didn't see Iran as a challenge, rather an opportunity to atone for America's past sins. He has always blamed America for the collapse of Iranian prime minister Mohammad Mossadegh's government in 1953. Obama appears convinced that we maliciously strangled Iranian democracy in its cradle. He wrote about it in his 2006 campaign book. He said it in his Cairo speech. He repeated it at the United Nations as his nuclear diplomacy went public in 2013. In his recent memoir, he used the episode to indict America's anti-communist policies throughout the Cold War. Obama has a deep conviction that America wronged Iran.

The only problem is, it's dead wrong. Mossadegh was no democrat and America mostly had tried to play honest broker between the British and the Iranians. As the unpopular Mossadegh cracked down on rivals and communists gained strength, the Eisenhower administration indeed encouraged the shah to remove Mossadegh—which the shah had the legal right to do. But Mossadegh refused to leave, so the Iranian military and the clerics mobilized against him. If anything, it was Mossadegh who mounted a coup by clinging to office and the mullahs—not the CIA—who were most responsible for his removal. Obama and the progressive left's account of America's "coup" is nothing more than a left-wing fairy tale to blame America yet again. On top of that, they blamed America for supporting the pro-American shah over the next quarter century.

This Blame America First view of Iran explains Obama's early moves on the campaign trail and in office. During the 2008 campaign, he offered to meet with the ayatollahs without preconditions. In return, Mahmoud Ahmadinejad, Iran's extremist president, sent Obama a congratulatory note after the election, the first such note to a president-elect since the 1979 revolution. I guess the ayatollahs knew a mark when they saw one. Things got worse after Obama took office. He asked the ayatollahs to "unclench their fist" in return for "an extended hand" of American friendship. He echoed this spirit of cooperation in a secret letter to Iran's supreme leader, who replied with a blistering rant about the 1953 "coup" and the shah. Maybe he and Obama read the same history books.

But Obama wasn't deterred and he continued to conciliate Tehran. In June 2009, a rigged presidential election sparked the largest protest movement in Iran since the revolution. Fearful of antagonizing the murderous regime, Obama impotently remained silent and refused to support the protesters in the critical early days. In a moment when our vital interests of weakening an implacable enemy regime aligned with the aspirations of the Iranian people, the Citizen of the World president did nothing.

Three months later, our intelligence agencies revealed another secret underground nuclear facility in Iran. The ayatollahs acknowledged the facility, but humiliated Obama by agreeing to his latest diplomatic entreaty, only to reverse course the next day. Secretary of Defense Bob Gates later quipped, "Nine months of the 'extended hand' had produced zero progress."

At this point, Obama acquiesced to European allies and members of Congress, including some Democrats, demanding tougher sanctions on Iran—but only to a point. He watered down sanctions drafted at the UN or imposed by executive orders. In Congress, the Obama administration habitually worked behind the scenes to weaken or block new sanctions laws. Only when Congress rebuffed him with overwhelming, veto-proof majorities did he relent and, of course, take credit for the tough sanctions.

Yet, Obama also had secret negotiations underway with Iran. In 2011, John Kerry, then a senator and later Obama's secretary of state, traveled to Oman with Obama's blessing to meet its sultan and explore the possibility of Oman hosting the secret talks. He also passed messages via Oman's sultan to the Iranians hinting at a softening in America's opposition to Iran's nuclear program. Obama himself called the sultan twice. These overtures of course suggested to the ayatollahs that, despite the sanctions, Obama would ultimately throw them a lifeline, just as he did with Cuba.

The Oman channel was central to Obama's ideological ambitions with Iran. Direct talks began in the summer of 2012, led by Jake Sullivan, then a top aide at the State Department and later Joe Biden's national security adviser. More meetings followed soon after Obama's reelection and accelerated after supposed "moderate" Hassan Rouhani won Iran's presidential election in June 2013. In the "official" story about Obama's nuclear deal, Rouhani's victory was a turning point. But the president of Iran is little more than a figurehead; the supreme leader holds the real power in the regime. Obama and his team understood this reality. But I suspect they cite Rouhani's election because they don't want to admit the election that really mattered: Obama's reelection. As with Cuba, once Obama was safely reelected, he could pursue his grand plans without political constraint. Indeed, just a few months before Sullivan's secret meeting in Oman, Obama was caught on a hot mic telling Russian president Dmitry Medvedev that he would have "more flexibility" after the election. One must wonder if Sullivan delivered a similar message to the Iranians.

In any case, the negotiations heated up in 2013 and Obama's

team hammered out many details, still keeping Congress, Israel, our Arab allies, and even our supposed European negotiating partners in the dark. Meanwhile, at the United Nations in September 2013, John Kerry became the first secretary of state to meet with an Iranian foreign minister since the revolution and Obama became the first president to speak by phone with an Iranian president. Only then did Obama reveal the secret talks. Within two months, an interim nuclear deal was reached, despite an effort by the French to slow it down and toughen it up. The French! Most American presidents would fear looking weaker than the French, but everything was going according to plan for Obama. The interim agreement gave Iran sanctions relief and, as Kerry had suggested in Oman, recognized Iran's right to enrich uranium—contrary to America's long-held position and several UN resolutions.

The final nuclear deal with Iran, reached in July 2015, was even worse. Obama had promised to "end their nuclear program," but the deal put Iran on the path to the bomb with merely temporary and feeble limits on Iran's enrichment of uranium and other nuclear activities. The deal didn't address Iran's ballistic-missile program, and it even lifted the embargo on conventional arms such as tanks. Iran got as much as $150 billion in sanctions relief from the deal, which it naturally used to support terrorists and its proxies in Iraq, Syria, Lebanon, and Yemen. In the final year of Obama's presidency, far from moderating its behavior, an empowered and emboldened Iran demanded pallets of literal cash—$400 million, to be exact—for the release of four American hostages, while also unjustly detaining American sailors. As usual with Democratic presidents, our enemy got everything and we got essentially nothing.

Was Obama surprised or disappointed at this turn of events? I doubt it. He never evinced much interest in confronting Iranian aggression anyway. His singular priority was always a rapprochement to atone for America's sins against Iran and to empower Iran against our traditional allies, Israel and the Arab states, thinking it would allow him to lead an American retreat from the Middle East.

Bob Gates put it well: "By 2009," he wrote, "Iran had become a kind of national security black hole," exerting a gravitational pull on all other issues. Why did Obama stand passively by while the ayatollahs butchered those protesters? Why did he reject a plan to arm Syrian rebels that was supported by his CIA director, secretary of state, secretary of defense, and chairman of the Joint Chiefs of Staff? Why did he refuse to enforce his own "red line" against Syria's use of chemical weapons? Why did he alienate Israel, our Arab allies, and our European negotiating partners? Why did he appease China and Russia in a dozen different ways? A big part of the answer at every turn was Iran.

ARAB SPRING, AMERICAN WINTER

In early 2011, mass protests toppled Tunisia's government, which sparked similar demonstrations throughout North Africa and the Middle East. The so-called Arab Spring expressed legitimate grievances against repressive governments and yielded overdue and constructive reforms in some cases. Sadly, another common result was chaos, disorder, and violence that emboldened Islamic extremists and threatened America's interests. Obama's reaction was famously incoherent, especially in three countries with the largest and most consequential uprisings: Egypt, Libya, and Syria.

But his Blame America First instincts reveal a deeper consistency. He toppled pro-American governments in Egypt and Libya, yet he coddled the anti-American, pro-Iran regime in Syria. As a result, the Middle East erupted into violence, harming our interests in the region to this day.

Egypt

By 2011, General Hosni Mubarak had led Egypt's military regime for nearly thirty years. Mubarak was a key American ally and Israel's partner for peace and stability in the region. No doubt Mubarak was authoritarian and repressive, but he largely supported America's interests and he led the Arab world's largest nation and cultural heartland. Four American presidents had found a way to work with him, as previous presidents had worked with his predecessors. Moreover, the Egyptian military was likely the only governing alternative to the Muslim Brotherhood, an ideological forerunner to al-Qaeda.

But Obama jettisoned that decades-old partnership in a matter of days. He gave Mubarak no opportunity to address the protesters' concerns with political and economic reforms, an approach that succeeded in other Arab countries. Instead, he dispatched an envoy to tell Mubarak to plan for an orderly transition of power. Facing massive demonstrations and the loss of American support, Mubarak did just that, announcing that he would amend the constitution, retire when his term expired a few months later, and open a dialogue with the opposition. Yet Obama moved the goalposts, nagged by his young Wilsonian aides "to be on the right side of history." Against "the unanimous advice of his senior-most national security advisers," Gates wrote, Obama called Mubarak and told him to resign "now"— and announced it publicly. Mubarak initially resisted, but the protests only grew until he left a few days later. The military established an interim government until elections could be held later that year. Obama celebrated in a speech that "the wheel of history turned at a blinding pace."

As Gates and many others predicted, though, events in Egypt spiraled out of control and hardly to America's advantage. Anxious allies across the region wondered if America would abandon them next. As the only organized party, the Muslim Brotherhood won almost half the seats in the parliamentary election; another Islamist party took another quarter. The Brotherhood also broke a pledge not to field a candidate for president and elected Mohamed Morsi in 2012. He was an anti-American fanatic, hardly a big improvement on Mubarak. He had called Jews "blood suckers" and "the descendants of apes and pigs," vehemently opposed Israel, and supported Sharia law—exactly what one would expect from the Brotherhood. Morsi cracked down on dissent and began consolidating the Brotherhood's hold on power, while badly mismanaging the Egyptian economy. As the chaos deepened in 2013, the Egyptian military intervened and removed Morsi from power.

The "wheel of history" indeed turned quickly—against America, thanks to Obama's progressive infatuation with "History" and his haste to abandon a pro-American government. After barely a year, military rule had returned to Egypt. Only now, the military regime mistrusted America, as did the Egyptian people and our partners in the Arab world.

Libya

Libya was up next for Obama. Days after Mubarak's resignation, protests engulfed Libya and immediately turned violent, in contrast to Tunisia and Egypt. Libya's strongman, Muammar al-Qaddafi, had no desire to follow in his neighbors' footsteps. But he would. Obama intervened militarily in Libya, an ill-advised decision that he later admitted was one of the worst mistakes of his presidency.

Unlike Mubarak, Qaddafi hadn't always been an American partner—far from it. During much of his forty-year reign, Libya was a rogue nation, a sworn enemy of America, and a sponsor of terrorism.

Indeed, Ronald Reagan bombed Libya in 1986 in retaliation for targeting our soldiers in Europe.

But Qaddafi was scared straight after we invaded Afghanistan and Iraq. In 2003, he turned over his weapons of mass destruction. He also cooperated with our counterterrorism efforts. In return, the Bush administration lifted sanctions, removed Libya from the State Sponsors of Terrorism list, and reestablished diplomatic relations. Qaddafi remained an eccentric dictator, but he had become a de facto American partner and an example for how rogue states could come in from the cold.

The military intervention in Libya was a mistake. America didn't have vital national-security interests in Libya. Perhaps our main interest was preserving the thaw with Qaddafi to encourage other rogue nations to follow his path. The attack on Libya sent the opposite signal: they could never trust America. In fact, these signals worsened two years later with the Iran deal. The contrast indicated that unrepentant hostile regimes got rewarded, while contrite and cooperative regimes got toppled. Our military was also badly stressed at the time from fighting two wars; we hardly needed a third. Further, given Libya's complex tribal politics, the aftermath of a military intervention was highly unpredictable.

But Wilsonian war fever was running high in Obama's White House. Samantha Power, then a White House staffer and later Obama's UN ambassador, harped on the supposed "responsibility to protect," an academic theory that America has a duty to intervene to protect other peoples from war and oppression. Taken literally, this fantastical theory would obligate American troops to wage war solely for the benefit of others in dozens of nations at any given time—including against China, for the genocide it's committing against the Uighur people.

In a rare departure from his aversion to using force, Obama sided with his Wilsonian advisers, while also displaying some familiar liberal tendencies. He waited until both the Arab League and the UN approved military action—though he didn't get congressional approval, a typical disregard for American sovereignty. And like other Democrats acting tough, his heart wasn't in the fight. Our military initially suppressed Libya's air defenses and struck some of its ground forces preparing to attack civilians, but then Obama headed for the exits. After fewer than two weeks, he turned over command to Europe and receded into the background. An anonymous aide infamously explained that America was "leading from behind," a far cry from the motto and mode of leadership we learned at the Infantry School: "Follow me!"

Predictably, the military campaign lasted longer than expected and the mission shifted from protecting civilians to regime change. When Qaddafi was captured and killed, Obama celebrated in a Rose Garden speech and Hillary Clinton cackled, "We came, we saw, he died!" While I've lost little sleep over Qaddafi's death, I do wonder what rogue regimes thought when they saw the viral video of Qaddafi dragged from a ditch, brutally beaten as he begged for mercy, and then shot in the head. I suspect the lesson was, never give an inch, especially to America.

"Libya is a mess." Those were Obama's words years later, yet still an understatement. Obama turned Libya into a failed state and we're still living with the consequences. Jihadists flooded into Libya and weapons flooded out. Nearly a year after Qaddafi's death, terrorists killed four Americans, including our ambassador, during an attack in Benghazi. The anarchy in Libya has unleashed massive waves of migrants from across Africa into Europe, destabilizing European nations with a refugee crisis. In some corners of Libya, the slave trade has even returned. A "mess," indeed.

Syria

But the dangerous consequences radiating from Libya are modest compared to the "geopolitical Chernobyl" that is Syria, in the words of General David Petraeus, who also served as Obama's CIA director. Whereas Obama quickly intervened in Egypt and Libya, he stayed on the sidelines in Syria. Many critics on the left and right have accused Obama of passivity, indecision, even fecklessness. On the contrary, I believe that Obama was resolute in abstaining from Syria with one goal in mind: to mollify and reassure Iran.

Unlike Libya, we had clear and vital interests in Syria. Bashar al-Assad's regime was a committed enemy of America and ally of Iran. Assad supported Hezbollah, the Lebanon-based terrorist group with much American blood on its hands, and funneled Iranian assistance through Syria to Hezbollah as well. Syria was also a Russian client state. It would've been a huge strategic blow to these adversaries had they lost their grip on Syria. By the same token, our allies encircled Syria and would've benefited significantly from Assad's defeat: Turkey, a NATO ally; Israel, our closest ally in the region; Jordan, a key military ally and Israel's partner for peace; and Iraq, a fragile ally whom Syria had destabilized for years. Saudi Arabia and the United Arab Emirates also wanted to weaken Iran and supported opposition forces in Syria. By contrast, Libya was a strategic backwater.

Moreover, the Syrian opposition was probably the most organized and capable force of any Arab Spring uprising. Within four months of Assad's crackdown, large numbers of Syrian army officers and troops had defected. In these early days, too, Islamic extremists hadn't gained a significant foothold in the Syrian opposition, partly because Assad, a minority Alawite Muslim ruler of a large Sunni population, hadn't tolerated Sunni extremists in his country before the war.

Despite our clear interests and the emerging proxy war, Obama refused to act. After calling for Mubarak and Qaddafi to depart just days after the uprisings began, Obama waited six months before making the same demand of Assad. It would be another year before Petraeus presented a plan to covertly arm and support the Syrian opposition. Secretary of State Hillary Clinton, Secretary of Defense Leon Panetta, Chairman of the Joint Chiefs of Staff Martin Dempsey, and Director of National Intelligence Jim Clapper unanimously supported the plan. But Obama rejected it, later ridiculing the opposition forces as "a farmer, a carpenter, an engineer who started out as protesters."

This moment was a key turning point in the war. Although we shouldn't have intervened directly as we did in Libya, much less with ground forces, it was obvious that only battlefield losses for Assad could shape an outcome favorable to our interests. Having seen what happened to Mubarak and Qaddafi, Assad wasn't going to relent until he suffered combat losses that even Iran and Russia couldn't underwrite. Obama should've approved the Petraeus plan in the summer of 2012, before the opposition had radicalized. After all, he approved a similar plan later in the war under pressure from Congress and regional allies when the odds of success were worse. Even better, Obama should've armed and supported the opposition from the earliest days of the war, instead of his Libyan misadventure.

Around the same time he declined the Petraeus plan, Obama also laid the groundwork for making the Syria debacle even worse. Facing growing calls to act, Obama said that "a red line for us is we start seeing a whole bunch of chemical weapons moving around or being utilized." A year later, that's exactly what happened when Assad killed more than one thousand Syrians, including women and children, with a large-scale chemical attack. Surely Obama would attack now, even if limited strikes wouldn't alter the deteriorating strategic situation in Syria. But no. Obama punted to Congress, seeking authorization for the kind of strikes that presidents had conducted unilaterally for decades—that he himself had conducted in Libya.

I was home in Arkansas when Obama recalled Congress from recess for the vote. As I began the unexpected trip back to Washington, I strongly believed that Obama should've already attacked. Whatever one thinks of drawing the red line in the first place, any president must enforce his red lines once drawn. Thus, I wrote an op-ed with my fellow congressman, Mike Pompeo, laying out the case for the strikes. But we could all tell Obama's heart wasn't in it. So could Russian President Vladimir Putin, who swooped in with a disingenuous offer to remove Assad's chemical weapons. Obama jumped at it and Congress called off the vote.

The red-line fiasco permanently damaged our interests in Syria and beyond. Seeing no consequences, Assad and Iran redoubled their brutality. As predicted early in the war, this brutality against the Sunni population empowered jihadis in the opposition; the rise of ISIS is hard to imagine without Assad's brutality. Within four months of the red-line fiasco, ISIS had declared the Syrian city of Raqqa as its capital, captured the Iraqi city of Fallujah, and was on its way to establishing a caliphate in Syria and Iraq. Obama was compelled to return troops to Iraq and even send them to Syria—but not to fight Assad or Iran's proxies. As Assad's regime teetered in 2015, we fought ISIS, helping Assad and Iran. Meanwhile, Russia surged troops into Syria, demonstrating to friend and foe alike that Putin's Russia was a reliable security partner, unlike Obama's America. The butcher's bill in Syria is as many as half a million dead, with nearly six million Syrians displaced and destabilizing Jordan, Turkey, and many European countries.

I cannot overstate how badly the red-line fiasco undermined

confidence in America. In the final years of the Obama administration, I met in Washington or abroad with senior leaders from Israel and nearly every Arab country. Obama's inaction was still on the top of their minds. Why, they asked, wouldn't Obama enforce his own red lines? Why did he go to Congress for Syria, but not Libya? Why would he topple friendly governments in Egypt and Libya, yet help preserve Assad's regime? To them, the only explanation for Obama's baffling choices was Iran.

I believe they were correct. Aside from the obvious fact that Assad was Iran's ally, we now know that the Petraeus plan and the red-line fiasco coincided with Obama's secret diplomacy with Iran. As Jake Sullivan and John Kerry were coaxing the Iranians to negotiate, Obama repeatedly stayed his hand against Iran's most valuable partner. When Obama initiated military action against ISIS, he wrote yet another secret letter to Iran's supreme leader, reassuring him that our operations in Syria wouldn't target Assad.

Put simply, the "geopolitical Chernobyl" of Syria gets back to Obama's Blame America First ideology and his relentless drive for a grand bargain to atone for America's sins against Iran and to empower Iran in the Middle East. Obama wasn't paralyzed by the Syrian civil war. He wasn't indecisive or irresolute. On the contrary, Obama had a plan all along and he resolutely stuck to it.

OBAMA ACTS TOUGH

It's no exaggeration to say Iraq made Obama president. He opposed the war from the start, calling it a "dumb war" as a state senator in 2002. His early opposition gave him a clear contrast with Hillary Clinton on a central issue in the 2008 Democratic presidential primary. Without that, he probably wouldn't have won; indeed, he might not have run at all. Yet Obama's position exposed him to charges of weakness, as often happens with Democrats. Obama responded by saber-rattling on Afghanistan, treating it as the smart war, and criticizing George W. Bush for "taking his eye off the ball." As we saw in Chapter Five, Democrats often act tough to mask a deeper weakness, and Obama's aggressive campaign rhetoric on Afghanistan was mostly a smoke screen to conceal his planned retreat from Iraq. But he began to sour on the Afghanistan War, too, almost as soon as he took office. His combined, politicized approach to these two wars is a classic example of what happens when Democrats act tough: half measures, hasty retreats, and growing danger.

Iraq

By the time Obama took office, the Iraq War was essentially won. Like any wartime leader, Bush made mistakes and took wrong turns in Iraq. I saw firsthand when I served in Baghdad in 2006 that we didn't have enough troops to defeat the growing insurgency. To his credit, though, Bush didn't cut and run. Instead, he surged 30,000 more troops into Iraq to conduct a counterinsurgency operation under Petraeus's command. As a result, our forces crushed the insurgency and created the conditions for political compromise. The success was so complete that the war was barely an issue in the fall campaign.

At first, Obama smartly took the win handed to him by Bush and our troops. He had campaigned on "ending the war," yet vaguely pledged only to remove "combat troops" within sixteen months. Our military commanders preferred a drawdown over twenty-three months, but Obama and Gates compromised at nineteen months. Obama also agreed to keep around 50,000 troops in country afterward to train and advise the Iraqi military. Those troops were scheduled to stay through 2011, when the status-of-forces agreement negotiated in the Bush administration's final days would expire. A few left-wing critics grumbled that Obama broke his campaign promise for a sixteen-month deadline and kept too many troops after the new deadline, but Obama didn't suffer politically. Rather, he benefited by preserving Iraq's positive trajectory and by appearing to prioritize national security over arbitrary political pledges made under sharply different circumstances.

But Obama's rigid ideological approach returned in 2011. Gates, the military, and Obama's own ambassador all recommended a new status-of-forces agreement to permit a residual force of around 10,000 troops in Iraq beyond 2011. As important, Iraqi politicians wanted us to stay, even if they didn't want to say so publicly. Such political posturing had occurred throughout the war about the status of American forces. For that matter, it's commonplace in Congress and just about any legislature for politicians to hope for an outcome yet not want to take the heat for it. The Bush administration had always resolved these tensions. But Obama just wanted to get out of Iraq and his administration didn't undertake the intense diplomacy needed for a new agreement.

Unfortunately, we didn't "get out" of Iraq in 2011; we only took a costly and unwise break. When I returned from my Iraq deployment in late 2006, I often got asked if we'd still be there in five years. I answered yes, the only question was whether we'd have to fight our way back in. Even that early, I recognized that an abrupt withdrawal would lead to disaster. Thanks to the surge, we averted disaster. But the dynamic I predicted back then is what happened when Obama withdrew our troops. Without a small military presence to fortify our diplomatic efforts, Iraq's government reverted to its sectarian ways, Iran's meddling increased, and the fallout from the Syrian civil war crossed into Iraq. Barely two years after our troops departed Iraq,

ISIS captured Fallujah and Ramadi. Obama responded, incredibly, by calling ISIS the "JV team." Within six months, ISIS seized Mosul and threatened to topple the Iraqi government. Obama rushed troops back into country and steadily added more; when he left office, we had more than 5,000 troops in Iraq.

One can only wonder what might have been. If we had maintained a small residual force of a few thousand troops in Iraq in 2011, we might have ended up with fewer Americans there by the end of Obama's presidency than those 5,000. More important, we might have averted the terrorist attacks inspired by ISIS, the carnage in Iraq and Syria, and the damage to America's interests and reputation.

Afghanistan

As it was with Iraq, so it was with the "smart war" in Afghanistan. Obama's tough rhetoric during the campaign resembled John Kennedy's critique of Dwight Eisenhower and Richard Nixon in 1960 for losing Cuba. As we saw in Chapter Five, however, Kennedy vacillated once he took office, resulting in the Bay of Pigs fiasco. Obama suffered similar indecision and doubts. "His fundamental problem in Afghanistan was that his political and philosophical preferences... conflicted with his own pro-war public rhetoric," Gates wrote, "especially during the presidential campaign." A classic example, in other words, of a Democrat acting tough.

This tension between ideology and security colored Obama's approach to the war. Having promised during the campaign to send more troops, Obama sat for two months on a request for 21,000 more troops that Bush had approved, but deferred out of respect to Obama. I was serving in eastern Afghanistan at this time and the paralysis was noted by both our troops and the Afghan people. I had several conversations with Afghans who asked when the new president would make good on his promises. More than once I heard the old Afghan proverb: "you have the watches, but we have the time." Sadly, this proverb would be proven true.

In another telling episode, as he dithered on a larger troop request, Obama refused an interim request for around 5,000 more troops to protect our forces already in country. These "enabling" troops had skills such as bomb technicians and medevac, critical to supporting and caring for the frontline troops. But Obama saw the request solely through the lens of domestic politics, leaving Gates so "deeply disturbed" that he "came closer to resigning that day than at any other time."

All told, Obama took ten months to commit to his new strategy, and then only half-heartedly. Obama's new commander, General Stanley McChrystal, among the most dynamic generals from the Iraq War, undertook a review of battlefield conditions when he arrived in country. He recommended a surge of 40,000 troops to win what Obama still publicly called "a war of necessity." But an infuriated president, egged on by Joe Biden, exploded at the request. He accused the military of trying to box him in. Indeed, these months saw the scenes of the mistrust directed by Obama and Biden at the military that we saw in Chapter Four. In the end, Obama arbitrarily slashed the request to 30,000 troops, partly for political benefit. Obama admitted to his secretary of defense that "my poll numbers will be stronger if I take issue with the military over Afghanistan policy." Worse, Obama publicly limited their deployment to eighteen months, which would conveniently remove them before the 2012 election.

The Taliban indeed had the time. By announcing in advance his withdrawal deadline, Obama undercut his own strategy. The Afghan government and people hedged their support and the Taliban waited us out. Our troops fought bravely, sacrificed much, took significant ground, and put the Taliban back on their heels. Our success was short-lived, though, and our gains receded as Obama rushed for the exits.

Obama didn't want to get tough with the Taliban; he only wanted to act tough. As a result, the Afghan government was soon back on the defensive. Obama had effectively squandered our last chance of durable victory. And he set the stage for America's humiliation at the hands of the only administration official more consistently wrong about Afghanistan than he was: Joe Biden.

A TWENTY-FIRST-CENTURY MAN IN A NINETEENTH-CENTURY WORLD

A thoroughgoing progressive, Obama believed that "History" had transcended great-power politics with nations like Russia and China. He simply couldn't understand aggressive nationalist leaders like Vladimir Putin and Xi Jinping, nor why they obsessed about retrograde matters like nuclear weapons or territorial expansion. To Obama, such things were outmoded, even illegitimate national priorities. The "arc of history" had moved beyond them to globalist priorities like climate change. Obama's secretary of state, John Kerry, captured this mindset when he said of Russia's invasion of Ukraine, "you just don't in the twenty-first century behave in nineteenth-century fashion by invading another country." Putin apparently thought otherwise. But Obama was an enlightened twenty-first-century man stuck in a messy, dangerous nineteenth-century world.

Russia

Obama inherited a tense relationship with Russia, for which he naturally blamed America, or at least George W. Bush. In reality, Bush had conducted extensive personal diplomacy with Putin, but Putin has always wanted to reassemble the Russian Empire. Putin used Russia's economic collapse in the 1990s, NATO expansion in the 1990s and 2000s, and popular uprisings in Georgia, Ukraine, and Kyrgyzstan in the mid-2000s as pretexts to consolidate power, suppress dissent, and threaten his neighbors. In 2007, Putin declared a newly aggressive, confrontational approach during an infamous speech in front of the assembled leaders of the West. Then, in 2008, Russia reignited a frozen conflict in Georgia, matching words with actions.

Obama brushed all this away, however, and declared a "reset" with Russia, which sounded to Putin like a willingness to make one-sided concessions. Obama dispatched Secretary of State Hillary Clinton with a gimmicky red button with the word "reset" written on it next to a Russian translation. The translation turned out to be "overcharge," but the meaning wasn't lost in translation to the Russians: they repeatedly got concessions from Obama, while paying nothing in return. Obama halted a missile-defense system in Poland and Czechia that the Russians opposed—partly to buy their cooperation with Iran. He also reached a new arms-control deal that allowed Russia to expand its nuclear forces even as it constrained ours. And that treaty happened while the Obama administration knew Russia was cheating on another arms-control treaty, which the administration conveniently kept secret. In 2011, Obama also helped Russia join the World Trade Organization. We got little in exchange for these acts of goodwill.

Putin regained the presidency in 2012, after four years as prime minister but de facto leader, and ran circles around an oblivious Obama. As Obama sat on the sidelines of Syria, Putin rushed weapons to the Assad regime and protected it at the UN with Russia's veto. During the red-line fiasco, Obama actually sought out Putin at a summit and asked for his help to avoid a military strike by removing Assad's chemical weapons. Putin happily obliged to humiliate Obama, while of course violating the deal to enable future chemical attacks in Syria.

Two incidents above all illustrate Obama's philosophical aversion to power politics. First, Putin invaded and annexed Crimea in 2014, then fomented a separatist rebellion in eastern Ukraine. Obama responded with the mildest of sanctions and refused lethal military aid, even as Ukraine pleaded for weapons, especially Javelin anti-tank missiles. Instead, Obama sent blankets and meals-ready-to-eat. By contrast, the Ukrainian president understood power; he quipped in his speech to Congress, "one cannot win a war with blankets."

So did the Ukrainian soldier who told me the following year during my trip to Dnipro, "Mr. Senator, we don't need to destroy every Russian tank; we only need to destroy one Russian tank." Even when we voted to authorize tougher sanctions and lethal aid, Obama still refused because it might "draw a more forceful response from Moscow." And it might interfere with Obama's single-minded pursuit of the Iran deal, which wasn't yet settled. To add one final insult to injury, Obama put Joe Biden in charge of Ukraine policy, which solved none of Ukraine's problems, but did allow Hunter Biden to cash in.

Second, as the Assad regime tottered in 2015, Putin surged troops into Syria to save his client. Obama once again did nothing, other than predict that Putin would get "stuck in a quagmire." On the contrary, Putin stabilized the Assad regime with a modest but well-timed military intervention. In return, Putin received decades-long leases to military bases in Syria, new customers for his arms industry, and newfound influence for Russia across the Middle East for the first time in four decades. Obama had sniffed that Putin's intervention was "not a smart, strategic move" and "not some superpower, chessboard contest." But the results and reactions proved that's exactly what it was—checkmate, Putin.

Yet Obama insisted that Putin's military adventurism came "not out of strength, but out of weakness." To think otherwise "is to fundamentally misunderstand the nature of power in foreign affairs or in the world generally. Real power means you can get what you want without having to exert violence." And that's indeed one measure of power. But when it fails, the willingness to "exert violence" to achieve national objectives is also a measure of real power. And the proof of Putin's growing power could be seen when leaders of friendly countries like Israel and the United Arab Emirates began trekking to Moscow to meet with Putin.

Then again, maybe Obama was tipping his hand. As we've seen, Obama wanted America to break the bad "habits" of strength and global leadership. His steadfast refusal to use force or merely to arm our friends against our enemies advanced that goal. Besides, Obama had his own idea of "real power," which a nineteenth-century relic like Putin didn't understand. Putin's intervention in Ukraine and Syria "doesn't suddenly make him a player" according to Obama. "You don't see him in any of these meetings out here helping to shape the agenda. For that matter, there's not a G20 meeting where the Russians set the agenda." What's really important to the Citizen of the World is who drafts the agenda at a useless globalist gabfest.

During his reelection campaign in 2012, Obama had famously laughed at the idea that Russia was a top geopolitical foe of America, snarking that "the 1980s are now calling to ask for their foreign policy back." It's too bad that Obama didn't pick up the phone, because Reagan's hard-nosed policies toward the Russians were exactly what America needed.

China

From the beginning, Obama viewed Communist China not as an enemy or even a rival, but as a "partner," as he said when welcoming Chinese leaders to Washington early in his tenure. He envisioned a future "where China is a strong, prosperous, and successful member of the community of nations." Obama also reassured his guests that the "most pressing dangers we face no longer come from competition among great powers."

The Chinese Communists probably couldn't believe their good fortune. For millennia, China had viewed itself as the Middle Kingdom—the nation at the middle of the world—with a mandate to rule all under heaven. Although China had fallen far from this lofty self-image, its leaders had long plotted China's return to prominence. For decades, they practiced Deng Xiaoping's maxim: "hide our strength and bide our time." By 2009, China had grown strong by preying on America's workers, businesses, and inventors for two decades. Yet Obama celebrated their success and deprecated great-power competition as old-fashioned, nineteenth-century politics. No doubt the Chinese Communists in attendance grinned and nodded; the next eight years would be very, very good for China.

Obama had talked tough on China at times during the campaign, but like Bill Clinton before him, he didn't deliver. He criticized Beijing for currency manipulation, unfair trade practices, and human-rights abuses. Yet the very title of his campaign's white paper foreshadowed his presidency: Obama promised to "engage China," not to "confront China." And so it went. In his first months, he refused to designate China as a currency manipulator despite his Treasury Department finding that it was indeed manipulating its currency, hurting American manufacturers. In her second month as secretary of state, Hillary

Clinton shrugged off China's brutal repression because "we pretty much know what they're going to say" and, besides, she didn't want such minor matters to interfere with "the global climate change crisis." At the same time, Obama gave his first address to Congress and mentioned China only once—to praise it for its energy efficiency.

China's leaders hardly reciprocated. On Obama's disappointing first visit to China, they both harangued and ignored him. They arrested dissidents and refused his request to broadcast his town hall. As Hillary Clinton recalled, "hide and bide" had turned into "show and tell," an attitude which continued throughout Obama's first term. China's rapid military buildup proceeded, and its navy began to harass our ships at sea. Beijing also thwarted the Obama administration on its professed goals, from climate change to nuclear nonproliferation to its North Korea strategy.

Matters only got worse when Xi Jinping took over as Obama's second term began. Obama tapped Joe Biden to manage the relationship. In Washington, it's often said that "personnel is policy." If that's true, then Obama's appointment of Biden may have been his worst China policy of all. When Xi visited the United States, Biden rolled out the red carpet and proclaimed, "we believe that a rising China is a positive development." Xi naturally applauded in agreement. Xi had big plans in store, but the main thing Biden got from China was business opportunities for his son. Hunter Biden had already forged relationships with Chinese oligarchs and helped them secure White House meetings. Now Joe could bring Hunter with him to Beijing on Air Force Two for more shady business deals. We deserved a better negotiator with Xi Jinping than a man whose son was compromised by Chinese influence. We still do.

Xi bested Obama and Biden at every turn. China's massive military buildup accelerated. In 2013, Xi declared China's control of the airspace over the East China Sea, a direct threat and affront to Japan, our treaty ally. China also began building islands in the South China Sea. Xi promised Obama that he wouldn't militarize these islands. He lied. Today, these garrisons host runways, aircraft, ships, radars, missile batteries, munitions stockpiles, and Chinese troops. Xi matched these military moves in 2013 with the so-called Belt and Road Initiative, a trillion-dollar global infrastructure network to ensnare strategically vital nations in China's web. And the hits kept coming. Chinese warships entered America's territorial waters in 2015. At a White House summit, Xi promised Obama to stop cybertheft of America's intellectual property. Once again, he lied. China continued to target American companies and government agencies with cyberattacks. The next year, China began constructing its first overseas base in Djibouti, just miles from America's base in that geographically critical country on the Horn of Africa.

For every provocation, every affront, every lie, Obama and Biden turned the other cheek. Perhaps Obama was desperate for China's cooperation with the Iran deal or the Paris Climate Accords; perhaps Biden looked the other way to enable his son's business deals. Maybe Obama truly could not understand the mindset of an assertive, nationalist dictator like Xi who still believed in and practiced old-fashioned power politics. Or maybe Obama saw an opportunity to hand off some of America's leadership responsibilities.

Whatever the case, Obama never did see China as a threat. In his final year in office, he still believed that China was "on a peaceful rise" and he looked forward to China "sharing with us the burdens and responsibilities of maintaining an international order." Xi, on his way to becoming the most powerful Chinese leader since Mao Zedong, must've laughed when he read those words. He certainly intended for China's rise to continue, but he didn't plan to share anything with

America. On the contrary, he intended to restore China to its rightful place as the Middle Kingdom.

AFTER EIGHT YEARS of being led by the Citizen of the World, America was in retreat around the globe. It's hard to think of a single place where our strategic position had improved, our allies respected and appreciated us more, or our enemies feared us more. With the possible exception of counterterrorism, where Obama benefited from rapidly advancing drone technology for strikes against terrorists, Obama had weakened America on every front. (I only say "possible" because even with drone warfare, Obama hobbled our counterterrorism efforts with legal rigamarole and bureaucratic red tape, which I fought on the Armed Services and Intelligence Committees, but most of which I'm still not at liberty to discuss.)

Yet Obama embraced the decline of a "world order that elevates one nation." He regretted little, for he only saw the success of his ideological plans. Our "enemies"—nations wronged by America— got rewarded, while our "allies"—freeloaders likely to drag us into war—got put in their place. Like an American Ozymandias, he wanted proud, patriotic citizens to look upon the ruins of his work and despair.

What he should've done is apologize to Americans for the most ideological, Blame America First foreign policy in our history. Because if you ask me, Obama's Apology Tour came eight years too early.

But as bad as Obama's foreign policy was, four years later, things would somehow get worse.

CHAPTER 7

Biden Stumbles

A MERICA'S RELATIONSHIP WITH Taiwan is critical to our
security and prosperity, but the relationship requires delicate
handling because China considers Taiwan a part of China. Just look
at the State Department's website: "The United States has a long-
standing one China policy, which is guided by the Taiwan Relations
Act, the three U.S.-China Joint Communiques, and the Six Assurances." Put simply, this means we acknowledge our friendship with
Taiwan and China's claim to Taiwan without resolving the claim.
These esoteric nuances go back to 1979, when we shifted our diplomatic relations from Taiwan to China. Although we no longer have
official diplomatic relations with Taiwan, we have "an abiding interest
in maintaining peace and stability in the Taiwan Strait," as State puts
it, and we "encourage the peaceful resolution of cross-Strait differences."
Another related, nuanced policy is "strategic ambiguity," by which America hasn't committed explicitly and in advance about whether and how
we would intervene militarily to protect Taiwan from a Chinese attack.

Most Americans have never heard of these obscure diplomatic
niceties. Frankly, a lot of congressmen and senators haven't, either.
But it's reasonable to expect the president to understand the complexi-
ties of the world's hottest flash point, lest he ignite it.

Thus, when a new president was asked if we would defend Taiwan and he said, "Yes, I would," he upset the delicate, nuanced policy. Yet when pressed if the president meant "with the full force of the American military," he insisted, "whatever it took." Within a few hours, presumably after his staff explained his misstep, the president backed away from his chesty assertions.

But he couldn't unspeak his words, as an experienced senator later lectured. The president had made a "startling new commitment," the senator criticized, and the about-face only created a dangerous new "policy of ambiguous strategic ambiguity." The president's "inattention to detail has damaged U.S. credibility with our allies and sown confusion throughout the Pacific Rim." The senator condescended in conclusion: "Words matter."

The president was George W. Bush and the senator was Joe Biden.

If only President Biden would heed Senator Biden's advice. Not once, not twice, but three times in nine months as president, Biden did the exact same thing for which he criticized Bush. In August 2021, during the Afghanistan withdrawal disaster, Biden contrasted that country to our NATO allies, whom we're bound by treaty to defend, adding "same with Japan, same with South Korea, same with Taiwan." Yet we have no mutual-defense treaty with Taiwan, unlike Japan and South Korea. Within hours, an anonymous aide said, "our policy with regard to Taiwan has not changed."

Two months later, Biden twice answered "yes" when asked during a town hall if we would come to Taiwan's defense, adding, "we have a commitment to do that." Again, an anonymous aide quickly denied the president's own words: "The president was not announcing any change in our policy."

In May 2022, Biden again answered "yes" when asked if America would "get involved militarily to defend Taiwan" because "that's the commitment we made." This miscue was especially careless because it happened in Japan, so the cleanup brigade again rushed to the rescue: "As the president said, our policy has not changed." Perhaps since he said the exact opposite, Biden himself felt compelled the next day to stress that "the policy has not changed at all."

As it happens, Biden stumbled onto the right answer for once—or three times, as it were. The policy of strategic ambiguity dates to an era when China was too weak to invade Taiwan, but those days are over. With changed circumstances should come changed policies. Yet Biden's "ambiguous strategic ambiguity" is the worst of both worlds: provoking China without deterrence. Biden's confused and inconstant rhetoric had once again cost our nation.

No one has ever accused Joe Biden of being a rigorous, disciplined, systematic thinker. Even Biden's friends and supporters—even Biden himself!—defend him as "Uncle Joe" or "Scranton Joe," a masterful old-school politician guided by fingertip feeling and gut instincts. Biden and his defenders add that his finely honed instincts keep him lashed to the nation's political center.

But Biden is no centrist, or he's a centrist only in this respect: for fifty years, with his eyes on presidential primaries, Biden positioned himself at what he perceived to be the center of the Democratic Party. His shifting political positioning makes Biden a reliable weathervane of progressive foreign policy. He usually reflects the bad progressive tendencies and impulses in vogue at the time. And since progressives are reliably weak and wrong, so is Biden. As former Secretary of Defense Bob Gates, who worked closely with Biden in the Obama administration, famously wrote, Biden was "wrong on nearly every major foreign policy and national security issue over the past four decades."

Today, we can add another decade. But now Biden's bad judgment is far more dangerous. It's one thing to be wrong as a senator or a vice president, but another thing altogether as president. Look no further than Afghanistan and Ukraine.

THE DOVE, THE HAWK, AND THE OSTRICH

You've probably heard politicians with muscular and aggressive foreign-policy views called "hawks" and those with timid or hesitant views called "doves." As a third avian category, I would add the "ostriches," who stick their heads in the sand to ignore gathering threats. Most politicians belong to one of these flocks. But not Joe Biden.

Even by the low standards of a politician, Joe Biden has changed positions dramatically and frequently. Elected to the Senate in 1972, in his own words, "as a twenty-nine-year-old kid against the war in Vietnam," he expressed dovish views for the last two decades of the Cold War. But after the Persian Gulf War and well into the Iraq War, he was reborn as an avenging Wilsonian hawk. After setbacks in Iraq, however, he reverted to his dovish past. Along the way, he has also exhibited ostrich-like tendencies, simply sticking his head in the sand about threats, especially those coming from Russia and China. Biden's erratic, inconsistent views seem hard to square with a coherent, integrated worldview. "I wish I could say Biden was a student of history," said one senior Obama administration official during the debates about the Afghanistan surge, but "that's not Biden. He has gut instincts." Unfortunately, these instincts tend to line up with Democratic political trends, not America's national interest.

Having campaigned against the Vietnam War, a young Biden reflected his party's Blame America First mindset. As North Vietnamese forces advanced on Saigon in April 1975, Biden voted against a bill to give last-minute aid to South Vietnam and to authorize the use of American troops to evacuate our citizens. In an eerie preview of his misjudgments about Afghanistan forty-six years later, Biden concluded that "the time has come—perhaps it is past—for a swift, uneventful evacuation of all Americans from South Vietnam before the situation develops wherein it would take large numbers of American troops to bring out our citizens." Biden understood that an evacuation was necessary, but he opposed the military measures necessary to conduct a safe evacuation. The Senate passed the bill but it failed in the House, and Saigon fell a few days later. American helicopters scrambled to evacuate our embassy. The desperate scenes on a rooftop in Saigon would only be surpassed by those at an airport in Kabul.

The humiliating evacuation of the U.S. embassy in Saigon would be repeated nearly half a century later in Kabul, Afghanistan. Getty Images.

That same month, Biden also foreshadowed his lifelong hostility to defense spending. He proposed to slash more than 10 percent from the Ford administration's defense budget, dangerous under any circumstances but especially during a foreign-policy crisis. The amendment was defeated easily, with even liberal stalwarts like Walter Mondale opposing it. "The Congress decided against the war in Vietnam," Mondale explained. "We did not vote to become an isolationist country." But Biden did, complaining that defense spending took priority over social spending and that we shouldn't base the defense budget on "everything our adversary can do"—which is of course exactly how we should craft the defense budget.

For the rest of the Cold War, Biden took conventional dovish positions. He opposed higher defense spending, new missiles, and advanced weapons, fretting that we would gain the upper hand against Soviet Russia. By the same flawed logic, he opposed missile-defense systems. Biden also championed deeply flawed arms-control agreements such as the Strategic Arms Limitation Talks of 1979, which died politically with Russia's invasion of Afghanistan that year, but which Biden tried to resuscitate for years. Biden opposed the deployment of medium-range missiles to Europe in the 1980s and called for a nuclear freeze, which would've only frozen Russia's advantage in place. He detested the Somoza government in Nicaragua and opposed Reagan's funding of the Contra rebels in the 1980s, just as he opposed Reagan's backing of the pro-American government of El Salvador against a Marxist insurgency. At every turn, Biden hewed to the Democratic mainstream of Blame America First policies.

Biden's vote against the Persian Gulf War concluded his first flight as a dove. Though it's largely forgotten now, the vote to authorize military force to evict Saddam Hussein from Kuwait was very close, 52–47, with a few Democrats joining nearly all Republicans. Biden asked, "What vital interests of the United States of America justifies sending young Americans to their death in the sands of the Arabian Peninsula?" The way Biden phrased the question is telling. Kuwait isn't really on the Arabian Peninsula, so Biden apparently presupposed Saddam might not stop there but rather invade more neighboring countries. That threat was a centerpiece of the case for war, as was the threat to the region's oil supply, on which our prosperity depended more in those days. Yet Biden seemed indifferent, condemning "a precipitous war that will divide and weaken our nation." Biden was wrong as usual: after a punishing six-week air campaign, our troops destroyed what was then the fourth-largest army in the world in four days.

After the war, Biden shed the soft white down of a dove for the razor talons of a hawk. Perhaps he had recognized the error of his ways. More likely, he recognized that Bill Clinton had at least claimed to support the war and had chosen Al Gore as his running mate, one of the few Democratic senators to vote for the war. In any event, Biden espoused bellicose interventionist views for the next decade.

Biden began his transformation by overcompensating for his misjudgment on Iraq. He acknowledged his error, but that wasn't enough. He criticized President George H. W. Bush for not removing Saddam from power altogether, which he called a "fundamental mistake." Biden also affirmed that Iraq had a program for weapons of mass destruction, stating in one Senate hearing that inspections and sanctions couldn't stop the program—only "taking Saddam down" could. These words later came back to haunt him in the 2008 and 2020 Democratic presidential primaries.

Next, Biden was particularly belligerent about the Balkan Wars in the 1990s. He bragged that he was "the first guy to call for air strikes in Bosnia," without articulating a vital American interest to get involved in that country's civil war. He boasted that he "was suggesting we bomb Belgrade," the Serbian capital, and also "blow up all the bridges" between Serbia and Bosnia. Biden condemned "the bankrupt policy in the former Yugoslavia, begun by the Bush administration and continued with minor adjustments by the Clinton administration." He added that Clinton had a "policy of despair and cowardice." Even worse in his eyes were our European allies, whom he accused of "moral rape."

Finally and most notoriously, Biden supported the Iraq War in 2003—until it became politically inconvenient. Again, it's largely forgotten now, but this vote wasn't close, 77–23. Besides Biden, among the Democratic senators who voted for the war were Hillary Clinton, Tom Daschle, John Kerry, Harry Reid, and Chuck Schumer. Four months after the war started, Biden stood by his vote. "I would vote that way again today," he declared, while adding "the cost of not acting against Saddam I think would have been much greater." A year later, he maintained that his "vote was just" even if the war itself was "unwise." But by late 2005, as he prepared again to run for president, Biden finally recanted and admitted his vote was a "mistake." And he's spent the rest of his career falsely denying his early support for the war.

Biden has followed the Democratic Party back to its dovish, Blame America First roots. He opposed the Iraq surge, which he called a "tragic mistake," even when it turned out to be a smashing success. As vice president, he stridently opposed a similar surge in Afghanistan as well, subjecting Obama to what Secretary of Defense Bob Gates characterized as constant "Chinese water torture" about the decision as we saw in Chapter Four. He opposed the operation to capture or kill Osama bin Laden, alone among Obama's senior team. Biden also didn't join other senior members of Obama's war cabinet in advocating the Petraeus plan to arm Syrian opposition fighters in 2012. To be fair, Biden did counsel against the ouster of Hosni Mubarak in Egypt and the military intervention in Libya; even a stopped clock is right twice a day.

Whether dove or hawk, over the years Biden also has behaved like an ostrich, sticking his head in the sand about threats, especially those from Russia and China. Biden is particularly allergic to acknowledging geopolitical competition and rivalry, and heaven forbid a "cold war"—even during the actual Cold War. In 1983, Biden asserted that "we're not in a cold war," but as a result of Reagan's policies, "we're a whole heck of a lot closer than we were two years ago." When Mitt Romney cited Russia as a chief "geopolitical foe" in 2012, Biden mocked his "Cold War mindset."

The same goes for China. In 2019, Biden defended the Chinese Communists as "not bad folks." Even after decades of Chinese crimes and aggression, Biden incredibly declared that "they're not competition for us." Biden's ostrich routine continued as president. At his first speech to the United Nations, Biden insisted that "we are not seeking a new Cold War." Of course we're not and we never did, with Russia or China. Yet China has waged a cold war against us for decades, so our choice isn't whether to seek one, but whether to win. Biden was so timid, however, that he couldn't even bring himself to mention China's name in the speech. Biden has always struggled to see China as a competitor or a threat. He summed up his own long-standing views in 2011 when he recalled a trip to China in 1979 as a junior senator: "I believed then what I believe now: that a rising China is a positive, positive development, not only for China but for America."

Talk about sticking your head in the sand.

But Biden's ostrich-like tendencies aren't limited to Russia and China, as witnessed with the disastrous withdrawal from Afghanistan.

THE AFGHANISTAN FIASCO

Biden nursed a grudge about Afghanistan for more than a decade. In 2009, when the military recommended a surge of troops, he ridiculed the proposal, questioned the motives of senior military leaders, and urged a scaled-down mission with an eye on the exits. As we saw in Chapter Four, Biden harangued Obama about the generals, poisoning the well between the new president and his commanders. But Obama rejected Biden's counsel, leaving Biden to sulk and brood. Once he took the helm in 2021, though, Biden planned to show everyone he had been right all along. With his characteristic and deadly combination of supreme confidence and rank incompetence, Biden stuck his head in the sand about the threats of the withdrawal and set the stage for one of America's worst strategic debacles in modern times.

The agreement with the Taliban that Biden inherited wasn't without flaw, though at least it imposed conditions on the Taliban for the final withdrawal of American troops. But the Taliban didn't meet those conditions in the final months of the Trump administration or first months of the Biden administration. On the contrary, the Taliban planned for rapid assaults across the country. I know that Biden received these warnings because I did as well on both the Intelligence and Armed Services Committees. While initial assessments predicted that the Afghan government could defend itself for more than a year, that time frame seemed to shrink with every briefing we received. After Kabul fell, Biden subsequently lied that he hadn't received this intelligence.

Yet Biden kept his head in the sand. He ignored the warning signs and heedlessly plunged ahead with his withdrawal planning. He demanded nothing of the Taliban and rejected the advice of his senior military leaders to keep about 2,500 troops in country. He later lied about getting this advice too: our four-star commander in Afghanistan, our regional commander for the Middle East, the chairman of the Joint Chiefs of Staff, and his own secretary of defense all contradicted him before my committee. In a grotesque twist, he also announced that our troops would withdraw by the twentieth anniversary of the 9/11 attacks, as if that were an appropriate way to commemorate and honor those who died that day and in the wars since. Worse still, this new date put our withdrawal right in the middle of the summer fighting season when the threat from the Taliban peaked.

As conditions deteriorated during the summer, Biden stubbornly refused to budge. The administration briefly paused the withdrawal before handing over control of Bagram Air Base, a massive complex about fifty miles outside Kabul. Bagram would've been a superior evacuation site compared to the Kabul airport, but Biden had arbitrarily capped the number of troops in country at a level too low to secure both. When the military assessed that 5,000 troops would need to deploy temporarily to secure the base, Biden refused. In a sad irony, that's about how many troops he had to rush to Kabul in August to secure the airport there.

Biden also lied to the American people as the dangers gathered. Barely five weeks before Kabul collapsed, when asked about parallels between Afghanistan and the fall of Saigon in 1975, he scoffed, "none whatsoever, zero." Biden added, "there's going to be no circumstance where you see people being lifted off the roof of an embassy." At that moment, though, Biden was hastening this outcome. He insisted on the withdrawal of civilian mechanics who kept the Afghan Air Force flying. Without air support, the Afghan army crumbled.

Perhaps worst of all, Biden had virtually no plan to evacuate thousands of American citizens and green-card holders, to say nothing of Afghans who had served alongside our troops. The State Department is responsible for noncombatant evacuations, yet they dithered as the Taliban advanced. Once Kabul collapsed, all those Americans were left on their own to reach the Kabul airport and our troops were exposed to grave danger at the small urban airport. The Biden administration even relied on the Taliban for an outer security perimeter.

Tragically, perhaps inevitably by that point, a suicide bomber passed through the Taliban lines and killed thirteen of our finest young troops. Thanks to Joe Biden's prickly pride and incompetence, America had its deadliest day in Afghanistan since 2011. And to make matters worse, we abandoned our countrymen and partners behind enemy lines while evacuating thousands of Afghans who had no right to enter our country, some of whom proved to have terrorist ties.

Yet Biden proclaimed the whole operation an "extraordinary success."

I think "utter fiasco" is a better term. Biden's shameful execution of the withdrawal from Afghanistan was a human tragedy for those we lost, for their families, and for those we left behind. But it was more; it was a massive strategic defeat. As Kabul fell, a Chinese propaganda outlet mocked America and predicted an "Afghan effect" as our enemies perceived new opportunities amid Biden's weakness and our allies questioned our resolve. You can bet that Vladimir Putin was watching.

Early in the Obama administration, Biden argued that in Afghanistan "we had to do what we did in Vietnam." And that's what he did—though Afghanistan was worse. In Vietnam, our combat troops had departed years before Saigon fell to a regular army backed by our communist enemies. In Afghanistan, our troops had to evacuate under attack from a band of medieval savages. The Afghan effect is real and will haunt us for years, at least as long as Biden is president. But it didn't take years, or even months, to see its first impact: shortly after the last American troops left Afghanistan, Russian troops began to mass around Ukraine.

THE WAR ON UKRAINE

Biden's impotence in Afghanistan doubtless encouraged Vladimir Putin to believe he could get away with invading Ukraine. But from the moment he took office, Biden also signaled weakness to Putin, resulting in the worst war in Europe since Nazi Germany and Soviet Russia invaded Poland.

Biden should've realized the danger. Putin has never concealed his desire to reassemble the Russian Empire, especially in Ukraine.

Putin subscribes to the view expressed after the Cold War by Zbigniew Brzezinski, Jimmy Carter's national security adviser: "It cannot be stressed strongly enough that without Ukraine, Russia ceases to be an empire, but with Ukraine suborned and then subordinated, Russia automatically becomes an empire." Putin has never wavered in this conviction. In 2008, when George W. Bush proposed NATO membership for Ukraine, Putin erupted at Bush that "Ukraine is not even a country!" In July 2021, Putin published a long essay on the "historical unity" of Russia and Ukraine, warning that he would "never allow our historical territories and people close to us living there to be used against Russia. And to those who will undertake such an attempt, I would like to say that [in] this way they will destroy their own country." Biden seemed to understand Putin's ambitions after Russia invaded Ukraine in 2014. To his credit, Biden actually wanted to arm Ukraine back then, though Obama refused. And during the 2020 campaign, Biden always talked tough about Putin.

Yet the tough talk was just that—a way to score political points against Donald Trump. He appeased Putin from the beginning. In his first week in office, Biden agreed to extend the New START Treaty. This badly one-sided arms-control agreement, negotiated by Obama, allowed Russia to expand its strategic nuclear arsenal and ignored Russia's large advantage in tactical nuclear weapons. Putin had wanted to extend the treaty for years; it was his top priority with the United States. The Trump administration refused to extend it without concessions or modification. Yet Biden gave in without getting anything in return. Of course, this concession didn't satiate Putin, it only whetted his appetite.

Biden also conceded Putin's second-highest priority by waiving sanctions on the Nord Stream 2 pipeline. This pipeline under the

Baltic Sea would've allowed Russia to deliver gas to Germany without transiting Eastern European NATO members or Ukraine.

The appeasement continued. In April 2021, Putin deployed tens of thousands of soldiers, tanks, and munitions to the Ukrainian border. In response to this provocation, Biden rushed to propose a glitzy presidential summit in Geneva, his first with a foreign leader. Putin accepted the invitation, which confirmed his global stature. While Putin withdrew most of his troops, much of their equipment and infrastructure stayed behind at the border.

A month later, Russia-based hackers attacked the Colonial Pipeline, threatening fuel supplies for tens of millions of Americans. Biden blamed Russia, but reverted to his dovish ways and took no action. In fact, he soon after released a notorious Russian hacker from federal prison and returned him to Russia without explanation. Biden received nothing of consequence for these concessions.

And then came Afghanistan, where Putin saw a feeble American president overmatched by events and in denial of reality. Just weeks after America's humiliation in Kabul, Russian troops returned to Ukraine's border under the cover of unusually large annual military exercises—and never left. The Biden administration was well aware of the troop movements from the beginning; I received multiple briefings from administration officials in early autumn. I monitored this intelligence, while also searching for news reports or even social-media videos with which I could ring the alarm. The Biden administration finally leaked the story in late October, and I published a *Wall Street Journal* op-ed entitled "Russia Is Biden's Next Foreign Policy Test" that I had drafted weeks earlier. I called for immediate action to deter Putin: shipping weapons to Ukraine, sanctioning Nord Stream 2, and demanding that our European allies join us in threatening further sanctions. Biden ultimately did all these things, but only months later, when it was too late.

This weak passivity continued for months, until the invasion itself. In December, Biden explicitly ruled out the deployment of American troops to Ukraine. I agreed with this decision, believing that we should help Ukraine defend itself, but not send our troops to fight the war. By announcing it publicly, however, Biden simplified Putin's war planning. Ronald Reagan, by contrast, didn't seriously consider deploying troops to Afghanistan even as we supported the Afghans against Russian occupiers, but he never ruled it out publicly. Indeed, he hardly ever spoke about our efforts there; actions speak louder than words. Biden's needless announcement started a foolish trend of saying all the things he wouldn't do, never helpful in a contest of wills.

In January, Biden even speculated that a "minor incursion" by Russia into Ukraine might be met with a collective shrug. I was sitting at my desk in the Senate with Biden's press conference playing in the background when I heard those words and froze. The words echoed Secretary of State Dean Acheson's infamous speech in 1950 when he excluded South Korea from our "defensive perimeter" in East Asia; North Korea invaded the South just a few months later. I figured it wouldn't take Putin nearly so long.

Privately, too, Biden and his administration continued their dovish posture. In the Senate, some Democrats were working with Republicans to draft a tough, pre-invasion sanctions bill. The Biden administration lobbied furiously against it, killing its chances. And I sat through too many briefings to count in which one senior administration official after another dutifully insisted, "we don't have intelligence that Putin has made a decision to invade." Call me crazy, I said to them, but putting 200,000 troops on the border seemed like pretty good evidence, especially when those troops included medical units with fresh blood supplies to treat wounded soldiers. I planned my share of exercises in the Army and I never arranged for blood at the training ranges.

The concessions, the denials, the wishful thinking—none of it worked. Putin went for the jugular in Ukraine, as I had predicted for months. Even then, Biden hesitated. He apparently believed Russia would seize Kiev in just days and President Volodymyr Zelensky would surrender or flee. Indeed, the Biden administration offered to evacuate him, which the plucky president refused. "The fight is here," he rejoined, "I need ammunition; not a ride."

To be brutally frank, I believe some administration officials and European leaders actually hoped Russia would win in lightning fashion so they could slap on a few cosmetic sanctions and get back to business, as had happened after the 2014 invasion. Zelensky and the heroic Ukrainian army shamed the West into action.

Yet Biden equivocated many times in the early days of the war. We heard excuse after excuse in Senate briefings about which weapons were "defensive," and thus suitable for delivery to Ukraine, versus "offensive," and thus dangerously "escalatory." Again, call me crazy, but I observed that Russia invaded Ukraine and Ukraine was defending its own territory, so it seemed to me like all weapons were inherently "defensive." These lawyerly distinctions spilled into public when Secretary of State Antony Blinken gave "the green light" to Poland to deliver MiG fighters to Ukraine, only to have Biden bizarrely reverse the decision within days. Biden also refused to provide much actionable intelligence to the Ukrainians at first, only doing so after congressional oversight and further shaming by Ukraine's battlefield successes.

It was the same story on the economic front. The first sanctions against Russia were pathetically weak. Only once Ukraine repelled Russia's initial assault did the administration get more serious—and even then, Congress and Europe tended to drag Biden along. He refused to ban oil imports until it had unstoppable momentum in Congress. Similarly, he only called to strip Russia of its most-favored nation trading status once Congress had already begun to act.

Biden then sounded the hawkish trumpet in another one of his erratic swings. But in classic Democratic fashion, his tough talk was only talk. Three weeks into the war, he blurted out that Putin "is a war criminal." No question Russia has committed war crimes in Ukraine, but it's a little strange to extemporize about such a serious matter. Moreover, Biden put the cart before the horse: victory in war must come before accountability for crimes. At the very moment Biden condemned Putin, he was denying Ukraine fighter aircraft, armored vehicles, artillery, rocket launchers, and anti-ship missiles. Wars are won with such things, not with lawyers filing complaints at The Hague.

Biden made matters worse a few days later in Warsaw when he called for regime change in Russia. Again, seemingly at random, he yelled at the end of a speech, "For God's sake, this man cannot remain in power." The sentence wasn't in his prepared remarks and for good reason. Putin had long claimed that America wanted to remove him from power. He could now point to Biden's intemperate verbal outbursts as proof positive. Further, Biden dangerously raised the stakes of the war. If regime change and a war-crimes trial awaited a defeated Putin, then he had nothing left to lose in the war—not a good place to put a man who controls the world's largest nuclear arsenal.

Reagan provides a good contrast here again. Reagan confronted the Russians aggressively and successfully around the globe. Indeed, Democrats like Biden hysterically criticized him for risking a nuclear war. Yet Reagan never called for the ouster of Leonid Brezhnev or

Mikhail Gorbachev. Strength and resolution aren't the same thing as prattling rashness, but this difference is lost on Joe Biden when he starts acting tough.

Throughout the war, Biden has shown all his feathers—his dovish, hawkish, and ostrich-like instincts—sometimes all at once. And while things haven't turned out how either Putin or Biden expected, make no mistake, this tragic war came about because Biden's weakness offered Putin "temptations to a trial of strength," to borrow from Winston Churchill. The trial may be won, but Russia never should've been tempted.

IT's COMMON THESE days to dismiss Joe Biden as incompetent and confused. And he may be that—but he's not only that. Across his career, Biden has reflected and acted on the progressive conventional wisdom of the time. He often has blamed America for the world's problems, contending that we needed to retreat from the world and accommodate our enemies. When he could bring himself to employ American power, he usually has done so in half-hearted fashion and typically on behalf of abstract ideals, not to defend our core interests.

Amid all Biden's inconsistency, though, his record consistently demonstrates the progressive distaste for American strength. Fortunately, Biden lost many critical national-security debates as a senator and vice president.

But now he's the president. China is on the rise. Russia is on the march. Iran, Cuba, and Venezuela confidently wait for the latest round of concessions. The gap with our enemies is closing and "temptations to a trial of strength" are multiplying.

America can't afford much more of this weakness. It's time to be strong again. In Part II, I'll explain how to do it.

PART II

The Way Forward

CHAPTER 8

Restoring American Strategy

IN 1988, PRESIDENT Ronald Reagan warned the Islamic Republic of Iran by word and deed not to impede commercial shipping
or threaten U.S. Navy vessels in the Persian Gulf. But the ayatollahs
foolishly tested Reagan's resolve. The resulting naval battle was the
largest since World War II; it lasted only nine hours and destroyed
half of Iran's navy.

The backdrop was the long-running Iran–Iraq War. Both regimes
were vile and America didn't really have a dog in the fight. Henry
Kissinger quipped, "it's a pity both sides can't lose." And he wasn't
wrong. But we did have interests at stake. We didn't want the Shiite
ayatollahs to expand their anti-American empire into Iraq's Shiite-
dominated south. Nor did we want Soviet Russia to regain influence
in the region. Most important, America depended in those days on
Persian Gulf oil much more than we do today. Threats to the massive
oil tankers transiting the gulf hit every American family's wallet at
the gas pump.

By 1987, Iranian attacks on commercial tankers had increased so
much that Kuwait appealed to the superpowers for help. Reagan bested
Russia by offering to reflag Kuwaiti tankers under the Stars and Stripes
to allow U.S. Navy warships to escort them through the gulf.

The ayatollahs still didn't get the picture. In October, an Iranian missile struck a reflagged tanker. The next day, Reagan issued an ominous warning: "Any risk to that naval presence or to U.S. flag commercial ships operating peacefully in the waters of the gulf will be dealt with appropriately." Two days later, the Navy retaliated "appropriately" by destroying an Iranian oil platform used to facilitate Iran's attacks on tankers. When asked if America was "now in a war with Iran," Reagan scoffed, "No, we're not going to have a war with Iran. They're not that stupid."

Indeed, Iran ceased its attacks on reflagged tankers, though its attacks on other nations' tankers and its reckless mining of the Persian Gulf continued. The ayatollahs were playing with fire and they got burned on April 14, 1988. The USS *Samuel B. Roberts* struck an Iranian mine that blew a massive hole in its hull, nearly sinking the ship and wounding ten sailors. Iran had directly attacked our ship and harmed our sailors. America's credibility and honor were on the line.

Reagan didn't hesitate. Four days later, the Navy sent out nine destroyers, supported by Marines and air power. The first targets were two more "oil platforms" used to plan and facilitate Iran's attacks. An American commander bluntly warned one platform's crew: "You have five minutes to abandon the platform; I intend to destroy it at 0800." And that's what he did, with the second platform following the first. Much of Iran's navy raced out to engage our forces, only to end up at the bottom of the sea. America sank five Iranian ships that day and badly damaged another. When asked permission to sink the final ship, the chairman of the Joint Chiefs of Staff replied, "I think we've shed enough blood today." Iran towed the damaged ship back to port, a smoking symbol of the ayatollahs' humiliating defeat.

Reagan, in his understated manner, briefed Congress on the largest naval battle in four decades and concluded, "we have completed these self-defense actions and consider the matter closed." Iran, in no position to disagree, didn't target another American ship. Just four months later, the grinding eight-year war came to an end.

Peace through strength didn't lead to "endless war"—it led to victory.

SO FAR, WE'VE seen how the left has taken a wrecking ball to American power over the last century. They've repudiated America's founding, even America itself. Ambivalent and diffident about American power, they constrain and limit our freedom of action. The result is a weakened, chastened America, less fearsome to our enemies and less reliable to our friends. Of course, that was the left's goal all along.

But there's an older, prouder tradition of American strength and honor. This tradition teaches that the goal of American strategy is the safety, freedom, and prosperity of the American people. How we achieve that goal may differ from age to age, but the goal remains the same: America must come first. Our founding generation and statesmen like George Washington, Thomas Jefferson, and John Quincy Adams acted in this tradition, as did Ronald Reagan throughout his presidency, including when he destroyed half of Iran's navy. And we can too.

RECOVERING THE FOUNDERS' WISDOM

Many Americans sense our foreign policy suffers from aimless drift, but it's actually worse than that. Liberals haven't drifted away from our founding principles; they consciously turned away. We got to this point not by accident, but by design. By looking back to our Founders, we can recover their wisdom about American strategy and how to craft foreign policy in today's world.

As we've seen, Woodrow Wilson and the Progressives repudiated the Founders, including their foreign policy. Recall how Wilson lamented that Americans exhibit "the narrowness and prejudice of a family" because we put our own nation and interests ahead of other nations. Or how Wilson entered World War I not to avenge the deaths of Americans or to protect our territory and commerce, but for abstractions like "the rights and liberties of small nations." The Wilsonian streak is alive and well among progressives today, whether in Bill Clinton's foolish attempt at nation-building in Somalia or Barack Obama's reckless intervention in Libya under the incautious banner of the "responsibility to protect."

The Blame America First Democrats didn't just repudiate our founding principles, but virulently—and violently—rejected America itself. John Kerry defamed his fellow veterans for war crimes without evidence—until it became inconvenient for his political ambitions. George McGovern was willing to abandon our prisoners of war since "begging is better than bombing." Jimmy Carter abandoned long-standing allies in Latin America and the Middle East to anti-American zealots. And Obama didn't just deny American exceptionalism, he apologized for the "narrowness and prejudice" of his countrymen. These views are also alive and well on the left today, from the 1619 Project to the socialist Squad in the House of Representatives to the Biden administration's repeated confessions of America's supposed racism.

Joe Biden reflects both strains of left-wing thinking—sometimes at the same time on the same topic, as we saw with Ukraine in the last chapter. Early in Russia's war on Ukraine, he canceled a routine missile test because he didn't want to appear "provocative," as if America was somehow to blame for Russia's war of aggression. Vladimir Putin repaid this deference by proceeding with his own tests, even as he issued nuclear threats. Similarly, when our diplomats returned to the American embassy in Kiev, the Marines didn't return with them; Biden apparently feared it might violate his no-troops-in-Ukraine pledge—even though we have Marines at our embassy in Moscow. At the same time, Biden rashly called for Putin's ouster, a dangerous and unwise outburst.

These warped views are alien to the Founders' way of thinking. As we saw in Chapter One, the Founders put America first. In a fallen and dangerous world, they knew no one else would. And they were right— then and now. This maxim may be true of all nations, but it's especially true for America. We are a free nation with a government explicitly dedicated to our "Safety and Happiness," as the Declaration puts it, and to "secure the Blessings of Liberty to ourselves and our Posterity," in the words of the Constitution's preamble. Because these are the objectives of our government, they're also the objectives of our foreign policy.

What are the "blessings of liberty" when it comes to foreign policy? The phrase may strike some as general or vague. But I think the Founders' example and some common sense can mark out its meaning as what most Americans rightly expect their government to provide and protect: safety, freedom, and prosperity.

Safety was the Founders' paramount concern and responsibility. They had to protect our infant nation at a time of great vulnerability and danger. Old World empires like Britain and Spain violated our sovereign borders, threatened our commerce, and impressed our sailors into military service. We also shared a frontier with American Indians, some of whom fought an insurgency for control of the land. We shared the seas not only with rival nations but also outlaw pirates. Putting a foot wrong under these circumstances might have ended the American experiment before it really began.

Safety, though the first end of government, is not its highest end, and certainly not for America, a nation "conceived in liberty," in Abraham Lincoln's words. The purpose of a free government and a free society is the freedom of its people. Our people expect to live freely in the most basic ways. Freedom in this practical sense is worshiping your God, raising your kids, earning a living, and speaking your mind, all without leave of the government. The surest way to preserve freedom is self-government and the surest way to lose it is defeat in war and foreign domination.

At this most elemental level, that's what the Founders fought for in the Revolutionary War. Levi Preston was a young soldier at the Battles of Lexington and Concord. Seventy years later, a young historian asked Preston if he felt oppressed by the Tea Act and the Stamp Act, or perhaps inspired by the writings of John Locke. Preston said, no, he didn't use those stamps, he never drank tea, and he hadn't read Locke. The flummoxed historian pressed for an answer. "Young man," an exasperated Preston explained, "what we meant in going for those Redcoats was this: we always had governed ourselves, and we always meant to. They didn't mean we should." That's a succinct statement of how freedom is central to our foreign policy.

Finally, the Founders wanted to set the conditions for prosperity by harnessing all the abundance and potential of the New World. Our farmers needed fertile land to grow their crops, our manufacturers needed skilled workers and investment for their factories and mills, and our merchants needed markets for their goods. But widespread prosperity meant more than a higher standard of living for Americans, as vital as that was. In our infancy, America depended on imports from Great Britain, France, and other foreign powers for everything from cloth to guns. This dependence exposed us to coercion and exploitation. The Founders worked steadily to nurture and protect our own industry to achieve political and economic independence.

For some, a foreign policy of safety, freedom, and prosperity may still seem too vague as a guide for specific cases, but our Founders understood that foreign policy is foremost the domain of prudential judgment and reasoning about circumstances. Rigid doctrine and ideology are poor guides when going out to face the world. In any given case, there might be a hundred and one different practical considerations. Working through these considerations can be hard and fraught, but it must be done and the guiding question remains the same—what course of action best secures our safety, freedom, and prosperity?—even if the answers appear to differ from case to case.

The case of the Barbary pirates illustrates how much circumstances matter in foreign policy, even though ultimate goals remain the same. For centuries, pirates from the Barbary States—basically, modern-day Morocco to Libya—had threatened commercial vessels in the eastern Atlantic and Mediterranean. They demanded ransom in return for captured ships and crews. Our ships became common targets after they lost the British navy's protection following the revolution. Thomas Jefferson, then our ambassador to France under the Articles of Confederation, recommended war against the Barbary States. He feared, reasonably enough, that paying ransom would only encourage more attacks. John Adams, then our ambassador to Great Britain, sympathized with Jefferson, but concluded our Navy was too weak and the government too burdened by debt to risk a war. He reluctantly encouraged paying the ransom. Though Congress was too divided and broke under the Articles of Confederation to do either, once the Constitution was adopted and George Washington became president, he agreed with Adams and began to pay annual ransom. This policy continued during Adams's own presidency.

But then Jefferson became president. His views hadn't changed but circumstances had. Our naval power had grown steadily during the first decade under the Constitution. So too had the pirates' demands, which Jefferson now refused. Instead, he deployed the Navy and Marines to battle the pirates, free our citizens, and redeem America's honor. And that's exactly what they did; still today, the "Marines' Hymn" celebrates their valor on "the shores of Tripoli."

Yet circumstances changed again near the end of Jefferson's tenure. The pirates renewed their attacks after our Navy departed the region due to rising tensions with Great Britain that led to the War of 1812. Jefferson and then James Madison had to endure the pirates' attacks until the war ended. At that point, Madison again dispatched the Navy, which finally ended the piracy threat once and for all.

Neither the Barbary pirates nor America's core group of statesmen changed over thirty years, but our military strength and geopolitical conditions did. And as the times and circumstances changed, our leaders shifted course, though always guided by the same lodestar: safety, freedom, and prosperity.

Washington's Farewell Address also captures this prudential element of the Founders' foreign policy. The great statesman warned against "permanent alliances" and recommended "as little political connection as possible" with other nations. These policies were well suited for our circumstances in 1796: a young, weak, and fragile America; a Europe convulsed by the French Revolution; and fairly primitive military and communications technology. But he also foresaw a future when America would gain strength, stand up, and assert itself:

> With me, a predominant motive has been to endeavor to gain time to our country to settle and mature its yet recent institutions, and to progress without interruption to that degree of strength and consistency, which is necessary to give it, humanly speaking, the command of its own fortunes.

Washington understood, in other words, that our policy might change, probably should change, as circumstances changed.

A good example came a quarter century later, with John Quincy Adams and the Monroe Doctrine. Circumstances had changed a lot since 1796. We had settled our territorial and diplomatic disputes with Great Britain after the War of 1812. We had obtained Florida from Spain in 1821. And reactionary European monarchies were threatening to recolonize the newly independent nations in our hemisphere. Adams, who was then secretary of state for James Monroe, sought to deter this threat with the doctrine, which stated that attempts to recolonize the New World would be treated as hostile acts. In Washington's time, we lacked the strength to pursue such a policy, which wasn't really needed anyway. But by Monroe's presidency, we had gained enough strength and stability to announce a new policy that was plainly needed given the new threats in our neighborhood.

Our Founders were shrewd and skilled statesmen who guided our infant nation safely through turbulent, dangerous waters. They understood that the "blessings of liberty" are precious and rare, and they adapted methods and policies to protect our safety, our freedom, and our prosperity. Their principles and practices should still guide us today. It was a mistake, for instance, when Obama intervened militarily to topple Muammar Qaddafi precisely because it did nothing to advance these principles, unlike Jefferson's war against Tripoli.

But can the Founders' wisdom really guide us today? Let's consider the statesmanship of Ronald Reagan.

On the surface, Reagan's foreign policy seems to break sharply with Washington and Adams. Washington warned against permanent alliances. Reagan added Spain to NATO and fortified our alliances and partnerships across Eurasia. Adams cautioned against going abroad in search of monsters to destroy. Reagan attacked monsters in Afghanistan,

Grenada, Libya, Iran, and Central America, to name just a few. Everywhere you turned, he confronted and challenged our enemies.

But at a deeper level, Reagan had the same foreign policy as Washington and Adams, all things considered—again, as they must be. He surveyed the world and acted to secure the blessings of liberty for America. We faced Soviet Russia, a traditional Old World power with a godless, globalist ideology grafted on top of it. Military and communications technology had advanced to the point that we couldn't count on time to gather our strength and rally our allies when a war began. In fact, thanks to the rise of weapons with global reach, we might not even realize a war had begun.

Under these circumstances, Reagan did what Washington and Adams would've done. He rebuilt our military strength from its shocking lows of the 1970s. Reagan reinforced the beachheads and lodgments of freedom around the world to confront the enemy on their turf, not on our turf. He supported the forces of freedom to pressure Soviet Russia, which tried to undermine them everywhere. Reagan never confused America's friends with our enemies, nor drew a moral equivalence between the two.

But Reagan also never confused means with ends. He acted foremost to protect our safety, freedom, and prosperity. For example, he supported the Solidarity movement and the Contras not primarily for their sake, but for ours. Yes, he admired these anti-communist heroes and he wanted Poland and Nicaragua to live in freedom, but his prime motive was always America's freedom. He didn't see tools and methods like alliances, negotiations, and treaties as ends in themselves, but as means to achieve our ends.

Reagan recovered the Founders' wisdom and we can too. Their wisdom is alive and well in the common sense of the American people. During an Armed Services Committee hearing early in the war on Ukraine, a Democratic senator lamented that the American people focused more on Russia's invasion of Ukraine than on Ethiopia's civil war, implying that racism was the difference. I observed to him that the real distinction was between invasions and civil wars. In the early 1990s, the American people similarly cared more about Iraq's invasion of Kuwait than they did about the civil wars in the former Yugoslavia. Most Americans seem to believe intuitively that naked wars of aggression, even a world away, threaten our interests more than civil wars, especially when the invader is an old adversary like Russia. And they're right to believe it—not just intuitively, but historically, as we learned from the 1930s. This kind of practical wisdom captures the thinking of the Founders and Reagan.

Though the world has changed a lot from the founding era—and, indeed, from Reagan's days—the central purpose of America's foreign policy hasn't. With hard-nosed and clear-eyed thinking, we can return to the position of strength, to borrow again from Washington's Farewell Address, "when we may choose peace or war, as our interest, guided by justice, shall counsel."

AMERICA'S INTERESTS

When we move from "the blessings of liberty" to our vital national interests, it's good to be specific. How we define our interests, after all, determines why, when, and with whom America will confront other nations, to the point of war. This is deadly serious business. We ought to be clear and concrete, both for ourselves and for those other nations.

But the progressive left does the opposite. At times, progressive do-gooders appeal to "national interests" for any nation but our own, as when they convinced Obama to intervene militarily in Libya for no good reason—indeed, contrary to our interests. Ask Wilson or his heirs the reasonable question of, "what's in it for us?" and they'll respond, "nothing!" And they think that's a good thing. Or Blame America First Democrats define our "interests" so narrowly that there's no insult or abuse they think we shouldn't suffer in silence. They say interest, but they mean surrender.

So let's examine how we understand our vital national interests. Our interests aren't abstract, arbitrary, or made up. They're based on the real, tangible, specific circumstances of our country; these circumstances include our geography, our economy, and our people and their special way of life. America is a large commercial republic in the Western Hemisphere. Our prosperity depends heavily on our ability to transport goods by sea and by air. Our people travel and live across the globe, not only for commerce but also as bighearted missionaries, charitable workers, and students.

This reality points to some obvious conclusions about America's interests—indisputable, really, to anyone but a left-wing ideologue. For instance, our geography gives us especially strong interests in Latin America and the Caribbean, since problems there can quickly arrive here. As serious geopolitical thinkers like Nicholas Spykman long understood, "geography is the most important factor in foreign policy because it is the most permanent." Similarly, we have strong interests in the freedom of the seas for our commerce and strategic choke points like the Panama Canal or the Strait of Malacca. Why is America's only military base on the African continent in tiny Djibouti? In no small part because that country sits on the narrow Bab el Mandeb Strait, which connects the Red Sea (and hence the Mediterranean Sea) to the Indian Ocean. By contrast, we have less interest in landlocked and out-of-the-way places, unless they produce something of essential value or grave danger.

Let's build on these examples and look more closely at our interests.

Our Home

It should go without saying, but liberals discount reality so much that it perhaps needs saying: our first and most vital interest is to prevent an attack on America itself. Some of our nation's darkest moments have resulted from foreign attacks, from Great Britain's burning of the capital during the War of 1812 to Pearl Harbor to 9/11 in our own living memory. Blessed as we are by geography, these attacks are relatively rare, especially compared to what Old World nations have suffered.

But America isn't immune from attack. In the age of nuclear-armed intercontinental ballistic missiles, we're more vulnerable than we were a century ago. China, Russia, and even North Korea could strike us with nuclear weapons. The threat will only grow if we allow other rogue states like Iran to obtain nuclear weapons. In addition, these nations can threaten us with chemical and biological weapons; the damage caused by the Wuhan coronavirus pandemic is an analogue to the damage that an intentional attack could inflict. Iran also plots to kidnap and kill on American soil, as do terrorists. Our enemies, in other words, have ways to reach across the ocean and harm us, without warning.

The most immediate threat to our home is the slow-motion invasion at our southern border. A country without borders isn't a country. Thanks to Joe Biden and the radical left, our southern border is essentially open. In Biden's first year in office, Border Patrol encountered more than two million illegal immigrants at our southern border, a staggering number. Many are so-called economic migrants, who may not threaten our safety but do take American jobs and drive down wages. Border Patrol also caught twenty-three known or suspected terrorists in 2021 alone. ISIS recently plotted to smuggle hit men across the border to assassinate former president George W. Bush. Even if only a small percentage of illegal aliens are criminals, drug runners, and terrorists, it's still a large and dangerous number in absolute terms.

We all see the consequences of the Democrats' open-border ideology. More than 100,000 Americans died of drug overdoses last year, mostly from fentanyl and heroin trafficked across our southern border. In the last four years alone, more Americans have died of overdose than in the four years of World War II combined. And millions more suffered from drug addiction and its consequences for themselves and their families and friends.

This assault on our sovereignty has to stop. The security of our southern border is an overriding national security concern and should be the paramount priority for our relationships with Mexico and Guatemala (the geographic choke point for other nations to Mexico's south).

Our Citizens

After the safety of our citizens at home, America has a vital interest in the protection and liberty of our citizens abroad. Millions of Americans live and travel overseas. These citizens are a source of strength and pride, acting as unofficial ambassadors whether they're spreading the Gospel, selling American goods, or just seeing the world. The same goes for the nearly 175,000 troops stationed overseas; they protect America, and they deserve our protection in return. A strong, proud country protects its citizens and punishes those who harm them.

Yet too many enemies target our citizens because they believe they can get away with it. Iran's mullahs, for instance, held fifty-two Americans hostage for more than four hundred days, unafraid of the feckless

Jimmy Carter, only to release them within hours of Ronald Reagan taking office. Iran continues to take Americans hostage and the Democrats continue to appease the ayatollahs. Obama negotiated his nuclear deal with Iran even as it held Americans unjustly; indeed, he paid $400 million in ransom for four American hostages the day after the deal took effect. Within a month, Iran was back at it, unlawfully detaining another American, who had traveled there to visit his son, yet another American hostage. Biden also has refused to link nuclear negotiations with Iran—much less concessions from Iran—to the release of hostages.

Liberals never learn. Obama, after all, had run the same playbook with Cuba, swapping legitimate prisoners who got due process in our judicial system for American hostages, all as a precursor for his capitulation to the Castro regime. Biden lightened sanctions on Venezuela in a desperate scramble for oil despite the outlaw Maduro regime holding six Americans hostage. Russia and China also get in on the action by detaining Americans on trumped-up criminal charges or by denying them exit visas.

We should learn the lessons of the past. Jefferson put an end to the Barbary pirates' hostage-taking only with military force, not with ransom. Reagan punished Qaddafi with retaliatory strikes after Libyan operatives bombed a West Berlin nightclub popular with American troops. To go back further, in ancient times, a Roman citizen could safeguard his rights across the empire simply by stating *civis Romanus sum*—"I am a Roman citizen." Acts 22 informs us that the fearsome phrase saved Paul the Apostle from an unjust flogging for his ministry. So it should be today with us: *civis Americanus* ought to ensure justice for our citizens wherever they venture, and retribution ought to follow wherever it's denied.

Our Commerce

A core interest of American foreign policy is to support our trade and commerce with other nations, ensuring American workers and businesses get a fair shake from foreign governments. Those nations may—indeed, probably will—benefit from their trade with us, but their benefit is incidental. Our priorities are the jobs and wealth of our own people.

As the world's great maritime power, positioned between its two largest oceans, freedom of navigation on the high seas has always been among our most vital interests. If an enemy could restrict our freedom to travel and trade, they could bottle us up in the Western Hemisphere and strangle our economy by restricting our access to seven-eighths of the world's population and most of its resources. The same logic has also extended to freedom of air travel for the last century.

It's hard to overstate the significance of freedom of navigation in our foreign policy. Historian Walter Russell Mead has observed that "infringing on our freedom to travel by sea and air remains the fastest way to start a war with the United States." Similarly, the normally pacific Jefferson launched the Barbary Wars over freedom of travel and sounded unusually bellicose notes about it: "Our commerce on the ocean and in other countries must be paid for by frequent war."

In our times, this logic also extends to the movement of information and data across undersea cables and satellites in space. As a New World power, we depend on these cables and satellites much more than do Old World powers, who can rely on terrestrial cables. Russian and Chinese threats to our cables and satellites, and threats of cyberattack against our government and businesses, aren't much different from old-fashioned naval threats to our commercial shipping, and in some ways worse.

Freedom of navigation doesn't mean much, though, without open markets across the seas where our farmers and factories can sell their goods. We have never shied from playing hardball. When Commodore Matthew C. Perry sailed into Japan's Edo Harbor in 1853 and told its negotiators to open their market to American merchants, he handed them a white flag so they could surrender if they defied him. Adam Smith's invisible hand may guide our commerce at home, but the mailed fist of the U.S. Navy has protected it abroad. While trade negotiators have (mostly) supplanted gunboats on these matters today, our negotiators should still drive hard bargains for our workers and businesses, being especially careful not to sacrifice our best sources of leverage, such as access to the world's largest market, our rule of law, and the protection of our world-class laws of contract and property rights.

A corollary to freedom to travel and trade is access to critical and strategic goods. Oil has been the bedrock of modern economies for more than a century, a fact which won't change any time soon, despite Democratic fantasies. Wars have started over oil, and access to oil figures prominently in most nation's war plans. That means American energy independence isn't just a political slogan—it's a strategic imperative. Its opposite is energy dependence, a dangerous and humiliating condition for a superpower, especially since so much of the world's oil is controlled by unsavory or unstable governments. Just look at Joe Biden's pathetic pleading to Venezuela after Russia's invasion of Ukraine.

Today, other goods such as rare-earth elements and semiconductors have joined oil as central to our national interest. Rare-earth elements are essential to everything from the smartphone in your pocket to the car you drive to our military's stealth aircraft. Although these elements aren't really rare in nature, what is rare is the mining and processing of them, which the world has mostly outsourced to China. That foolish decision has empowered our principal enemy to cut off access to the elements, as it did to Japan over a territorial dispute in 2010, or simply to prioritize supply to its domestic manufacturers. It's an urgent priority to reverse this self-inflicted wound and begin producing these elements here in America.

The same goes for advanced semiconductors, which today are produced primarily in Taiwan. That island is the world's hottest flash point for several reasons. One is Communist China's attempts to dominate Taiwan. Another is Taiwan's geographic position in the middle of what's known as the First Island Chain, the islands—from our Aleutians to Japan to Taiwan to the Philippines—which impede China's navy behind a wall of friendly territory. A third and newer reason is Taiwan Semiconductor Manufacturing Company's significance to the world economy. TSMC's chips power our computers, our communication networks, our cars, and our health care, among many other things. Imagine how it would affect our lives if China suddenly controlled those chips. That's why it's in our vital national interest to deter a Chinese invasion of Taiwan and encourage TSMC and its competitors to build new factories in America.

Our Friends

America has built a strong, durable network of allies and partners around the world over the last seventy-five years. In some cases, mostly NATO countries and a handful of nations in East Asia, we've committed through treaties to mutual defense. In many others, such as Israel and Taiwan, we've developed deep military, diplomatic, and political partnerships even without a formal treaty. These allies and partners don't always agree with us or support our goals or methods. They're a fractious lot, often disagreeing among themselves, sometimes to the point of armed conflict. And too many allies too often don't shoulder their share of the load; many NATO countries, for instance, have allowed their militaries to atrophy. But what Winston Churchill said of allies near the end of World War II remains true today: "There is only one thing worse than fighting with allies, and that is fighting without them."

Given these frictions and the costs, it's essential to recall that we have allies and partners for our sake, not theirs. As with trade agreements, our friends benefit from their relationship with America, but that's not the point. Nor is it to uphold the "liberal, rules-based international order," the kind of abstraction progressives love, but for which no soldier ever picked up a rifle and fought. No, the point of these alliances and partnerships is to fortify our own security.

How exactly do our alliances and partnerships benefit us? Bill Rood, a legendary strategist and combat veteran of Patton's Third Army, offered the simplest explanation of why America needs allies and overseas bases under modern circumstances. Rood built on Spykman's idea of the "Rimland," Eurasia's coastal regions and marginal seas, such as the South China Sea and the Mediterranean Sea. The Rimland contains most of the world's population, resources, and key terrain. The most serious threat to America has always been the rise of an adversarial nation or coalition that dominates the Rimland and turns these latent sources of power against us. Germany and Japan threatened just that in World War II, as did Soviet Russia and its communist satellites in the Cold War. China has similar ambitions today. And the threat is more serious than it once was because advances in military and communications technology over the last century might enable our adversaries to achieve their objective before we recognize the danger and send in the cavalry.

According to Rood, the answer to these challenges is to "defend forward." A dominant Rimland power would threaten our most enduring and fundamental interest, the prevention of an attack on America. The best way to prevent an attack by such a power, he contended, is to man the "distant ramparts," the beachheads and lodgments of freedom in the Old World. As I heard in the Army, our defense strategy is always to fight away games, keeping the awful destructive power of modern war as far from our shores as possible.

This strategy is why some of our most important overseas troop presence and bases—our distant ramparts—are located around the Rimland: Great Britain, Germany, Italy, Spain, Turkey, Djibouti, Kuwait, Bahrain, Qatar, Japan, and South Korea. Some of these nations are treaty allies, others are partners, but all possess vital territory necessary to retain access to the Rimland and a balance of power in Eurasia favorable to America. The same is often true for our allies and partners where we have no or minimal troop presence. Montenegro joined NATO in 2017, for instance, primarily because it had the last Adriatic coastline outside the alliance. Montenegro didn't add much military power to the alliance, but it closed off that coastline to Russian and Chinese warships.

No doubt this global network imposes real costs, Rood acknowledged. Some costs are tangible, such as the tax dollars we spend on overseas deployments and bases; our hosts offset some of those costs, as they should. Other costs are intangible, such as the risk of an unwelcome conflict provoked by a rash ally. But, he contended, these costs pale in comparison to another general war like World War II, especially a nuclear war. Further, our relationships with divergent allies and partners allow us to mediate their differences, which might otherwise spark conflicts that could disrupt our commerce and threaten our safety. We've played a constructive role, for example, in mediating some of the traditional tensions between Japan and South Korea. And our friendship with both Israel and the Arab countries has led to historic peace agreements like the Abraham Accords.

Americans benefit from our global network of friendly nations. Our allies trade with us, provide safe harbor for our ships and bases for our troops, and supply vital intelligence about what our adversaries are up to. Most important, our network of allies and partners helps us keep our enemies at bay on their side of the world. But to preserve these benefits, America must be a reliable and resolute friend. We need to keep our word.

AMERICA'S PROMISES

Even small children understand the importance of speaking clearly and keeping promises; if Mom and Dad threaten a punishment but don't follow through, children know they can get away with it. In the Army, we used to say, "the deficiency you walk by is the standard you set." What's true in raising kids and training soldiers is true in the world. Our credibility is an essential part of our security. No amount of wisdom or strength can succeed without credibility.

Unfortunately, America's credibility is in tatters today.

Obama damaged America's credibility in ways that harm us to this day. Two broken promises above all undercut our credibility: his refusal to enforce his own "red line" in Syria and his discarded pledge not to allow Iran to keep an industrial-scale nuclear capability. He viewed both as strategic masterstrokes, but when our credibility is at stake, it doesn't matter how we view things—it's how the world views them. And no one viewed them as anything other than shocking reversals.

I witnessed the fallout firsthand with foreign leaders. In one remarkable meeting, I sat down with an Arab head of state late in

Obama's presidency. At the last minute, he changed the venue from the palace to his home, which I paid no mind. He proceeded to savage Obama for the red line and the nuclear deal. America looked weak and unreliable, he explained, emboldening Iran and unsettling his nation and others. I couldn't disagree with him; after all, I was the deal's foremost critic in Congress. An hour into the meeting, our disheveled and frantic ambassador rushed into the room. She apologized for her tardiness, saying she didn't get word of the location change until she reached the palace. For the rest of the meeting, he was diplomatic, tactful, and appreciative of America's support. It was obvious to me what had happened. He switched the location at the last minute and didn't tell her because he wanted to convey how he really felt and how others viewed Obama without the ambassador tattling on him. It was a sad commentary on America's standing.

And it wasn't just in the Middle East; I heard similar anxieties from other foreign leaders. On a trip to East Asia, leaders from multiple nations inquired about the red-line fiasco and what it meant for them. These nations usually wouldn't care much about Syria, but they cared deeply about the word of the American president. In 2016, I attended international security conferences in Munich and Singapore. During many meetings with foreign leaders, a common theme emerged: could America be trusted any longer?

Because that trust is so central to American power, so easily lost, and so hard to restore, America should put its credibility on the line sparingly and only when our vital national interests are at stake. Bob Gates served eight presidents in many roles, including as secretary of defense for Obama. He learned from this lifetime of service that credibility is both critical and fragile. "A threat by the president of the United States," he wrote, "is a potent deterrent only if it is credible and the president is prepared to act upon it. For this reason, I always urged that we avoid 'red lines' and ultimatums." Tough talk feels good, but it harms America in the long run if it's not backed up with tough action. The commander in chief should draw red lines carefully, but enforce them ruthlessly, as Gates colorfully summed up: "Presidents should scrupulously avoid red lines and ultimatums unless they are fully committed to enforcing them militarily. Once a president cocks the pistol, he or she must be ready to fire it."

Our greatest statesmen understood the need to enforce our threats and to keep our promises if we want to preserve America's credibility. In his Farewell Address, Washington counseled against new commitments, but also stressed, "so far as we have already formed engagements, let them be fulfilled with perfect good faith." Reagan, despite his assertive foreign policy, didn't often put America's credibility on the line. But when he did, as with Iran's threat to our ships in the Persian Gulf, he followed through decisively.

Indeed, so important is a president's personal credibility to America's credibility that issues far removed from foreign policy can affect our standing in the world. Early in his first year, Reagan faced a strike by air-traffic controllers in blatant violation of federal law. He issued an ultimatum: return to work in forty-eight hours or be fired. Most didn't return, so Reagan fired them. His secretary of state, George Shultz, called it "the most important foreign policy decision Ronald Reagan ever made." Tip O'Neill, the Democratic Speaker of the House, traveled to Russia shortly after the firing and learned that Reagan's resolution in the controversy had "deeply impressed" Soviet leaders.

Such resolution in the face of danger is difficult, but it's a mark of true statesmanship and a critical part of America's credibility. When a president commits the military to preserve our credibility, he must accept the risks that come with that action. Winston Churchill, one of the great wartime statesmen of all times, cautioned about the inherent unpredictability of military conflict:

> Never, never, never believe any war will be smooth and easy, or that anyone who embarks on the strange voyage can measure the tides and hurricanes he will encounter. The statesman who yields to war fever must realise that once the signal is given, he is no longer the master of policy but the slave of unforeseeable and uncontrollable events.

Reagan's strikes against Iran in 1988 could have sparked a broader conflict. So could have Donald Trump's decision to kill Iran's terrorist mastermind, Qasem Soleimani, after Iran defied warnings not to attack our bases in Iraq. But a failure to back up our threats would've inflicted certain, immediate harm on our interests, as happened with Obama's red-line fiasco. That's why our leaders must be resolute in upholding our commitments and seeing them through till the end. "Resolution where others waver is the mark of leadership among nations," Bill Rood wrote. "The discriminate application of military power to serve the strategic interests of the United States is a warning to those who wish the nation ill and a reassurance to those whose alliance lends us strength."

We should be careful and judicious about the guarantees we extend and the threats we make. Once made, however, we have to be iron-willed until the business is finished. Otherwise, Jefferson observed, "an insult unpunished is the parent of many others."

OF COURSE, TO uphold our commitments and to enforce our red lines, America must have the strength to do so. Moral clarity, practical wisdom, and iron resolution don't amount to much if we can't impose our will on adversaries when needed. Even the Founders, as we've seen, had to suffer insults in the early days of our republic due to our weakness.

But our Founders also understood that weakness and dependence are pitiful conditions for a nation. They rapidly built our strength so America could take "command of its own fortunes," as Washington said in his Farewell Address. Sadly, our strength has declined in recent decades, even as China has built its strength, rapidly closing the gap between our two nations. Now that we have a better understanding of America's strategy, we must turn to how we can regain America's strength.

CHAPTER 9

Regaining American Strength

D URING JIMMY CARTER'S disastrous presidency, communism spread throughout Latin America. In the especially piv-
otal year of 1979, both Nicaragua and Grenada fell to communists. As
he returned from a celebratory trip to Managua, Fidel Castro boasted,
"now there are three of us." And the Cuban dictator had big plans to
add more captive nations to his anti-American axis in the hemisphere.

Grenada is a small, beautiful island in the southeast Caribbean—
and therefore was strategically vital to Cuba and Soviet Russia during
the Cold War. Barely 150 miles off the coast of Venezuela, the island
could serve as an offshore arms depot for communist rebels in South
America and other Caribbean nations. Russia could also use Grenada to operate submarines in the Caribbean basin. Most ominous,
Grenada's proximity to Africa made it the potential final linchpin in
a string of Soviet and allied air bases from southern Russia to North
Africa to West Africa to Grenada to Cuba. Soviet bombers and heavy
cargo planes could fly between these bases without refueling and
largely beyond American detection. This grave threat materialized
when Grenada welcomed hundreds of Cubans to construct a massive airport with a 9,000-foot runway. What Ronald Reagan called
the "suspiciously huge" runway was larger than needed for Grenada's

commercial aviation, but coincidently just large enough to support the largest Soviet bombers and cargo aircraft.

The air base posed a two-way threat. Russia could use Grenada to arm Cuba and other Latin American communists, and Castro could export revolutionaries to the bloody war in Angola and perhaps elsewhere in Africa.

Tensions reached a crisis point in October 1983 when even more radical communists toppled the ruling communists. The new government killed the former prime minister and instituted a twenty-four-hour shoot-on-sight curfew that threatened hundreds of American medical students on the island. The Reagan administration feared a replay of the Iranian hostage crisis. The Organization of Eastern Caribbean States pleaded with the Reagan administration to intervene and prevent communism from spreading further in the region.

Within days, Reagan had concluded that we had "no choice but to act strongly and decisively" and authorized an invasion. This wasn't an easy decision; we had only spotty intelligence on Grenada's forces and capabilities, we had little time to execute the mission, and many in Washington still hesitated to use military force due to a hangover from Vietnam. And just after Reagan authorized the invasion planning, a suicide bomber killed 241 Marines in their Beirut barracks, commanding the attention of Reagan and his team. But Reagan didn't let the crisis in Lebanon crowd out the crisis in our backyard. He declared, "there are Americans there and they are in danger. We are going!"

On October 25, barely a week after the coup, around 8,000 American troops embarked on Operation Urgent Fury. They had a clearly defined mission: save the endangered Americans, depose the communist regime, and reestablish order on the island.

Our troops had some setbacks, but they adapted, overcame, and prevailed. The incomplete intelligence hampered the operation, yet vindicated Reagan's judgment. Military leaders anticipated only 200 Cuban construction workers on the island; in reality, 700 well-armed Cuban soldiers awaited American forces. Our troops also discovered huge weapons caches at the air base, enough to arm the Cuban forces and thousands more communist rebels. Reagan had acted just in time. The war ended after four lopsided days. Our troops took fewer than 150 casualties, while the communists suffered nearly 500 casualties and more than 600 Cubans surrendered. Our citizens on the island were safe. Reagan hit hard and he hit fast. America won.

The Grenada operation was the first successful military rollback of communism during the Cold War. We had eliminated a deadly threat on our doorstep. And we had liberated a grateful people, who enjoy freedom and democracy to this day.

Reagan worked to stabilize the island and later traveled there in 1986. Tens of thousands of Grenadians lined the streets and welcomed Reagan as a liberator. Grenada's prime minister described Reagan as "our own national hero" and "our rescuer after God." Reagan passed banner after banner that read "God Bless America" and later wrote that "I probably never felt better during my presidency than I did that day." What Reagan felt that day was the joy of American success, made possible by American strength and confidence.

AFTER DECADES OF liberals squandering our power, such joy in victory can seem like a distant memory. American strength has declined as our rivals have gained ground, a dangerous situation. Rivalry among nations isn't a horse race; it's not enough to win by a nose. The narrowing gap between us and our enemies only gives them "temptations to a trial of strength," as Winston Churchill taught us. Today, we face the stark reality that we might be eclipsed as the world's superpower and that we won't be able to secure the blessings of liberty for our children.

Patriots recoil at the thought of losing our birthright. Yet we know, as Reagan said, "freedom is never more than one generation away from extinction." It's time to defend our freedom. It's time to reverse the left's plot to sabotage American power. We can start by getting rid of the liberal policies and mindsets sapping our nation of its strength.

While I can't catalog the solution to every failed liberal policy in these pages—this isn't *War and Peace*, after all—there are a few urgent things we can do to regain our strength and confront the challenges ahead.

To begin with, we have to rebuild our military, the foundation of our power. For too long, progressives have weakened our military by a thousand (budget) cuts and undermined its warrior culture.

Next, our wide-open border is a national-security threat. The uncontrolled migration of illegal aliens and influx of illegal drugs across the border harms American workers, endangers our communities, and poisons our kids. We have to secure our border.

We also have to achieve energy security. Energy is the actual power behind American power. Without affordable and reliable energy, our economy will collapse and our military will stall. Liberals want to destroy American energy; we have to protect it.

Turning our eyes abroad, we have to distinguish once again between friends and foes. It's no surprise that Blame America First Democrats also blame our allies for siding with us and truck with our enemies. But we need friends in a dangerous world, and we should have the moral confidence and clarity to ask a simple question: are you with us or against us?

These steps will prepare us for the final urgent task ahead, beating China in the new Cold War. Communist China is our gravest threat, perhaps the most dangerous threat America has ever faced. If we rise to the challenge, we can send the Chinese Communists to the same "ash heap of history" where Reagan sent the Russian Communists. But if we fail, as Reagan warned, "one day we will spend our sunset years telling our children and our children's children what it was once like in the United States where men were free."

I believe America will once again rise to this challenge. The great patriots of our great nation are ready for a new American Century. Let's take a look at a road map to renewal.

REBUILD THE MILITARY

Let's start with our military because military power is the foundation of all American power. For too long, we've allowed our military to atrophy, asking our troops to shoulder more tasks with fewer resources.

The world is far more dangerous than it was when Bill Clinton declared a peace dividend of reduced defense spending at the end of the Cold War. China poses a grave threat to America—and it openly aims to replace us as the world's dominant superpower. China has increased its military spending by more than 1,000 percent over the last two decades and shows no sign of stopping.

As Jimmy Carter's secretary of defense remarked of Soviet Russia, when we build, China builds, and when we cut, China builds. China today has the world's largest army, navy, ground-based missile forces, and arsenal of sea mines. And China is expanding its nuclear arsenal the fastest of all. China doesn't hide its ambitions or intentions; its military uses mock targets shaped like our aircraft carriers.

But China isn't alone. The war on Ukraine is a reminder that Russia, though a declining power, still has a military strong enough to threaten our interests in Europe and the Middle East, along with the world's largest nuclear arsenal. The war also illustrates the continued primacy of traditional military strength: Ukraine fought off Russia's initial campaign with missiles and guns, not cyberattacks and hashtags. Thanks to Obama and Biden, Iran is closer than ever to a nuclear weapon, and spreading more mayhem than ever. North Korea's nuclear arsenal continues to grow, straining our missile defenses. And these enemies meddle in our backyard in places like Cuba, Venezuela, and Nicaragua.

Yet our defense budget remains at historically low levels. In Biden's first year, we spent only 3.4 percent of our economy on national defense, well below the "hollow force" era of the late 1970s, when the budget bottomed out at 4.5 percent of the economy. And this low point isn't justified by some "peace dividend" after the wars in Iraq and Afghanistan ended because we haven't had large numbers of troops in those countries for years. Rather, as we saw in Chapter Four, Obama's budget cuts devastated the military. And while Donald Trump and Republican Congresses partially reversed those cuts, Biden has proposed even deeper cuts—so deep, in fact, that some congressional Democrats couldn't stomach them. Our military also has to contend with the historic inflation unleashed by Biden's failed policies, which hits our military's budget just like it hits your family's budget.

To meet the challenges we face, the defense budget needs to grow at least to 4 percent of the economy, and probably more than that. For perspective, it never fell below 5 percent and was usually near 6 percent during Reagan's presidency. The National Defense Strategy Commission is a congressionally directed bipartisan panel that acts as a sanity check on a new administration's defense strategy and budget. The commission recommends that the defense budget should grow annually by 3–5 percent over the rate of inflation. Such growth is necessary for the foreseeable future to rebuild our military. Many progressives will fret about an "arms race," but as I often point out, it's much cheaper to win an arms race than to lose a war.

How should we spend this new money? The military needs more of everything and it needs to stick to the basics: flesh and blood and steel. Too many politicians and more than a few generals get caught up with whizbang high-tech ideas, fantasizing that wars can be won with keystrokes. Technology is critical to war, of course, but battlefield technology is what matters most. The whole history of human warfare proves that wars are won by soldiers with guns, sailors on ships, and pilots in planes. This history is repeating itself today in Ukraine; hashtags and sanctions are fine, but the war has ebbed and flowed almost entirely based on the success of arms—rifles and artillery and missiles. Our Army and Marine Corps need to grow immediately to match the threats we face; as we learned in Iraq, it takes too much time to build the force for us to wait until the shooting starts. Our Navy has fewer than 300 ships, down from Reagan's 600-ship Navy. Our Air Force has begun to upgrade its fighters, bombers, and tankers, and these plans need to be completed. The same is true of the badly needed upgrades to our nuclear arsenal. Even things as basic as our munition stockpiles need attention. We've seen once again in Ukraine how munition shortages can hinder an army as surely as any enemy. And we're not immune: the Air Force, for instance, almost ran out of Hellfire missiles in 2015 during the bombing campaign against ISIS.

If we devote more of your tax dollars to defense, we should expect the military to spend the money wisely. Unfortunately, that's not always the case; the Pentagon has a spotty record of cost-effectiveness when it comes to major weapons programs, to say the least. Take the F-35, our new stealth fighter. This troubled program has been notoriously over budget and off schedule for years; I'm grappling today in Congress with flawed decisions made while I was still in school. Don't get me wrong: our pilots love the aircraft and it's vital to our national security. But we shouldn't repeat its mistakes. That's one reason why I've conducted extra oversight through my committee for the B-21, our new stealth bomber. This plane is absolutely essential in our struggle against China and I don't want questions twenty years from now about why the program failed. So far, the Air Force has run it smoothly—it's actually under budget—but double-checking their homework is part of my job.

I dedicate a lot of time to this kind of oversight to ensure our troops get what they need and you get good value for your tax dollars. Early in my Senate tenure, for instance, the Army had spent $6 billion on a battlefield communication system known as WIN-T, yet it remained ineffective, immobile, fragile, and insecure. I pressed the Army to cancel the program, which it ultimately did. This is just one example of my insistence that the Pentagon buy commercial off-the-shelf technology where available, especially information technology. America has the world's leading technology companies; we don't need defense contractors to duplicate their work. Just look at Ukraine, where Elon Musk's Starlink satellite-internet terminals enabled the Ukrainian army in the early days of the war to communicate and target Russian forces with artillery and drones—all for just a few hundred dollars each.

Beyond the money we spend and the things we buy, we also have to refocus our military on its warrior culture. Too many generals—to say nothing of political appointees—obsess about matters far removed from lethality on the battlefield. But that's the only standard our military should care about. Marine General John Kelly, who later served as Donald Trump's secretary of Homeland Security and White House chief of staff, once suggested to me a simple test: "Does it make us more lethal on the battlefield? If yes, do it. If no, don't do it. If you don't know, don't do it. Because the stakes are too high."

Consider recent peacetime losses in the Navy. In 2017, two destroyers ran into commercial ships, killing seventeen sailors and causing nearly a half billion dollars of damage. Investigations revealed disciplinary problems, "insufficient training," and "a lack of effective operational oversight." In 2020, a billion-dollar amphibious-assault ship burned up in harbor because the ship's firefighters were unprepared to stop the blaze.

These incidents were so alarming that I commissioned a study of the Navy's surface-warfare culture. A stunning 94 percent of sailors interviewed attributed the incidents to cultural and leadership failures, including inadequate focus on warfighting and insufficient training. One recently retired senior enlisted leader lamented, "I guarantee you every unit in the Navy is up to speed on their diversity training. I'm sorry that I can't say the same of their ship-handling training." A destroyer captain added, "where someone puts their time shows what their priorities are. And we've got so many messages about X, Y, Z appreciation month," he observed, yet "we don't even have close to that same level of emphasis on actual warfighting." Imagine the consequences of this mentality in a war with China.

These warped priorities persist today. In 2020, the Pentagon removed official photos from promotion and command-selection packets used to decide who gets promoted and command positions. They wanted to combat supposed "implicit bias." Just a year later, though, Navy leaders considered reinstating the photo requirement to improve their diversity initiatives. It's genuine whiplash to go from "photos cause racial discrimination" to "we need photos to discriminate by race" in just a year—and it does nothing for lethality.

It's not just the Navy, either. I served with a friend who recently took battalion command. He asked sarcastically, "where do you think company commanders take risk on the training calendar? The 'healthy sexuality' briefing is tracked closely by higher headquarters on a spreadsheet. You think they cut that? Or do they shortchange team and squad tactics, hoping no one will notice?" Maybe those squads won't go to war and in fact no one will notice. But do we want to gamble our security on that? More to the point, do we want to gamble their lives on it?

It really comes down to that: if we deprive our military of the resources it needs or we tolerate distractions from the warrior culture, we risk the lives of our troops and ultimately our survival as a nation. In basic training, one drill sergeant above all reveled in his harsh, almost cruel persona. He never laughed or joked, except at a messed-up soldier's expense. He quickly imposed collective punishment for the slightest deficiency. We all dreaded the days when he led a training event. But one day, he dropped the facade and spoke to us like an uncle or a football coach:

> You all think I hate you. I don't hate you. You're here to take my place so I can retire and sit on my porch with a beer. But I have to train you first. I know you think I'm a mean son of a bitch, but I don't care. Hate me, love me, I don't care. All I care about is you'll still be alive to hate me or love me. And I'll have done my job.

I wouldn't say that I ever grew to love him, but I've always respected him and thought the military could use more of him.

Historian and Korean War veteran T. R. Fehrenbach cautioned that every society ultimately gets the military it wants and deserves. The credit or the blame, he wrote, rests with us. What was true of our military's shockingly high casualties in the early days of the Korean War, after Harry Truman hollowed out the force, remains true for us today:

> No American may sneer at them, or at what they did. What happened to them might have happened to any American in the summer of 1950. For they represented exactly the kind of pampered, undisciplined, egalitarian army their society had long desired and had at last achieved.... They had been raised to believe the world was without tigers, then sent to face those tigers with a stick. On their society must fall the blame.

The world is full of tigers. We cannot arm our warriors with sticks.

SECURE THE BORDER

The most basic and indispensable kind of national security is border security. No country can long survive if it can't protect its borders. We can take control of our southern border and end the damage caused by the Biden border crisis with a few critical actions.

That damage is severe, as we saw in Chapter Three. More than two million illegal aliens have crossed our southern border since Biden took office, threatening American workers' jobs and wages. Some of these illegal aliens belong to vicious drug cartels or criminal gangs. I've hugged too many Angel Moms who've lost a child to criminal aliens. These cartels and criminals also smuggle in most of the drugs that are killing more than 100,000 Americans each year. Terrorists, too, exploit our open southern border.

The first step is a physical barrier—a wall, a fence, whatever you want to call it. Walls work; they always have. There's a reason why human beings have built defensive walls for as long as we've lived in organized societies. Progressives may condemn walls and fences at the border, but their actions speak louder than words. Barack Obama and Joe Biden voted as senators to build 700 miles of new border fence. Obama admitted the bill would stop "immigrants sneaking in through unguarded holes in our border." Nancy Pelosi kept a fence around the Capitol for six months after the Capitol riot, without any credible threat. Biden hasn't removed the fence around the White House; same for Kamala Harris at the Naval Observatory.

Israel's security fences also disprove the liberals' irrational hostility to walls. Since their construction, terrorist bombings from Palestinian–controlled territories have plummeted. Construction of a fence along Israel's southern border also has virtually eliminated illegal immigration from Africa. That hasn't stopped liberals from comparing these fences to the Berlin Wall, as they do with our partial border wall. Blinded by ideology, they can't see the obvious difference: Israel's wall and ours keep people out, the Berlin Wall kept people in.

Progressives sometimes pretend to want to use technology to secure the border, but this is just a smoke screen. No one spends thousands of dollars on a fancy home-security system without first locking the doors. Technology like cameras and ground sensors can complement a barrier, but they can't replace it. When I learned defensive operations in the Army, a central tenet was "an obstacle without overwatch isn't an obstacle," because any obstacle can be breached with enough time. That's why our bases in Iraq and Afghanistan had guard towers. Democrats often contend that taller fences lead to even taller ladders. The answer isn't to abandon physical barriers, but to add high-tech monitoring of them, along with more Border Patrol officers.

Yet a wall isn't enough, because illegal aliens are just as likely today to run to the Border Patrol as away from them. The word is out how to game our asylum system; often, left-wing nonprofits have coached migrants on the magic words they need to utter about fearing persecution in their home country. But I didn't hear such fears when I traveled to the border shortly after Biden took office; every migrant spoke about getting a job or how easy it was to get in under Biden.

We have to stop illegal aliens from taking advantage of our generosity. Asylum is intended for aliens already legally present in the country—for instance, a foreign student with a valid visa whose country collapses into civil war. There should be no claims of asylum at our borders. Instead, foreigners should apply for refugee status at our embassies with eligibility strictly limited to a genuine fear of persecution for legitimate reasons such as race, political views, or religion. Those aliens who do arrive at our border should remain in Mexico or return to Guatemala, the geographic choke point on Mexico's southern border and thus a "safe third country" under international asylum principles. Progressives complain that Guatemala isn't safe, but its murder rate is much lower than Democratic–run cities like St. Louis and Baltimore. They also complain that Guatemala can't possibly support the number of refugees who cross our border, which misses the point. Once economic migrants realize they won't get into America, but instead have to stay in Mexico or Guatemala, they'll stop coming in the first place.

In addition to a physical barrier and asylum reform, we have to turn off the jobs magnet inside our country. Fewer illegal aliens will come if we make it harder to get a job. The best method is to require all employers to use E-Verify, the government's free, quick, and accurate employment-verification website. Today, federal law only requires governments and federal contractors to use it. With mandatory E-Verify, employers wouldn't have excuses for employing illegals—and we could impose stiffer penalties on crooked employers who keep giving American jobs to illegals.

We also need to restart deportations, which have declined by nearly 80 percent since 2019, the last year of normal immigration enforcement before the pandemic. Biden has basically ended deportations by signaling to illegal aliens that unless you're the worst of the worst—terrorists or aggravated felons—it's olly, olly oxen free. But why should we allow any illegal to live and work with impunity in our country? They don't have a right to be here, after all. The word also gets out that if you can get here, you won't get deported, which only encourages more illegal immigration to begin with.

Most simply, we should speak clearly and confidently about the sanctity of our borders. The message is simple: do not come, you will not get in, and if you do, we will find you and send you home. Never underestimate the value of clarity. Border crossings declined early in Trump's tenure because would-be migrants assumed they wouldn't get in. But illegal immigration increased again as the Trump administration's policy initially didn't match the Trump campaign's rhetoric. Same thing with Biden. During his campaign and his first year in office, Biden practically invited foreigners to cross our border. Lo and behold, we got the worst border crisis in our history. Sending a clear message would itself be a big step forward.

Beyond defending the border, it's past time to go on offense against Mexican drug cartels, the worst threat from our open borders. These sadistic criminals unleash death and misery across our land. Each year, we lose far more Americans to the cartels' crimes and drugs than we did in the entire Vietnam War. Imagine how we'd react if al-Qaeda or ISIS set up camp in Tijuana, Juarez, and Monterrey. That's exactly how we should handle the cartels. We should target cartels with the same legal tools we use against terrorists: freeze their assets, kick them out of the international banking system, bar cartel members and their families from entering our country, and then apply all those penalties to anyone who assists them too.

As we would with terrorists, we should also literally target the cartels. There's plenty of precedent for taking the fight to them. Our military's special-operations forces and the elite tactical units of law-enforcement agencies like the Drug Enforcement Administration played key roles in the killing of drug kingpin Pablo Escobar in Colombia and the capture of El Chapo in Mexico. In 1989, we even invaded Panama and toppled its government in part to bring its military dictator, Manuel Noriega, to justice in America for drug trafficking. In coordination with Mexican authorities, our military and law-enforcement agencies are more than capable of killing or capturing drug kingpins and their key lieutenants, while also destroying their superlabs and other key infrastructure. We use these forces to target terrorists around the world—and rightly so—but the drug cartels have killed many more Americans than ISIS ever did. It's time to treat the cartels as the national-security threat they are.

ACHIEVE ENERGY INDEPENDENCE

Energy security is national security, because the opposite of energy independence is energy dependence, as we saw in the lead-up to and early days of Russia's war on Ukraine. European nations—especially Germany—had kneecapped their traditional domestic sources of energy and relied heavily on Russian oil and gas. Not surprisingly, they hesitated to confront Russia until shamed into action by Ukraine's early success. Even then, Europe slow-rolled sanctions against Russia's energy sector. Few things constrain a nation more than threats to its energy and few things give a nation more freedom of action than energy independence.

Yet during the 2020 campaign, Biden earnestly pledged, "I want you to look at my eyes. I guarantee you, I guarantee you, we're going to end fossil fuel." He has worked to make good on that promise. His policies have driven the price of gas and electricity through the roof, threatening the lifeblood of our economy and our security.

It's hard to overstate how vital energy is to the American way of life—indeed, to modern life. Our Founders didn't have a quality of life much better than did Jesus's disciples because energy hadn't changed much; the main sources were wind, water, fire, and muscle. Then came coal, next came oil and gas, and finally nuclear power. The Industrial Revolution sparked by fossil fuels has yielded economic abundance unparalleled in human history.

Affordable and reliable energy literally powers our way of life. America is the world's breadbasket partly because fertilizer made with natural gas reduces costs and increases crop yields. The automobile shaped modern America, and 99 percent of them run on fossil fuels; the few cars that don't plug into a grid powered mostly by fossil fuels and nuclear power. The smartphone in your pocket, the tablet on which you may be reading these words, the computer on your desk—all these devices and most modern technology require enormous amounts of energy to manufacture and operate.

Too often we take for granted that the power will come on when we flip the switch. But think how you feel during a power outage, and how much you appreciate the lineworkers when the power comes back. And speaking of those workers, more than eleven million Americans work in the energy sector in high-paying jobs.

Energy is equally vital to America's national security; anything so essential to our jobs and prosperity will inevitably factor heavily into our foreign policy. Few Americans would tolerate a foreign adversary who blocked our access to the energy that powers our economy. Even

Jimmy Carter understood the central role of energy to American life when he announced the so-called Carter Doctrine. "An attempt by any outside force to gain control of the Persian Gulf region will be regarded as an assault on the vital interests" of America, he declared, and "will be repelled by any means necessary, including military force." Ronald Reagan sank half of Iran's navy to protect the flow of oil through the Persian Gulf and George H. W. Bush waged war against Saddam Hussein to prevent him from controlling the Middle East's oil supply.

But Democrats want America to follow Europe's example. It's not just Joe Biden. Obama promised that "if somebody wants to build a coal-fired power plant, they can. It's just that it will bankrupt them." He also admitted that, under his plan, "electricity rates would necessarily skyrocket." Obama's energy secretary mused that "somehow we have to figure out how to boost the price of gasoline to the levels in Europe," or around eight to ten dollars per gallon. Hillary Clinton pledged that "we're going to put a lot of coal miners and coal companies out of business." Bernie Sanders and Alexandria Ocasio-Cortez want to ban hydraulic fracturing, the technology which enabled America to become the world's top oil and gas producer over the last two decades. They also have proposed a "Green New Deal" to eliminate fossil fuels and nuclear power entirely in the next decade.

These fantasies are divorced from reality. Fossil fuels and nuclear power account for seven-eighths of America's energy. Even among "renewable" energy sources, the combination of wood, water, and crops generates much more energy than do wind and solar. Put simply, the Democrats' energy dreams would impoverish America. Yet they would enrich China, the world's top importer of oil and gas but the dominant producer of "green" energy technology, thanks to its unfair trade practices. Progressives may march under the banner of climate change, but it looks an awful lot like Communist China's Five-Star Red Flag. That's not surprising: the statism and administrative bureaucracy needed to achieve their energy aspirations exceed even Woodrow Wilson's wildest dreams.

Perhaps that's why progressives are willing to put their ideology over your family's well-being and our national security. Just as the Blame America First Democrats prefer unilateral disarmament for the military, they also would unilaterally disarm our energy sector as well. Facing the political squeeze over high gas prices, Biden went to Venezuela and Iran—not Texas and North Dakota. Progressives look down their noses at coal miners and roughnecks while averting their gaze from Chinese slaves who make solar panels and African child workers who mine the rare-earth elements behind "green" technology.

Biden campaigned on an "irreversible" war on traditional sources of American energy, but progressives haven't yet killed the energy sector. Instead, they're slowly strangling it by limiting access to oil and gas reserves, blocking critical infrastructure, and demonizing the industry. We can resuscitate our energy industry by reversing these policies.

In the short run, we need to increase access on federal lands and waters, which account for about one-quarter of American oil production and one-tenth of our gas production. The Biden administration dragged its feet on a new five-year leasing program and quarterly lease sales, both mandated by law, while also canceling some current leases and delaying drilling permits for others. Biden has also designated millions of new acres of federal land off limits to the oil-and-gas industry. These actions should be reversed immediately. We can responsibly protect our environment and preserve the wonders of our natural world, while also harnessing the energy underneath. With the federal government owning 28 percent of the country's land, it's the only sane policy.

Over the long run, we need to build out new energy infrastructure. America needs more pipelines, the safest way to transport oil and gas. Yet Biden canceled the Keystone XL pipeline on his first day in office. That pipeline's future is now at risk, but it's far from the only needed pipeline. Biden also delayed the approval of several liquefied-natural-gas export facilities, which boost incentives for domestic production and support our allies who otherwise depend on Russian gas. For these and other energy-infrastructure projects, we need to expedite and standardize bureaucratic reviews across federal agencies.

Although Biden has waged war primarily against fossil fuel, don't forget nuclear power. America still gets almost one-fifth of our electricity from nuclear, but it could be much more. For example, France gets 70 percent of its power from nuclear. But thanks to hostility from the environmental lobby and bureaucratic red tape, nuclear reactors are regulary off schedule and over budget. With reforms to the Nuclear Regulatory Commission and technological advances that make new reactors safer and produce less waste, however, America could begin a new age of nuclear power, the only reliable source of carbon-free energy.

Finally, we should celebrate and champion our energy industry and its workers. The energy industry is capital intensive; many projects require billions of dollars and only pay off over decades. When Democrats threaten to "end" or "bankrupt" the industry, they discourage Americans from investing their savings in it—which, of course, is their goal. Instead, we should take pride in American energy. God has blessed our land with plentiful energy resources and skilled, ingenious workers who harness them for the rest of us. Liberals demonize these workers, but if we have their backs, then Americans will feel confident once again investing in them—and they'll flood the world with affordable, abundant energy.

DISTINGUISH FRIENDS AND FOES

In Plutarch's *Lives*, the historian ends his biography of Lucius Cornelius Sulla, the famed Roman general and consul, with the epitaph Sulla wrote for his own tomb: "no friend ever did me a favor, nor enemy an injury, that I have not repaid in full." Blunt, to be sure, but there are surely worse principles to guide our foreign policy—Woodrow Wilson's progressive idealism, for example. In fact, Sulla's maxim is the source for our Marine Corps's informal motto, "no better friend, no worse enemy." But liberals reverse the maxim, abandoning our friends and accommodating our enemies. The predictable result is diminished security for America—and usually even worse repression of the populations in our erstwhile allies.

America has always needed and will always need friends to help us protect our interests. Our best friends are mature, stable democracies like the United Kingdom and Israel, countries dedicated to freedom, representative government, and the rule of law. We share deep historical, cultural, linguistic, and religious bonds with both nations, as we do with a few other nations, such as Canada and Australia. We have also abiding friendships with democratic nations like Japan and South Korea, despite our cultural, religious, and linguistic differences.

But let's not kid ourselves: the world is a dangerous place, not a church picnic. The vast number of governments throughout history and still today are non-democratic. We may wish it were different and we may work to improve it, but that's the way the world is. If we only befriended nations that shared our system of government and our social and cultural sensibilities, we wouldn't have many friends.

In a fallen world, we take our friends where we find them. Sometimes, we work temporarily with truly dreadful regimes when our interests align against a greater evil. We partnered with Soviet Russia, for instance, to defeat Nazi Germany and then with Communist

China to contain the Soviets. Such temporary alliances may seem distasteful, but the urgent necessity of the moment serves a higher good.

We also have strong, durable friendships with pro-American but non-democratic countries. Morocco recognized the United States the year after we declared independence and our Treaty of Friendship of 1786 remains our oldest treaty relationship. America and Jordan established diplomatic relations in 1949, shortly after Jordan's independence. I've met with Jordan's ruler, King Abdullah II, on many occasions and can attest that few foreign leaders have such warm regard for America. While both nations are monarchies, they consistently support America's interests. Both nations, for instance, contribute to our efforts against Islamic extremism and both nations are peace partners of Israel.

No question, stable democracies make the most stable friends. But what matters, in the end, is less whether a country is democratic or non-democratic, and more whether the country is pro-American or anti-American.

Democrats turn this common sense on its head. For them, it seems the worst sin a nation can commit is being pro-American. We've already encountered many reliable American allies abandoned by Democratic presidents in their hour of greatest need. John Kennedy tolerated the coup against Vietnam's Ngo Dinh Diem, transforming a Vietnamese war into an American war. Over just a few months, Jimmy Carter withdrew support from the Somoza regime in Nicaragua and the shah in Iran as both confronted revolutionary movements. Barack Obama ditched Egypt's Hosni Mubarak after just a few days of protests, giving him no chance to address the protesters' concerns. Given this record, a foreign leader could be forgiven for recalling a reported Henry Kissinger quip: it's dangerous to be America's enemy, but it's fatal to be America's friend.

Actually, it's worse than that, because it's not really dangerous to be America's enemy when Democrats are in charge. It would be one thing to oppose all authoritarian governments, pro-American or anti-American alike—somewhat naive, but still a principled stand for democracy. Liberals don't take that stand. Instead, they consistently ignore, apologize for, or even defend left-wing dictatorships. Liberals obsessed about Somoza, yet they lost interest in Daniel Ortega's communist dictatorship—except those like Bernie Sanders, who applauded it. Ivory tower liberals hated the pro-American Augusto Pinochet in Chile, but they romanticized the virulently anti-American and brutal Castro regime in Cuba. Progressives insisted that the shah had to go in Iran, but they excuse the ayatollahs' chants of "death to America."

Democrats' sympathy for anti-American regimes doesn't just imperil our interests, but usually makes matters worse for normal people in those countries. No one ever mistook Diem, Somoza, the shah, or Mubarak for the Little Sisters of the Poor. But Ho Chi Minh, Ortega, the ayatollahs, and the Muslim Brotherhood are worse. They repressed their peoples, often brutally, and they usually destroyed the economy, leading to even more misery under socialism. Yet liberals never seem to care that their darlings make things worse. Sure, your average Cuban might starve thanks to the Castro regime, but at least liberal college kids get to wear a cool Che Guevara T-shirt.

At the same time, even as we support imperfect allies, we shouldn't overlook their imperfections. Pro-American authoritarians tend to be more open to reform because they care about American opinion and they're usually grounded in national traditions and cultures, which offer room for incremental improvements. By contrast, anti-American regimes are often totalitarian, destroying national traditions and cultures—even religion and the family—in the headlong pursuit of utopian ideologies like communism or Islamic theocracy. Jeane Kirkpatrick, later Ronald Reagan's UN ambassador, made these points in her famous 1979 essay, "Dictatorships and Double Standards."

Reagan acted on these views where circumstances permitted. Ferdinand Marcos, the longtime Filipino strongman, lifted martial law shortly after Reagan's election. Reagan worked with the anti-communist Marcos while quietly encouraging more reforms. When popular unrest with Marcos grew and he lost a fair election, Reagan urged him to accept the outcome. As a result, Corazon Aquino, the Philippines's "Mother of Democracy," took office—and continued to support America. Reagan also worked with the South Korean strongman, Chun Doo-Hwan, against the forces of communism, while prodding Chun to loosen his repressive grip and hold democratic elections. In 1987, Roh Tae Woo won and Chun agreed to the first peaceful transfer of power in South Korea. Roh continued Chun's pro-American foreign policy and further cemented his nation's democratic and free-market reforms.

More than ever, we need Reagan's model of prudent statesmanship and moral clarity. Abraham Lincoln's practical wisdom for life applies equally to foreign policy: "never sell old friends to buy old enemies." But that's exactly what liberals do, including Obama and Biden. In particular, they sold old friends like Israel and Arab nations like Saudi Arabia and the United Arab Emirates in a vain effort to buy Iran. All they had to show for it were disillusioned friends and an emboldened enemy. By contrast, the Trump administration treated our friends like friends and our foes like foes. What happened? The Abraham Accords—peace agreements for Israel with the Emirates, Bahrain, Morocco, and Sudan.

Even the language of Obama's supposed grand strategy—the "pivot to Asia"—illustrates the left's disregard for our friends. A "pivot" in sports or dance involves the act of turning your back. Obama may have meant he wanted to turn toward Asia, but our Middle Eastern allies heard that America was turning our back on them. Yet we need all the friends we can get in the fight against China, including in the

Middle East, where China gets almost half its oil. Instead of abandoning them, we should rally them to help us beat China.

Beat China

All roads to this point have led to China. Progressive failures for decades have weakened America and empowered China. The steps I've outlined thus far to regain our strength would put us on solid footing against China. But there's more to be done to win the new Cold War that China started years ago. And there's still time to do it, for Xi Jinping's signal mistake may have been to reveal China's ambitions too early.

The economy is the primary theater of conflict because China aspires to use the economic integration of America and China to replace us as the world's dominant power without a major war. Though the Chinese Communists are willing to risk military conflict to preserve their grip on power or if tempted by American weakness, they subscribe to Sun Tzu's maxim that the pinnacle of strategic excellence isn't to defeat the enemy in battle, but to subdue him without fighting. They prefer a gradual encirclement of America until one day we wake up to discover ourselves poorer, weaker, and compelled to submit to Chinese dominance.

Unfortunately, we've aided China's ambitions to our detriment for a long time. As we saw in Chapter Three, the China Shock resulting from our misguided trade policies turned China into the world's "factory floor" and cost hardworking Americans three million manufacturing jobs and 60,000 factories. China supplemented our foolhardy policies with its own predatory trade practices, currency manipulation, forced technology transfers, and outright theft. Our trade in goods with China has increased almost twentyfold over the last three decades—as has our trade deficit with China. As a result, China now has cornered the global market on goods as diverse as steel, basic medicines and medical devices, and rare-earth elements, among many others, giving it tremendous leverage over America and the free world.

To win the economic war against China, we have to start by disentangling our economies and ending our dependence on China. We may never separate our economies entirely, but it's one thing to depend on China for T-shirts and plastic toys, another thing altogether to depend on it for lifesaving medicine and medical equipment, as we learned in the early days of the coronavirus pandemic. It's an urgent priority of the highest order that we decouple our economy from China in strategic sectors, for instance, medical supplies and equipment, critical and rare-earth elements, telecommunications, semiconductors, and artificial intelligence and quantum computing.

Disentangling our economies begins with cracking down on China. Let's start by revoking China's permanent most-favored-nation status. As we've seen, this decision turbocharged China's economy and devastated ours. Why should we continue to allow our number-one enemy to trade on the same terms as our friends? Next, Chinese nationals who commit or benefit from predatory trade practices and intellectual-property theft should face sanctions and visa bans. Chinese businesses should also suffer sanctions and import duties if they commit or benefit from these practices.

We also need to curtail American technological and financial support to the Chinese economy. We already impose export controls on some American technologies, but we need to expand both the scope of the technologies and the number of Chinese businesses subjected to these controls. American investment funds, including public and private pension funds, should be restricted from investing in Chinese markets. Further, we should block American investments into Chinese corporate "national champions," companies tied to the Chinese

Communist Party or to human-rights abuses, and key technology companies in China. Wall Street shouldn't be funding our main enemy. We also have to work with our friends to do the same. For example, a single Dutch company makes the only machines in the world capable of producing the most advanced semiconductors and, partly at our request, our Dutch friends have agreed to deny their export to China.

As we prevent American investment into China, we also need to prevent strategic Chinese investments into America. The Committee on Foreign Investment in the United States, a federal interagency board, should scrutinize Chinese investments in strategic sectors and in any sector when control of a business is at stake. The burden should rest on the American company to seek approval and the presumption should be denial of the investment. We also need to remove Chinese companies from our stock exchanges if they refuse to abide by the same laws as our companies do. Some sectors are so vital that we simply need to ban Chinese investment. Just as we wouldn't allow China to own American defense companies, for instance, we also need to stop Chinese purchases of American farmland and food companies. We're the world's breadbasket and China can't feed itself. Why would we ever diminish this strategic advantage?

For too long, China has exploited our generous academic immigration policy, but it's time to stop training and aiding our enemy. Chinese nationals linked to the Communist Party or the People's Liberation Army ought to be barred from studying at our universities. All Chinese nationals should be excluded from advanced science and technology graduate and postgraduate programs. What China needs most from America is *The Federalist Papers*, not quantum physics. And American universities and professors who take your tax dollars—which is virtually all of them—should be banned from taking Chinese money. No man can serve two masters, as the Bible says, and you can be sure Chinese Communists insist that compromised professors serve them first. This threat is widespread and acute: the chair of Harvard's chemistry department was convicted in 2021 of crimes related to taking Chinese money, as was a former University of Arkansas professor the following year.

These American academics are just another example of the China Lobby, which we learned about in Chapter Three. The China Lobby is pervasive, a veritable fifth column of Chinese influence in our country. To beat China, we also have to break the back of the China Lobby. Several steps I've already outlined would curtail the China Lobby's influence by reducing the number of American industries, companies, and institutions with a financial stake in China. But there's more we can do. As we saw earlier, Hollywood and its affiliated media businesses are deeply exposed to the influence of Chinese money. The simple solution is to treat media businesses—film and television studios, streaming services, cable and satellite platforms, and so forth—as another strategic sector blocked from Chinese investment. We also can end federal support for any studio that allows Chinese Communists to censor its content. Good luck making your blockbuster war movie without the aid of the military.

We also have to evict the China Lobby from our nation's capital. Any person who advocates for a Chinese entity should be forced to register as a foreign agent because Chinese companies and organizations rarely operate outside the dictates of Beijing, especially when it comes to influence peddling. And I, for one, don't think anyone who performed substantial work for Chinese government entities should subsequently work in our government. Why should we bring our main enemy's agents inside our government councils? On the back end, too, former senior government officials should be barred from going to work for China. American think tanks, research organizations, and advocacy groups also should have to disclose publicly any Chinese financing. Finally, elected officials at all levels of government should be vigilant about Chinese approaches. When I learned that the Chinese government might try to indirectly influence me through Arkansas politicians, I sent a letter to every statewide official, legislator, and county judge to warn them: if a Chinese national approaches you about me, call me and then we can decide whether to call the FBI. That confrontational approach made some waves, but it should be standard operating procedure.

As we crack down on China and the China Lobby, we also need to take steps to prepare our own economy for strategic decoupling. Some policies are useful in their own right, such as slashing bureaucratic red tape and reducing regulatory burdens and uncertainty. But other policies specifically target our dependencies on China. For instance, if we want to get critical industries out of China, we'll need to provide incentives for companies to build new factories in America, especially in critical sectors like semiconductors. Those incentives can include tax breaks, grants, tariffs and other trade protections, and federal purchasing power. The federal government, for instance, purchases vast quantities of drugs and medical equipment through Medicare, the VA, and the military. We can ban purchases of Chinese-sourced goods and instantly create market incentives here at home. We can do the same for critical minerals and rare-earth elements. For that matter, we can also encourage the mining and processing of these minerals and elements here at home, where we have them in abundance.

Many of these proposals may not sound like traditional Republican ideas, and I suppose they aren't. But tough times call for tough measures. China has played hardball against America for decades. China started this new Cold War; it's up to us to finish it.

If some of my ideas seem too hard-nosed or far-fetched, I ask a simple question: would we have allowed Soviet Russia to get away with all this? I think the question answers itself. Soviet Russia didn't get most-favored-nation status during the Cold War and our trade with them was insignificant for much of that era. We obviously would've never allowed the

Soviets to invest in our defense industry, or any other critical industry. From *Red Dawn* to *Rocky IV*, Hollywood churned out patriotic, anti-Soviet hits. And betraying the country for Russia was something done by elite progressives like Alger Hiss, a top aide to Franklin Roosevelt and Harry Truman. To me, the question isn't whether we can disentangle from China, it's why we got so entangled in the first place. And there's no time to waste reversing the mistakes of the past.

One final, essential word about winning the new Cold War with China. While the primary theater of conflict is economic, it's not the only or most fundamental theater. As always, military competition underlies everything. China has undertaken "the largest military buildup in history since World War II," in the words of our commander in the Pacific. A bigger, stronger military is necessary to deter China, but we also need to take a few more specific steps, as well. First, we need to invest in the kinds of weapons and platforms suited for the highly dangerous and contested waters and airspace off China's coasts, for instance, submarines that China can't detect and inexpensive drones that we can afford to lose. Second, we also need to expand and defend our satellite systems, as well as other electronic-warfare systems and sensors, which allow our troops to communicate and target the Chinese, while denying the same to Chinese forces. Third, our defense industry urgently has to increase its build rate for missiles; China has a worrisome advantage in missile stockpiles. Fourth and for that reason, we need to increase our missile-defense capabilities in the Western Pacific, both for our ships and for our bases in Guam, Japan, and South Korea.

Finally, America needs to reinforce Taiwan immediately. As I discussed in the last chapter, Taiwan is the most dangerous flash point in the world. Xi Jinping will likely try to invade and annex Taiwan in the next few years—unless we stop him. First, Taiwan urgently needs the kind of asymmetric weapons that Ukraine used effectively to repel Russia's early lightning strike at Kiev. Anti-aircraft missiles, anti-ship missiles, and advanced sea mines are vital to deterring a Chinese invasion. Instead of a chicken in every pot, Taiwan needs a Stinger in every attic. We have to get these weapons to Taiwan before the shooting starts because, unlike Russia and Ukraine, China can blockade Taiwan once it does. Next, Taiwan needs to reform its military reserve forces. Our National Guard and Green Berets can help because they have deep experience in training reserves. Last, America needs to change our declared policy from strategic ambiguity to strategic clarity: we should tell Xi in advance that we will come to Taiwan's defense if China attacks—and China will suffer a grievous defeat. The point, as Reagan would've known, isn't to start a war or win a war, but to prevent a war in the first place.

THE PATH TO regain our nation's strength may be long and the price may be high, but it's a journey worth taking and a price worth paying. For the wages of weakness, like sin, is death—the death of the American dream and ultimately the death of our freedoms.

I still believe in a strong and confident America. More to the point, the American people do too. America doesn't deserve blame in the eyes of most Americans; it deserves pride and honor.

Americans are ready and more than capable of regaining our strength. Shortly after Pearl Harbor, Winston Churchill visited America and Canada. He observed of our character, "We have not journeyed across the centuries, across the oceans, across the mountains, across the prairies, because we are made of sugar candy." Churchill was right then, and he remains right now. We Americans aren't made of sugar candy; we're made of much sterner stuff. America deserves leaders made of the same stern stuff, leaders who take pride in our nation and who seek its preeminence in the world.

Only the strong can lead America back to glory.

Our Choice

I N J ANUARY 2020, while Washington obsessed over Nancy Pelo-si's first attempt to impeach Donald Trump, I studied the growing public-health crisis in Wuhan, China.

Early that month, a short news item that China had notified the World Health Organization of an unusual pneumonia outbreak caught my attention. I followed the story, casually at first, but intensely after a few days. I began to check East Asian news outlets, medical journals, and obscure social-media accounts each morning before I read the daily news.

Something didn't add up. China claimed the virus was under control, but used increasingly draconian measures to contain its spread— some reports indicated that they even nailed the exterior doors shut on high-rise apartment buildings. I never trust communists, especially when their actions contradict their words.

As the impeachment trial began, I sat at my desk on the Senate floor reading about the science of coronaviruses, the methods of vaccine development, and the history of pandemics. My aides delivered a steady flow of papers and photocopied books, hidden underneath a fancy cover sheet labeled "Supplemental Impeachment Materials" so nosy reporters sitting above us in the Senate gallery couldn't see what

I was reading. They probably would've reported that I wasn't paying attention to the trial.

But I was paying attention—to the story that mattered most. The outcome of the impeachment trial was a foregone conclusion, and it wouldn't impact the daily lives of normal Americans. This virus in China was different; it could dramatically affect our country, harm our citizens, and disrupt the economy. At that point, little was known about the virus because the Chinese Communists were already covering up the details. I did know, however, that this virus was spreading like wildfire and killing far more people than the Chinese authorities were admitting. China was building field hospitals from scratch and running crematories 24-7. You don't do that when a virus is under control.

A couple days into the trial, I wrote to Alex Azar, the secretary of Health and Human Services, urging caution about data provided by the Chinese and raising the possibility of a travel ban from China. The next day, China imposed its own travel ban on Wuhan and neighboring cities, locking down a population larger than our entire West Coast. Again, their soothing words didn't match their drastic actions. I called President Trump and urged him to stop air travel from China immediately. He naturally had been focused on the trial, though he shared my skepticism of Beijing and concern about the virus. He also understandably worried, however, about the economic impact of a travel ban.

I spoke to Eric Ueland, the president's chief liaison to Congress, during a break in the trial. Ueland was a seasoned pro. He understood the cross-pressures a president faces on any given issue and explained that the president's economic team were warning about the economic fallout. Ueland encouraged me to call Steven Mnuchin, the secretary of the treasury. Mnuchin laid out some of the reasonable fears about how a travel ban from China would disrupt supply chains and trade flows. He shared my concerns, but he didn't want to cause a recession. I sympathized with Mnuchin—care for the economy was his job— but I believed that this novel coronavirus from China had already sparked a worldwide recession, only no one had realized it yet.

What I heard next from Jared Kushner, the president's son-in-law and senior adviser, infuriated me. Kushner and I had developed a candid and trusting relationship over the last four years. He confided that, aside from the economic advice, public-health "experts" were also advising against a ban. Led by Anthony Fauci, these white-coat bureaucrats fretted that a ban violated "best practices" and would be seen as culturally insensitive.

I had heard this argument before and it brought to mind George Orwell's famous rebuke: "Some ideas are so stupid that only intellectuals believe them." When a disease breaks out in some distant place, of course a travel ban from that place will slow its spread here. It's common sense. Fauci's initial position defied logic. It was especially infuriating since Beijing had imposed its own travel ban from Wuhan. Fauci and other bureaucrats didn't want to appear insensitive for doing exactly what the Chinese Communists had already done. While I knew we couldn't stop the virus from eventually getting here, we could slow its widespread arrival, giving us more time to prepare and learn more despite China's cover-up. (Soon enough, Fauci flip-flopped on the issue of travel bans, as he did on pretty much every other issue too.)

I spent much of the next week urging the president and other administration officials to stop travel from China for all but American citizens. I badgered Ueland so often during the trial that eventually I just started making eye contact with him across the Senate floor and pointing down with my index finger, a wordless gesture to "ground the planes." At month's end, I called Kushner again during an evening break in the trial. I heard music and applause, and remembered that the president had a rally that night in Iowa. Kushner said, "I've got someone here who wants to talk to you." The president came on the line and by that point he didn't have to ask why I was calling. "Tom, we're about to do something you're really gonna like," he started. "I can't talk about it on this line, but it's gonna come tomorrow and you're gonna be very, very happy."

When I got off the phone, I sent a message to my senior staff to prepare to defend the travel ban. Though I wish the administration had acted sooner, the president made the right call and he deserved support. I knew the Democrats and their media wing would savage him. Like clockwork, Joe Biden accused him of "hysteria, xenophobia, and fearmongering."

IN THE COMING months, many Americans learned for the first time just how vulnerable we are to China. Doctors and nurses depended on Chinese factories for personal protective equipment like masks and gloves. China also manufactured critical medical devices; many nations had to turn to Beijing for ventilators. And China had cornered the global market for basic but essential drugs like penicillin, acetaminophen, and heparin. The Chinese Communists leveraged these advantages to the hilt. Beijing conducted "virus diplomacy," pressuring desperate nations to ease travel bans, minimize China's role in the pandemic, and join China's whitewash at the WHO.

We weren't immune from China's threats. Early in the pandemic, China hinted that it might withhold lifesaving medicines from America, Xinhua, its giant state-run news agency, proposed to cast us into "the mighty sea of coronavirus."

And how did the Democrats respond to these threats? Did they want to punish China?

No, Democrats punished the American people instead. They imposed extreme and intrusive lockdowns and mandates, long after these were proven unnecessary and ineffective. Governors arbitrarily dictated who could earn a living and who couldn't. Kids were kicked out of school indefinitely. BLM rioters rampaged in our streets while people of faith couldn't worship together. Powerful liberals dined mask-free at fancy restaurants while normal Americans couldn't even visit a dying parent or attend a funeral. Americans lost their jobs because they declined a vaccine that couldn't stop the spread of new variants anyway. At every turn, we were the problem—not the Chinese Communists who unleashed the plague on the world.

Democrats also acted as the speech police for the Chinese Communist Party. From the earliest days, I suggested the coronavirus probably originated in the Wuhan labs, not a food market—a theory now widely accepted as plausible, even probable. I expected the Chinese Communists and their WHO mouthpieces to attack me, but liberals also embraced China's propaganda.

The *Washington Post* ran a headline, "Tom Cotton keeps repeating a coronavirus conspiracy theory that was already debunked." The *New York Times* sniffed that I was peddling a "fringe theory" that "lacks evidence and has been dismissed by scientists." CNN's editor-at-large asserted that "this is the height of irresponsibility from a public official" and "Cotton obviously knows better."

Liberals also raced to condemn me and others for using geographically accurate terms like the "Wuhan coronavirus," even though CNN, MSNBC, and other media outlets had used the terms for weeks. But Fauci worried about the feelings of his Chinese buddies and China pressured its lackeys at the WHO to adopt the abstract name COVID-19 to absolve China of guilt. Liberals quickly fell in line. Nancy Pelosi huffed that such terms "make us all less safe,"

Chuck Schumer whined that they were "harsh, nasty, and bigoted," and Joe Biden later banned government officials from using them.

America's liberal elites had a clear message to China's critics: "shut up." Even after the Chinese Communists had unleashed the worst plague in a century and sparked one of the sharpest recessions in our history, liberals still tolerated, even indulged, Chinese leverage over America.

For years now, liberals have apologized for and excused Chinese wrongdoing. China has gotten off scot-free, while we remain as vulnerable as ever to China. I recall how, in those early days, several alarmed friends asked me what we could do. My answer was regretful: "Right now, not much. They've got us over a barrel."

THAT'S REALLY OUR choice for America's future: do we want to let China keep us over that barrel? The liberal sabotage of American power has exposed us to ever growing Chinese influence, manipulation, and control. Thanks to the outsourcing of American manufacturing to China, your access to basic antibiotics for your sick kid depends on Chinese goodwill. The corrupt and hapless WHO meddles in our business, while globalist liberals clap like seals. With each passing year, the People's Liberation Army closes the gap with our military, as Democrats worry if drill sergeants are using the right pronouns.

If we don't make a change and fast, our kids could grow up to live in a country unrecognizable from our own. It may not be a techno-totalitarian Chinese police state that compels them to speak Mandarin and renounce God—though maybe it will. But even if we remain a free and independent country in name, the world in reality will be a Chinese-dominated dystopia. China will get away with murder, as Western elites avert their gaze or even act as its lawyer—exactly as liberals did when I tried to hold China accountable during the pandemic. As Bill Rood taught, you run the show or the show runs you.

Don't expect the Democrats to rebuild our power or to beat China. They sabotaged American power to begin with and they remain ideologically opposed to a strong, dominant America. Barack Obama and Joe Biden both celebrated "a rising China" and viewed the Chinese Communists as partners. The standard Democratic line today is that criticism of China is xenophobic and racist. If anything, liberals sympathize ideologically with China. Tom Friedman, the prestigious *New York Times* columnist, has long fantasized about America being "China for a day." Friedman isn't some fringe figure, either; indeed, he's so mainstream among liberals that Joe Biden invited him to the White House for a private lunch when Biden's approval rating had collapsed and he needed a friendly boost.

You might wonder what Biden and the Democrats would do with the unfettered power of the Chinese Communists, but you really don't have to. We got a glimpse during the pandemic, when Democratic politicians and little Wilsonian scolds like Tony Fauci used "The Science" to justify their arbitrary control of our lives—and bullied Big Tech to censor anyone who disagreed. Yet the Democrats did nothing to reduce our dependence on and exposure to China.

BUT THERE'S A different way, a better choice. We can reverse the left's sabotage of American power and return to the tradition of strength, honor, and confidence. I've laid out the missteps that brought us to this point and some of the key steps to get America out from over that Chinese barrel. Just like Ronald Reagan turned America around after the disastrous presidency of Jimmy Carter, we can summon the same strength after Joe Biden's even worse failures.

Reagan often called America a "city on a hill." He popularized the metaphor, but he didn't create it. As Reagan knew, it comes from the Sermon on the Mount. Jesus told his followers,

> Ye are the light of the world. A city that is set on a hill cannot be hid. Neither do men light a candle, and put it under a bushel, but on a candlestick; and it giveth light unto all that are in the house. Let your light so shine before men, that they may see your good works, and glorify your Father which is in heaven.

Reagan also knew that he wasn't the first American to invoke Jesus's words. In 1630, John Winthrop preached to his small band of settlers aboard the *Arbella*, waiting to disembark in what became New England: "we shall be a city upon a hill. The eyes of all people are upon us." Americans have always seen ourselves as a city on a hill, and rightly so.

Let's think a little more about what it means to be the city on a hill. To start with, the city is on a hill—not an island. It must interact with the outside world. Its citizens must leave the city and descend into the valley to draw their water and into the fields to grow their crops and cultivate their herds. They must travel roads and build ports to cross the seas to exchange their goods for those they lack. And they will travel not only as merchants and traders but also as tourists, for beautiful though the city may be, its citizens will want to discover the world.

And when they watch the city, some foreigners will grow jealous and resentful, coveting its prime territory and its riches. And they may come to take those things.

Thus, the city on a hill can't live in splendid isolation, nor can it adopt a pacifist creed and hope to survive. Walls will be needed, as will guards to protect those walls. An army and a navy must be raised to defend the borderlands, guard the valleys and the fields, secure the ports and open the sea-lanes, and protect its citizens around the world.

The city can't easily do these things alone, so it must make alliances with other cities, some with alien cultures and customs, but shared interests. With those alliances may come new conflicts with still other cities. And so, the city must be prepared for those conflicts.

Put simply, the city on a hill isn't innocent or naive, and certainly not weak. The city elders know how the world works, as did Reagan and our Founding Fathers.

I believe America can once again restore the splendor of the city on a hill. Our people still take pride in our great nation. And they know that American strength is the foundation of American greatness. We must regain our strength to remain the city on a hill.

Only the strong can defend the city on a hill.

ACKNOWLEDGMENTS

FIRST OFF, I want to thank the people of Arkansas. I'm honored to serve you in the Senate. Many of the experiences and ideas in this book result from the opportunity to represent you. Arkansans are a strong and proud people; I work hard every day to keep you safe, advance your interests, and fulfill your aspirations for our great nation. I'm grateful for your confidence and support.

This book was a team effort, and I'm blessed with an outstanding team of advisers and assistants. Brian Colas first suggested the book while watching from afar the strategic catastrophe and human tragedy of the disastrous Afghanistan withdrawal. Brian served as a sounding board throughout the project—which frankly was the least he could do for getting me into this. Patrick MacDonnell and Blake Seitz were workhorses who spent countless hours with me crafting arguments, conducting research, and preparing the manuscript. Doug Coutts and Joni Deoudes, as always, helped me manage my Senate work, political activities, and family life with the added demands of writing a book. A. J. Schroeder handled operations and logistics. Caroline Tabler assisted with the book launch. Meg McGaughey oversaw the Senate's contract-review process. Drew Hudson assisted with fact-checking. Brian, Doug, Joni, and Caroline, along with Matt Downer, also reviewed the manuscript and offered helpful comments.

I'm grateful to several friends who went the extra mile to review the manuscript: Ted Dickey, Bart Hester, Jonny Hiler, Joe Kristol, Michael Lamoureux, Aaron MacLean, Brett O'Donnell, Chad Pekron, David Ray, and Alex Wong. I should add, of course, that responsibility for the book's ideas and arguments is mine alone, as it is for any mistakes that slipped through.

Javelin served again as my agent. I thank Keith Urbahn and Matt Latimer for their good offices from proposal to contract to launch.

Sean Desmond at Twelve was my editor. Sean responded enthusiastically to the book from the beginning and he improved the book at every step. I thank Sean for his confidence in the book and his hard work. I'm also grateful for the contributions of the whole team at Hachette Books and Twelve, including Zohal Karimy and Megan Perritt-Jacobson.

Many teachers, mentors, advisers, and friends helped to shape my thinking and ideas over the years. I especially appreciate the friendship and support of Elliott Abrams, Larry Arnn, Peter Berkowitz, Bob Gates, Charles Kesler, and Walter Russell Mead.

I also want to acknowledge others whom I cannot name: old friends and battle buddies still on active duty in the Army. Since our days together, these soldiers have taken high command positions or senior enlisted billets. For years, they've shared their perspectives on how Army training and mindsets have changed—in most cases, sadly, for the worse. Our conversations inform much of what I write about lethality and the warrior culture. I would like to thank them by name, yet I don't want to imperil their careers. But you know who you are. Thank you for your continued service. Help is on the way.

Finally, I want to thank my family. Once again, Cowboy was my little writing companion. A bit older and a bit slower, he still kept me good company during the long weekends and late nights. Gabriel and Daniel are old enough now to ask for "war stories" at bedtime, wonder whether Washington or Grant was the better general, and regret that children in other countries like China don't have the same freedoms they do. But they're still little boys who only play war. And like every kid, they deserve to inherit a safe, free, and prosperous America from their parents.

As usual, Anna shouldered more than her share of the task, one hundred percent and then some. While I worked on this book, she cared for our boys and managed our family's affairs, all while working on her own professional endeavors. On top of all that, she patiently listened to my ideas and always improved them. I sometimes say half-jokingly—but only half!—that Anna makes me look like the milquetoast moderate in the family. But there's no doubt that she's the strong heart of our family—for truly, only the strong can survive a house full of boys. Anna, I love you more than ever.

T HIS BOOK COMBINES history and current events, including my own experiences in the Army and the Senate. For the latter, I've drawn on my own recollections, research, notes, and writings for speeches, op-eds, and so forth. For recent events, I've also consulted news stories in traditional media sources such as the Associated Press, Reuters, the *New York Times*, the *Wall Street Journal*, the *Washington Post*, Fox, CNN, ABC, CBS, and NBC.

For my understanding and analysis of historic events, I've benefited over the years from hundreds of books, too many to name. But a few works merit mention here because I referred to them routinely while writing the book. *The New Cambridge History of American Foreign Relations* and George Herring's *From Colony to Superpower: U.S. Foreign Relations since 1776* are useful reference materials. Though I don't always agree with their interpretations—and sometimes strongly disagree—both books provide a helpful baseline for the history of American foreign policy. Bob Gates's *Duty* and *Exercise of Power* are rich insider accounts of multiple presidential administrations and indispensable studies of American foreign policy during Gates's remarkable life. Walter Russell Mead's *Special Providence* remains in my opinion the most definitive history of American foreign policy. Walter's scholarship and friendship over the years have immeasurably enriched me. Wilfred McClay's *Land of Hope* is an excellent survey of

American history and should be a standard textbook in high schools across our land.

What follows is a more detailed list of the specific books, essays, articles, and other sources I consulted for each chapter.

Prologue: Sabotaging a Superpower

While much of the material comes from my experiences and recollections, I also leaned on the recollections of aides and friends who helped during the evacuation of Afghanistan. I'm especially grateful to Doug Coutts, Matt Downer, John Noonan, and Kristen Trindle. I also appreciate Will Berry and Kent McCoy for sharing their recollections of those dark days.

Chapter 1: The Progressive Roots of Decline

I've studied the Progressives for a quarter century (sad to say) with my old friend and teacher, Charles Kesler. His books *I Am the Change* and *Crisis of the Two Constitutions* were especially helpful to understanding Progressive thought, as were our many pleasant conversations.

The best sources, of course, are the Progressives' own writings. I appreciate Hillsdale's David Azerrad for steering me toward useful primary material. *American Progressivism: A Reader*, edited by Ronald J. Pestritto and William J. Atto, collects many key sources. Pestritto's *Woodrow Wilson and the Roots of Modern Liberalism* and Eldon J. Eisenach's *The Lost Promise of Progressivism* are reliable interpretations of Progressive thought, along with interesting insights on their elite social background and, shall we say, disturbing views on race and society. Christopher Burkett's essay, "Remaking the World: Progressivism and American Foreign Policy" perceptively contrasts the Founders and the Progressives on foreign policy.

Likewise with the Founders: they left volumes of books, essays, letters, speeches, and other writings to understand their thinking. *The Federalist* remains the gold standard to explain the political philosophy of our Constitution. Probably the most famous essay about the conduct of foreign policy, to which Americans have returned for guidance ever since, is George Washington's Farewell Address. Two sources for much of the Founders' writings can be accessed online: The Founders Online (https://founders.archives.gov/)

and Hillsdale's Constitution Reader (http://constitutionreader.com/). The latter also contains useful material from the Progressives and other interpretative commentary. Kesler's *Crisis* is also helpful to understanding the Founders' thought in general, and Matthew Spalding's essay, "America's Founders and the Principles of Foreign Policy," lays out in particular their approach to foreign policy. Finally, Abraham Lincoln was the great defender and interpreter of the Founders and I've drawn frequently from his writings. I'm partial to the two-volume Library of America collection, but Lincoln's words are readily available online and in other anthologies.

Winston Churchill's sobering reflections on scientific versus moral progress are from his 1924 essay, "Shall We All Commit Suicide?" Colin Powell related his remarkable exchange with Madeleine Albright about the Balkan Wars in his memoir, *My American Journey*; surprisingly, Albright confirmed the story in her memoir, *Madam Secretary*.

CHAPTER 2: THE BLAME AMERICA FIRST DEMOCRATS

I relied on contemporaneous news accounts for much of the material in this chapter. Jeane Kirkpatrick's writings were also a treasure trove of insight, especially her essays in *Commentary*. "Dictatorships and Double Standards" and "U.S. Security and Latin America" are two of the most important, but all of her work is worth studying.

I referred often to Paul Johnson's classic, *Modern Times*. Two books informed my understanding of the "New Left." Peter Collier and David Horowitz's *Destructive Generation* is an eye-opening account of the left-wing fringe by repentant participants. Susan Braudy's *Family Circle* is the definitive work on the subversive activities of Chesa Boudin's parents and grandparents. Also helpful are Ann Coulter's *Treason* and Mona Charen's *Useful Idiots*.

For details about the military draft, I turned to Lawrence Baskir and William Strauss's *Chance and Circumstance*. James Fallow's infamous essay about dodging the draft was published in *Washington Monthly* under the title, "What Did You Do in the Class War, Daddy?" Public-opinion polling details are from the article "American Public Opinion and the War in Vietnam" by William Lunch and Peter Sperlick. Details about the Pentagon

Papers are from *The Trust* by Susan Tifft and Alex Jones. Mackubin Thomas Owens catalogued John Kerry's disgraceful anti-war activities in *National Review*.

I want to thank my friend Elliott Abrams for sharing his insight into American foreign policy especially during the late 1970s and 1980s. His prolific writings over the years are a treasure trove. He also pointed me to *Nicaragua* by Shirley Christian, which is a helpful account of the Sandinista takeover and Contra freedom fighters.

Chapter 3: The Globalist Surrender of Sovereignty

John Fonte's *Sovereignty or Submission* and Patrick Stewart's *Sovereignty Wars*, though argued from opposite perspectives, provide detailed histories of modern international organizations and agreements, along with the ideas and political movements that motivated their creation and maintain them today. I also referred to Rich Lowry's expertly written *The Case for Nationalism*, along with the writings and public speeches of Senators Henry Cabot Lodge, Daniel Patrick Moynihan, and Jesse Helms, among others.

For the sections on immigration and trade policy, I relied on my extensive work in the Senate on these issues, including my *Beat China* report, published in February 2021. I obtained most data from government sources such as the Bureau of Labor Statistics, Census Bureau, Customs and Border Protection, and the Commission on the Theft of American Intellectual Property. I also consulted Rush Doshi's book, *The Long Game,* which compellingly tells the story of China's malignant rise to global power and influence.

Chapter 4: Neutering the Military

I drew upon my own experiences in the Army and my work on the Armed Services Committee for much of this chapter. I consulted the Office of Management and Budget's *Historical Tables* for data about the defense budget over time. Mackenzie Eaglen and James Mismash of the American Enterprise Institute helpfully pointed me to other sources. Eric Edelman generously talked through the findings of the National Defense Strategy Commission, which he co-chaired.

For details on the sorry state of our military before the world wars, I drew upon General John Pershing's *My Experiences in the World War* and General George Marshall's 1941 report to the secretary of war. T. R. Fehrenbach's *This Kind of War* shows the high cost of underfunding the military before the Korean War. The Department of Defense's historical series provides an inside look at budget decisions in the postwar era. The shortcomings of military readiness under Jimmy Carter comes from the Congressional Research Service report *A Historical Perspective on "Hollow Forces"* by Andrew Feickert and Stephen Daggett. Details about the Clinton–era military are from Robert Patterson's *Dereliction of Duty*. I used Bob Gates's *Duty* and *Exercise of Power* as invaluable guides to events during the Obama administration.

My longtime advisers, Ryan Tully and Tim Morrison, both talked through how Democrats have weakened our nuclear forces. For insights into nuclear strategy during the Kennedy and Johnson eras, I drew from Richard Pipes's bracing 1977 essay in *Commentary*, "Why the Soviet Union Thinks It Can Fight and Win a Nuclear War."

Elaine Donnelly of the Center for Military Readiness shared her wealth of knowledge about social engineering in the military. James Hasson's *Stand Down* goes into great detail about the Marine Corps study of mixed-sex units in combat training. Finally, Captain Kristen Griest's thoughts on fitness standards are from her article "With Equal Opportunity Comes Equal Responsibility: Lowering Fitness Standards to Accommodate Women Will Hurt the Army—and Women," published by West Point's Modern War Institute.

Chapter 5: When Democrats Act Tough

For the vignette about Michael Dukakis's tank ride into electoral oblivion, I reviewed contemporaneous reporting along with more recent analysis on the infamous photo op, including Josh King's "Dukakis and the Tank" in *Politico*. I also appreciated the insights of Karl Rove, who is always a reservoir of political history.

For the Bay of Pigs, I relied on Howard Jones's *The Bay of Pigs*, Jim Rasenberger's *The Brilliant Disaster*, and Haynes Johnson's *The Bay of Pigs:*

The Leaders' Story of Brigade 2506. I also drew upon the CIA's multi-volume history of the Bay of Pigs, authored by its former historian, Jack Pfeiffer; these declassified materials are available at the CIA's online reading room. I want to thank my old friend, John Couriel, for sharing his own family's story, as well as insights into how the Cuban American community remembers this painful chapter of our nation's history. George Feldenkreis also shared his thoughts on the Bay of Pigs and its legacy.

For the Vietnam War, I consulted Mark Moyar's *Triumph Forsaken*, H. R. McMaster's *Dereliction of Duty*, and Michael Lind's *Vietnam: The Necessary War*. All three books are carefully reasoned, diligently researched, and compellingly written. These books are part of a growing body of "revisionist" scholarship in the best sense of the term: revising the false and slanted scholarly consensus about the Vietnam War after years of liberal smears.

For our misguided intervention in Somalia, I relied on Mark Moyar's *Oppose Any Foe* and Mark Bowden's iconic work, *Black Hawk Down*. Additionally, I consulted Gates's *Exercise of Power*; Bill Clinton's memoir, *My Life*; and Colin Powell's autobiography, *My American Journey*. I have spoken with several veterans of Mogadishu over the years and their experiences influenced my thinking. I also thank General Scott Miller for sharing his experience as a young Delta operator on the ground in Mogadishu. Mark Moyar reviewed this chapter and provided feedback; he also suggested helpful sources, as did Edward Gutierrez.

Chapter 6: Obama Apologizes

Much of this chapter comes from my own experiences in Congress fighting against Barack Obama's highly ideological foreign policy. But I also let Obama speak for himself. His third memoir, *A Promised Land*, and Ben Rhodes's *The World As It Is* did little to conceal Obama's thinking; after all, they viewed Obama's record as a great success. Jeffrey Goldberg's long essay, "The Obama Doctrine," in the *Atlantic*, based on countless hours as Obama's court scribe, is a kind of Rosetta stone into Obama's mindset and view of himself.

I relied on a wide range of secondary sources, too, including Mark Moyar's *Strategic Failure*, Colin Dueck's *The Obama Doctrine*, Bret Stephens's *America in Retreat*, Bob Woodward's *Obama's Wars*, and Gates's *Duty* and *Exercise of Power*. I'm indebted as well to my conversations with

Elliott Abrams, who pointed me to his many helpful writings in *Commentary*, *National Review*, *Politico*, the *Washington Post*, and on his Council of Foreign Relations blog. I also strongly recommend Michael Doran's two excellent essays, "Obama's Secret Iran Strategy" and "The Doctrine of American Unexceptionalism," which connect a lot of dots in the Obama-Biden worldview. For Iran in particular, I drew from Jay Solomon's *The Iran Wars* and Ray Takeyh's "The Coup against Democracy That Wasn't" in *Commentary*, based on his compelling book *The Last Shah*.

I appreciate my discussions of the Obama administration's foreign-policy legacy with Aaron MacLean of the Foundation for Defense of Democracy and Matthew Continetti of the American Enterprise Institute.

CHAPTER 7: BIDEN STUMBLES

Regrettably, we're still in the early stages of the Biden era, so most of this chapter comes from my own work in the Senate and contemporaneous news accounts from Biden's career as a senator, vice president, and now president. I believe the Afghanistan fiasco has its roots in the early days of the Obama administration, when Biden insistently counseled withdrawal. I depended here again on Bob Gates's *Duty* and *Exercise of Power* and Bob Woodward's *Obama's Wars*.

The ironic vignette derives from Biden's own op-ed "Not So Deft on Taiwan," from the *Washington Post*.

Mike Vickers offered useful insight about America's involvement in both Afghanistan and Ukraine.

CHAPTER 8: RESTORING AMERICAN STRATEGY

For the inside story of Operation Praying Mantis, I relied on Captain J. B. Perkins's account in the *Proceedings* of the U.S. Naval Institute. The Washington Institute for Near East Policy's "Gulf of Conflict: A History of U.S.-Iranian Confrontation at Sea" by David B. Crist provided a broader overview of events.

A few books in particular have informed my thinking about America's strategy. As I mentioned at the outset, Walter Russell Mead's *Special Providence* is an invaluable guide. Robert Kaplan's *The Revenge of Geography* is a helpful primer on geopolitics and the work of strategist Nicholas

Spykman. I regret that I never knew Bill Rood, perhaps even more that this famous teacher wrote so little. His only book, *Kingdoms of the Blind*, is a bracing introduction to his strategic thinking, as is his award-winning essay in *Proceedings*, "Distant Ramparts." Two of his students, J. D. Crouch II and Patrick J. Garrity, have synthesized his teaching in the outstanding *You Run the Show or the Show Runs You: Capturing Professor Harold W. Rood's Strategic Thought for a New Generation*. I also drew upon conversations with another Rood student and my friend, Larry Arnn. His essay "Three Lessons of Statesmanship for Americans Today" is a good primer on how to think about strategy, using Winston Churchill as a guide. Finally, I consulted the works of the late Angelo Codevilla, who advocated a uniquely American approach to strategy. In particular, I recommend his many essays in the *Claremont Review of Books* as an introduction to his thought.

CHAPTER 9: REGAINING AMERICAN STRENGTH

In researching the invasion of Grenada, I relied on Ronald Reagan's autobiography, *An American Life*, along with contemporaneous reporting and post-invasion military analysis. Crouch and Garrity's *You Run the Show or the Show Runs You* details Rood's novel analysis of the strategic importance of Grenada. Mike Vickers gave a similar account of the invasion and its necessity in our conversations. I appreciate the assistance of the Ronald Reagan Presidential Library in acquiring internal documents from the Reagan White House. Ambassador Bob Kimmitt, who served on the National Security Council during the invasion, also shared his insights with me.

For most of this chapter, I relied on my study of and work on these issues in the Senate. I drew most data from official government sources, including the Congressional Research Service, Energy Information Agency, and Immigration and Customs Enforcement, among others. I also relied on my *Beat China* report and a report on the Navy titled *A Report on the Fighting Culture of the United States Surface Fleet*, which I published along with Congressmen Jim Banks, Dan Crenshaw, and Mike Gallagher. I benefited from my conversations about the border and the drug cartels with Bill Barr, the two-time attorney general, and I recommend his memoir, *One Damn Thing After Another*. I thank Mike Sommers for his insights on energy policy.

Epilogue: Our Choice

I relied on my own recollections as well as those of my Senate staff and contemporaneous documents and news accounts to retell the story of the early days of the Wuhan coronavirus outbreak. I first explained what it means to be a city on the hill during a Veterans Day speech in 2015 at Washington National Cathedral and I have elaborated on the concept on many occasions since.

T OM COTTON IS a United States senator for Arkansas and best-selling author of *Sacred Duty*. He served in Iraq with the 101st Airborne Division and in Afghanistan with a Provincial Reconstruction Team. Between combat tours, he served with the 3rd Infantry Regiment ("The Old Guard") at Arlington National Cemetery. His military decorations include the Bronze Star, the Combat Infantryman Badge, and the Ranger Tab. He serves on the Senate Intelligence, Armed Services, and Judiciary Committees. Tom is married to Anna and they have two sons, Gabriel and Daniel.